# Citizen Critics

T0287852

THE HISTORY OF COMMUNICATION
Robert W. McChesney and John C. Nerone, editors

*A list of books in the series*
*appears at the end of this book.*

# Citizen Critics

## Literary
## Public Spheres

Rosa A. Eberly

University of Illinois Press

Urbana and Chicago

Publication of this book was supported by
    a University Cooperative Society Subvention Grant
    awarded by the University of Texas at Austin

Library of Congress Cataloging-in-Publication Data
Eberly, Rosa A.
Citizen critics : literary public spheres / Rosa A. Eberly.
    p.    cm.
Includes bibliographical references (p. ) and index.
ISBN 978-0-252-02513-6 (alk. paper)
ISBN 978-0-252-06867-6 (pbk. : alk. paper)
    1. American fiction—20th century—History and criti-
    cism—Theory, etc. 2. Authors and readers—United States—
    History—20th century. 3. Public opinion—United States—
    History—20th century. 4. Criticism—United States—History—
    20th century. 5. Miller, Henry, 1891– Tropic of Cancer.
    6. Ellis, Bret Easton. American psycho. 7. Joyce, James,
    1882–1941. Ulysses. 8. Reader-response criticism. 9. Dworkin,
    Andrea. Mercy. 10. Canon (Literature) I. Title.
PS379.E36    2000
813'.509'01—dc21    99-6743
CIP

1 2 3 4 5 C P 6 5 4 3 2

To the memory of my father, Austin H. Eberly,
and in honor of my mother, Hope

Knowledge of future events is not possible, given our human nature. We are so far removed from this prescience that Homer, who has the highest reputation for wisdom, has pictured even the gods at times deliberating among themselves about the future—not that he knew their minds but that he desired to show for humans this power lies in the realms of the impossible.
—Isocrates, "Against the Sophists"

For, d'ye see, rainbows do not visit the clear air; they only irradiate vapor. And so, through all the thick mists of the dim doubts in my mind, divine intuitions now and then shoot, enkindling my fog with a heavenly ray. And for this I thank God; for all have doubts; many deny; but doubts or denials, few along with them, have intuitions. Doubts of all things earthly, and intuitions of some things heavenly; this combination makes neither believer nor infidel, but makes a man who regards them both with equal eye.
—Herman Melville, *Moby-Dick*

What I propose, therefore, is very simple: it is nothing more than to think what we are doing.
—Hannah Arendt, *The Human Condition*

Oh, Mama, can this really be the end?
To be stuck inside of Mobile with the Memphis blues again.
—Bob Dylan, *Blonde on Blonde*

# Contents

# Preface

"You know you're on your way to the hospital," Keith Diehl has said, "when you see the hospital signs." To be sure, interdisciplinary work requires a different way of knowing. In writing *Citizen Critics,* I felt I was driving around in a place I had never been, using a map I had never seen. And I was never sure whether the map had not yet caught up to the road signs or the signs to the map.

I began writing this book a few years ago as a way of suggesting that criticism desiring to make claims about the effects of literary texts on social practices and on actual readers might do so by rhetorical and empirical rather than rationalistic means and that the condition of our public discussions about literary and cultural texts had something to tell us about the condition of our democracy. These exigences have not passed. About a year ago an expert literary scholar visited the campus where I teach to speak on the topic "Joyce and the Common Reader." His talk, while offering interesting interpretations of *Ulysses*'s "Scylla and Charybdis," "Nausicaa," and "Ithaca" chapters, neglected to mention the oral or written words of even one actual reader of the novel, other than himself. The critic claimed that Joyce had an interest in addressing the "common" reader because "the quotidian experience of common readers is manifested in the novel." The "common reader," in other words, was merely standing in, rationalistically, for the critic, as "the reader" has done in so many kinds of literary criticism, from high new criticism through reader-response and into cultural criticism. Commodified through instrumental public opinion polling, "the public" functions in reports on polls in structurally similar ways that "the reader" has functioned in criticism. Both reductions have consequences for our shared democratic practices.

In that context, *Citizen Critics* reports on the public arguments of literally hundreds of actual readers of four controversial novels in this country during this century. Many of these readers have no credentials other
than concerned citizen, writing to other citizens in newspapers and magazines to attempt to have some impact on their shared futures. Their arguments were public opinions, though no Roper or Gallup or Yankelovich
or even Fishkin would be able to measure them. I suggest it is what people
do with their judgments about books and other cultural products, not the
books or even the authors in and of themselves, that enables books to affect our shared worlds. *Citizen Critics* thus relies heavily on a body of work
I have referred to as "publics theory," some of which was introduced into
speech communication in the 1960s and into English studies only after the
1989 translation into English of Jürgen Habermas's earliest book, *Structural Transformation of the Public Sphere.* My reliance on publics theory,
along with my disciplinary identification as a teacher of rhetoric, suggests
that I am interested in reinvigorating this country's public discourse and
interrogating popular and corporate uses of *public*—for instance, "the
flying public" and, true oxymoron, "the investing public." Such uses of
the word *public* defame the concept by ignoring the intimate connections
among publics, rhetoric, and participatory democracy.

I argue that the public discourses written in response to *Ulysses, Tropic
of Cancer, American Psycho,* and *Mercy* might have affected—through the
acts of citizens choosing whether or not to read and then write publicly
about those books—certain social practices in this country during the
twentieth century. When citizen critics have been active participants in literary public spheres, I have followed their discourses in choosing which
*topoi* and *stases* to focus on. This method reflects my understanding of
rhetoric as an architectonic theoretical, productive, and practical art. Although I believe that my critical method is part of the news of this book,
the discourses of the citizen critics and the effects of those discourses are
the lead, particularly my study of the Chicago literary public sphere that
grew around *Tropic of Cancer.* Reading and writing in public about books
of common concern to them, citizen critics produced arguments that attempted to exert cultural force alongside the discourses of legal and aesthetic experts and in media controlled first by cultural and then by corporate elites. Thus the discourses of these citizen critics not only were *in*
public; they *were* public discourses in that they shared a concern for the
future of a common world and reflected an ethos of citizen participation
in common or public issues.

Throughout the twentieth century, however, the power and agency of citizen critics have diminished, as have the power and agency of citizens in general, largely through the mechanisms of commodified public opinion and corporate capitalism. *Citizen Critics* also tells the story of how marketing has turned texts usually considered literary into commodities and how legal, aesthetic, corporate, and other expert discourses have come to determine which books are published, who reads them, and how they are read. *Citizen Critics* is thus another call for reclaiming democracy, since truly public discussions of novels and other cultural products are necessary to a healthy democracy. In fact, as I discuss in the final chapter, public discussions of all kinds of cultural texts can be one means of fostering public discourse and hence democracy more generally. Thus, this critical book shares the same end as my scholarship on classrooms as protopublic spaces: to deepen our understanding of the relationship between the quality of our discourses and the quality of our democracy.

# Acknowledgments

The seeds of this project were soaked and sown in the early 1990s, when I was a student in Jerry Hauser's rhetoric and publics seminars at Penn State. Conversation with Professor Hauser remains my favorite inventional pleasure. Also at Penn State, Lester Faigley's visiting seminar on rhetoric and composition after poststructuralism, Jack Selzer's seminar on reader-response theories, Marie Secor's seminar on the history of rhetoric and composition, and Jeffrey Walker's seminar on rhetoric and composition prompted me to begin asking what were for me new questions about the chasm between intention and affect. Marie Secor, Jack Selzer, Jeff Walker, Jim Rambeau, Jennifer Jackson, and Michael Begnal read early drafts of this book, and completing it would not have been possible without their help. Kathleen Domenig, David Dunlap, Grace Fala, Per Fjelstad, Paul Ford, Kate Hastings, Gabrielle King, Susan Ross, and other graduate student colleagues across the mall in the Speech Communication Department at Penn State opened my mind to ways of reading that I had not encountered before; Ted Armstrong, Dominic Delli Carpini, Ben Click, Ann George, Nancy Lowe, Gigi Marino, Judith Storey, Keith Waddle, Janet Zepernick, and other graduate students in the Department of English at Penn State were wonderful kindred space travelers in the wormhole between literature and rhetoric. Stephen H. Browne's 1990 summer reading group on literary theory, in which I was a capricious participant, introduced me to the discipline of speech communication through the back door, and I will always be grateful for his willingness to float.

In Austin, copious friends and colleagues in various schools and departments and in the community supported me during the process of revising this book. For this I thank Michael Adams, Phil Barrish, Asenath Bartley,

Sabrina Barton, Tom Buckley, Kermit Campbell, Anna Carroll, Mia Carter, Evan Carton, Davida Charney, Olin Clemons, John Downing, Lester Faigley, Linda Faigley, Linda Ferreira-Buckley, Jim Garrison, Ron Greene, Becca Guerney, Barbara Harlow, Lester Harrell, Lucille Harrell, Elizabeth Harris, Rod Hart, Kurt Heinzelman, Susan Sage Heizelman, Jackie Henkel, Bob Jensen, Theresa Kelley, Sara Kimball, Sandy Levinson, Carol MacKay, Chuck Meyer, Lisa Moore, Katie Pearl, Wayne Rebhorn, Sue Rodi, John Ruszkiewicz, Madison Searle, John Slatin, Peg Syverson, John Trimble, Michael Winship, and Jorie Woods. Students at the University of Texas at Austin, in particular Virginia Anderson, Jonathan Ayres, David Barndollar, Scott Browning, Buddy Burniske, Sharan Daniel, Billy Earnest, Ben Feigert, Christy Friend, Mary Grover, Annie Holand, Adam Kohlhepp, David Lapides, Linc Leifeste, Jennifer Lehman, the late Prentiss Moore, Susi Paterson, Altrivice Revis, Courtney Robertson, Susan Romano, Cathy Ross, Lynn Rudloff, Gina Siesing, and Josh Yumibe talked with me about many of these ideas. I am grateful to the College of Liberal Arts and the Division of Rhetoric and Composition at the University of Texas at Austin for a Dean's Fellowship and a Summer Research Award, both of which helped me make coherent the connections between my critical method and my pedagogical practices.

I read earlier versions of sections of chapters 4 and 5 at the Rhetoric Society of America meeting in 1992; of chapter 1 at the Conference on College Composition and Communication in 1994; and of chapter 6 at the Modern Language Association in 1997 and at the Conference on College Composition and Communication in 1998. An earlier version of chapter 5 was published as "Andrea Dworkin's *Mercy:* Pain, Ad Personam, and Silence in the 'War Zone,'" in *Pre/Text* 14 (1993): 273–304, and sections of an earlier version of chapter 6 were published in *Rhetoric Review.* I am grateful to faculty at the University of Illinois at Chicago, Carnegie Mellon University, and the University of New Mexico for offering suggestions on chapter 2 when I read it at their campuses. Gina Siesing's editorial assistance—and friendship—have energized and blessed the final stages of this project. Emily Rogers at the University of Illinois Press has been a constant help and comfort through the editorial process. And the two anonymous reviewers for the Press not only helped me improve the "final" draft of *Citizen Critics* but also reenergized my enthusiasm for the book's arguments and potential consequences.

Wilma R. Ebbitt, my first rhetoric teacher, continues to inspire me through the memories I have of her passionate rigor for teaching and learning. My teachers at Dallastown Area middle and high schools—in particular Robert Hildebrand, Ann Skilton, and Jim Filizzi—taught me to believe in myself. Thank you for your care. I am grateful to Anne Matthews Conners for listening to me read, over the phone, the earliest drafts of each of these chapters. She remains my inspiration for public life and public service. My colleague and friend Dana Cloud continues to give me the gift of a scholarly role model and source of affirmation, support, and fun. Perhaps τύχη is the best therapist. Finally, Keith Diehl deserves my deepest thanks for being consistent in his faith that all will be well. He has, after all, made his own applesauce for his own baked apples.

# Citizen Critics

# 1

# Citizen Critics in Literary Public Spheres

What do I mean to suggest by the term *citizen critic?* Not *public intellectual*—because those who write under that name find their bylines more often in elite national or expert academic magazines than they do in local or city newspapers[1] or their names and voices on local talk radio. Public intellectuals are more experts than citizens—though *expert* and *citizen* are not antitheses but rather counterparts: points from which to understand and judge the other. Public intellectuals are generally more concerned with being intellectuals—in explaining the views of experts to nonexperts—than they are with forming publics or reinvigorating public discourse.[2] I do not mean to suggest that public intellectuals are bad. Rather, I mean that they are not the same as citizen critics. By *citizen critic* I mean a person who produces discourses about issues of common concern from an ethos of citizen first and foremost—not as expert or spokesperson for a workplace or as member of a club or organization.[3] *Citizen critic* is thus as much normative as it is empirical: it is as much hope as it is reality.[4] In any case, this book presents four studies of the relative presence of citizen critics in four literary public spheres in the United States across the twentieth century. The case studies proceeded from a concern about the usefulness of literary and cultural criticism and with the future of our shared discourses and hence our democracy. The case studies proceeded as well from a resilient conviction—bruised and bloodied but still on its feet—that cultural texts have some role to play in reinvigorating participatory democratic practice.

Though criticism has begun to move away from focusing solely on the formal aspects of literary texts, academic critics—even those who practice criticism that focuses on readers or on the cultural effects of texts—still rely on assumptions about the uniformity of readers and the univocality of discourses. Especially before works of literature become canonical, however, public acts of interpretation by citizen critics can reveal the very unsettled and polyphonic nature of texts as well as the widely divergent judgments of actual readers. By studying the interpretive acts of private people connected through their public discourses and shared interests, I will construct an empirical basis on which to build probabilistic theories about the discursive processes through which cultural works—both literary texts and critical texts written in response to them and to each other—affect society.[5] As more and more academics from various disciplines turn their attention to the history and purpose of public intellectuals, this book offers—through a study of literary public spheres and the discourses of nonexpert citizen critics—an account of some of the different forms public criticism has taken in this century. Further, I aim for *Citizen Critics* to be part of a reinvigoration of public life in this country in two ways. First, by contextualizing this study in the twentieth century's move away from participatory democracy, I suggest that citizen critics writing in literary public spheres may be able to reclaim some of the public arenas lost to corporate capitalism.[6] Second, I offer in chapter 6 a model of the classroom as a protopublic space that can foster literary public spheres and through which students may choose to form and enter publics and public spheres and to become citizen critics.

In the chapters that follow, I will suggest that four complex and controversial novels in twentieth-century literature—two that were censored in the United States and thus led to important court decisions and two whose noncensorship was a public issue—have fostered forms of what Jürgen Habermas has called "public spheres in the world of letters," or literary public spheres. In these four literary public spheres, interpretive arguments were made and, at least temporarily, lost or won by private citizens who came together through writing and reading in rhetorically constructed public spaces. These people came together because, in John Dewey's terms, they recognized—through the work of literature—that they had common interests; these individuals wrote publicly about literature and thus endeavored to persuade others because they felt they would share with others certain consequences of its publication. Further, studying public discourses of actual readers reveals that theories of texts and readers need to be much more complex. In addition, I suggest that rhetorical approaches to the study and practice of interpretation—and to the teaching of interpretive practices, including writing—need to reflect the observation that interpretations involve speaking and writing as well as reading and are shaped not only by broad cultural assumptions but also by the inventional strategies of other public arguments.[7] Ultimately I suggest through my study of discourses within literary public spheres in which actual readers argued over interpretations not only of literature but also of specific social and political practices—especially in response to books considered obscene, indecent, or pornographic—that rhetorical theory offers literary criticism, political science, and social theory possibilities for articulating how fictional texts and the public discourses written in response to them can influence social practices by fostering public debate about values and actions.

To construct a more serviceable account of how fictional texts might create literary public spheres and affect social practices, I have analyzed public discourses written in response to the incomplete serial publication of James Joyce's *Ulysses* in 1918 in the *Little Review;* the three-year battle for legal distribution of Henry Miller's *Tropic of Cancer* in Chicago in the early 1960s; and the nearly contemporaneous U.S. publication in 1991 of Bret Easton Ellis's *American Psycho* and Andrea Dworkin's *Mercy* amid calls for boycotts and censorship. Instead of assuming a univocal text or a highly theorized "ideal" reader, I study actually existing literary public spheres and employ a rhetorical lexicon that has allowed me to describe the interpretive practices of actual readers writing publicly about these problematic literary texts, a critical practice that shares some assumptions with what Steven Mailloux has called rhetorical hermeneutics[8] and is similar to what Gerard A. Hauser has used in studies of the Solidarity movement, the Meese commission on pornography, and the Iranian hostage crisis.[9] In each of the four cases, I have endeavored to provide a thick description of the public discourses written in response to the fictional text and to use the language of rhetorical invention and analysis to describe how certain inventional strategies, *topoi* in particular, shaped the contours of each literary public sphere. I suggest that political and social questions that should be subject to public debate in a democracy are very often decided by experts in aesthetics or law: whether Joyce or Miller or Ellis or Dworkin write "well," for example, or whether any of them is a "true artist." I also suggest that whereas institutionalized literary critics, lawyers, and judges have accepted the criterion of "literary merit" as warrant for no longer censoring or suppressing most works of fiction, citizen critics are less settled about whether "literary merit" (or the more pedagogical "good writing") is in itself a legitimate or ultimate criterion for making judgments about works of fiction.

More specifically, in chapter 2 I suggest how the argumentative strategies of the *Little Review* editors Margaret Anderson and Jane Heap, who consistently moved questions of obscenity and intelligibility to questions of "true art," set the discursive stage for the Woolsey decision, which gained *Ulysses* the right to legal publication and distribution in the United States in the early thirties. Focusing on a public sphere that was as much bourgeois as literary—merely to question Joyce's genius was to mark oneself as a tasteless outsider—I demonstrate in chapter 2 how political and social issues entered even a relatively elite public sphere when a controversial book was under discussion.[10] Focusing on a literary public sphere delimited by geography rather than class or education, I suggest in chapter 3 that public arguments in Chicago's four major daily newspapers about attempts to distribute *Tropic of Cancer* in and around the city helped shape legal decisions and further debates on issues of censorship and social change. Again, the criterion of "literary merit," while ultimately successful in courts of law, was not adequate to persuade the vast majority of Chicagoans that Miller's novel deserved to be published and distributed legally. In chapter 4 I argue that, amid intense publicity, a March 1991 *Vanity Fair* article by Norman Mailer changed the *locus* of argumentation about *American Psycho* from questions of corporate censorship and femicide to questions of aesthetics. Finally, I argue in chapter 5 that Andrea Dworkin's conception of publicity as a phenomenon in the "war zone"—warranted as it may be—so personalized public discourse about *Mercy* that only a very few reviewers—and no letter writers—were willing to participate in the limited literary public sphere that grew up around her novel.

Led by recurring inventional structures, or *topoi,* I have located, read, and studied public discourses about each of the works of fiction in question. As a general point of departure, I have used the analysis of argumentative structures Chaim Perelman and Lucie Olbrechts-Tyteca formulated in *The New Rhetoric* to determine how people reason about values. Jeanne Fahnestock and Marie Secor's *stases-* and *topoi*-oriented approach in "The Rhetoric of Literary Criticism"—in which they examine journal articles about interpretations of literature in order to initiate the study of "the rhetoric of literary argument" (77)—suggested a rhetorical method for studying arguments about literary texts. Like Fahnestock and Secor, I have found "special literary *topoi*" (84) in each of the four cases I studied; unlike professional literary criticism, however, citizen criticism—especially letters written in response to articles or reviews—is more explicitly argumentative and more deliberative than epideictic (Fahnestock and Secor 78, 94). More importantly, the *topoi* of citizens' arguments in literary public spheres are less concerned with aesthetics.

What does the rhetorical concept of *topoi* offer that contemporary notions of "thematics" or even simply "topics" do not? First, from their initial codification in the interstices between Aristotle's *Topics* and *Rhetoric,* *topoi* have been, by definition and function, inventional. Writing in the inaugural issue of *Rhetorica,* Michael C. Leff distinguishes topical systems that focus on the processes of inference from those that focus on the matter of the subject itself. Leff's study of Aristotle's, Cicero's, Quintilian's, and Boethius's topical systems implies a continuum from topical systems that, at one extreme, enable "the construction of a theoretically coherent art of rhetorical topics" (those focusing on the matter of the subject itself) and, at the other extreme, enable "the application of topics to public argument" (those focusing on the processes of inference). By the end of antiquity, Leff argues, "the inferential approach to topics leads to a theory that overwhelms the material conditions relevant to the art, while approaches based on the matter of the art refer to categories and situations that are anachronisms" ("Topics" 41). Leff's conclusions about the continuum of topical systems in antiquity can be generalized to contemporary accounts as well, Perelman and Olbrechts-Tyteca's in particular. What I want to emphasize by using the concept of *topoi* is that even within an enterprise that is critical or analytical, *topoi* allow the focus of the analysis to remain on rhetoric as an art concerned centrally with the production—invention and judgment—of discourses. The *topoi* I trace in *Citizen Critics,* then, serve as both source and limitation for further discussion and deliberation.

Second, and very much related to Leff's continuum, *topoi* are architectonic in that, particularly when they manifest themselves as propositions (Leff, "Topics" 25), they serve as probabilistic foundations for the invention and judgment of arguments. I have in mind here something similar to what Richard McKeon describes:

> The commonplaces of creativity operate in the interpretation of texts as well as in the writing of texts, in the interpretation of experience as well as of statements, in the interpretation and formation of character, thought, actions, and things. . . . Commonplaces of invention may open up the perception of new meanings and applications even in a familiar text, which in turn uncovers previously unperceived lines of arguments to unnoticed conclusions which were not there until they were made facts by discovery. (36)

Like McKeon, Perelman and Olbrechts-Tyteca range across the wide history of topics and commonplaces. Revising and elaborating on Aristotle's and Quintilian's formulations of *topoi* (the Greek) or *loci* (the Latin), Perelman and Olbrechts-Tyteca stress the function of *loci* as bases for constructing values or hierarchies (83–84). My use of the term *topoi* combines these ancient and contemporary notions: in tracing the recurring *topoi* of public arguments about texts usually considered literary as well as the ways different writers associated or dissociated different *topoi* or changed *stases* when using these *topoi,* I reveal for study the rhetorical and discursive processes through which actual people, reading and writing publicly about provocative novels, endowed fictional texts with the capacity to effect social and political changes.

In his article on *topoi* and *loci,* Leff notes that

> even when limited to its technical use in rhetoric, the term "topic" incorporates a bewildering diversity of meanings. . . . Traditional formulations tell us little more than that a topic is a resource for an argument, or a seat of an argument, or a region in which an argument resides. Further explanation, when it occurs at all, is not of much theoretical value. Normally it takes the form of an allegory, where, to cite the classic example, the rhetor is a hunter, the argument his quarry, and the topic a locale in which the argument may be found. In short, the classical lore of topics is as confused as the modern efforts to revive it. (23–24)

Instead of adding to the confused efforts Leff describes, my bricoleur's use of *topoi* in *Citizen Critics* endeavors to add to the store of metaphors by which rhetoricians talk about topical invention. Leff himself sees propositions as the "atomic" unit of topical discourse. In addition to "atoms" or "seats" or "stores" or "the hunt," however, I would offer a more agricultural trope. The practice of *Citizen Critics* suggests that *topoi*-in-use are organic and, at least potentially, sustainable. They disclose argument from the common ground up. Rhetorical *topoi* are bioregions of discourse. Accordingly, my "methodology" in *Citizen Critics* has been to make judgments about which *topoi* were significant and which were not in each of the four literary public spheres I studied. Instead of approaching my case studies with guesses about what the significant *topoi* might be, I looked to the citizen critics themselves. When they engaged and responded to the particular *topoi* of other writers—when the *topoi* "grew"—I understood those *topoi* as significant.[11] In that sense, all literary public spheres are, at least potentially, local.

This study focuses on how the available means of persuasion open to citizen critics were limited and narrowed by the *topoi* of other discourses as well as by differences in power and cultural authority. Thus, Michel Foucault's discussion of systems or rules of exclusion, of silences, and of the agency of discourse in *The Archaeology of Knowledge* and "The Discourse on Language" provided another starting point. A statement of the theoretical assumptions behind Foucault's case studies or archaeologies,

*The Archaeology of Knowledge* adds to rhetorical analyses this question: "How is it that one particular statement appeared rather than another?" (27). In "The Discourse on Language" Foucault offers systems or rules of exclusion that limit what can be spoken and written; the analyses in the following chapters rest in part on the first of Foucault's rules of exclusion, prohibition: "We know perfectly well that we are not free to say just anything, that we cannot simply speak of anything, when we like or where we like; not just anyone, finally, may speak of just anything" (*Archaeology of Knowledge* 216).

Interpreting the causes and consequences of silence as well as of speech and writing depends on a view of discourse as itself having agency, a view Foucault reveals in two ways. First, through his syntax in the various archaeologies, Foucault reflects a view of discourse as both cause and consequence: often in *Madness and Civilization,* for example—in addition to a persistent use of the passive voice—he uses *meanings* as agent: "it is by comparing their work, and what it maintains, with the meanings that develop among their contemporaries" (31); "The new meanings assigned to poverty . . . determined the experience of madness and inflected its course" (64). Writers did not intend these meanings; these meanings developed, Foucault argues, and his archaeologies support his claims.

Foucault reveals this view of discourse also through explicit discussions of silence. For example, the silence of the listening psychoanalyst, because it is "an attentive silence," reproduces the distinction between madness and reason (*Archaeology of Knowledge* 217). It is the silence rather than the psychoanalyst that reproduces this one aspect of society. This view of discourse as having agency—what Foucault at one point refers to as "the great anonymous" (*History of Sexuality* 95)—avoids the finger-pointing analyses of who silenced whom and allows an interpretation of the process through which certain discourses allowed and disallowed certain responses.[12]

For Foucault, discourse itself has agency; for rhetoricians, *topoi* are known to have lives of their own. By combining contemporary continental theories (Habermas and Foucault) with classical rhetorical methods of analysis (*topoi, stases*) reiterated by new rhetoricians (Perelman and Olbrechts-Tyteca), *Citizen Critics* serves also as a performative argument that rhetorical theories can benefit from contemporary theories sensitive to historicity and power and that contemporary theories benefit from rhetoric's consistent concern with and lexicon for strategies of language use and its origins in democratic praxis and public life. In the following chapters, instead of giving a solely chronological account of the public discourses, I examine what arguments were made about each of the books, what interpretive principles were assumed or made explicit, and how those arguments might have helped determine which interpretations emerged as legitimate and authoritative. In chapter 6, I cull from the four case studies a sense of the shape of public criticism about literature, censorship, and social change that emerged as authoritative over the course of the twentieth century and argue for a pedagogy that might reinvigorate our democratic discursive practices. Again, instead of arguing for an interpretation that conjectures about how "the reader" should read or will react to *Ulysses, Tropic of Cancer, American Psycho,* or *Mercy,* I have focused on the public discourses written by citizen critics in response to these novels—and in response to one another—to affect public opinion about the books as well as about the issues their publication raised.

I end *Citizen Critics* by arguing that studying and participating in the discourses of literary public spheres has several advantages over traditional literary criticism and English studies pedagogy, both in protopublic classrooms and beyond, in wider, nonacademic publics. First, however, what are literary public spheres?

In a section of *The Structural Transformation of the Public Sphere* called "The Basic Blueprint," Habermas argues that early eighteenth-century family discussions of literary texts in the private sphere prefigured not only literary public spheres but also the bourgeois public sphere. Habermas argues, "Before the public sphere explicitly assumed political functions in the tension-charged field of state-society relations . . . the subjectivity originating in the intimate sphere of the conjugal family created, so to speak, its own public. It provided the training ground for a critical public reflection still preoccupied with itself—a process of self-clarification of private people focusing on the genuine experiences of their novel privateness" (29). These familial structural predecessors to what would become the literary and political public spheres of salons and coffeehouses created a public-oriented subjectivity.

What Habermas is suggesting, through his critical-empirical method, is that discussions of novels within the private sphere allowed for the formation of the kinds of public-oriented subjectivities that later found themselves comfortable engaging in rational-critical debate in those salons and coffeehouses we have heard so much about—so much so, in fact, that people moved from criticizing ideas in literary public spheres to criticizing state actions in bourgeois public spheres. At least locally, literary public spheres have existed in one form or another since before the rise of the bourgeois public sphere and can exist today—but not without effort from teachers, students, and other citizens.

Where might we look to find literary public spheres? Literary public spheres are discursive spaces in which private people can come together in public, bracket some of their differences, and invent common interests by arguing in speech or writing about literary and cultural texts. They are able to do so because, by moving from reader to rhetor, they have begun to manifest a public-oriented subjectivity, that is, a self that is more or less able to turn private reactions about literary or cultural texts into discourses that address some shared concerns. Among Habermas's many commentators, Peter Uwe Hohendahl has focused on literary public spheres' ability to foster certain kinds of subjectivity. In Hohendahl's words, "What Habermas used to call literary public spheres is precisely the locus where problems of identity and difference have been articulated" (108). Literary public spheres have nothing de facto to do with aesthetics; historically and contemporarily, literary public spheres reflect various publics' common concerns about the consequences of the news of literary and cultural texts for their collective lives.

In the twentieth century, literary public spheres have been most robust when institutional, expert literary critics have had the least cultural authority. The rise of English studies and the professionalization of something called first "literary critic" and then "literary theorist" relegated the opinions of nonexpert or citizen critics to a position of relatively little cultural authority. My studies of the discourses of literary public spheres suggest that nonexpert citizen critics have argued in public about literary texts— sometimes about whether those texts should be banned, but much more often about how what they defined as the news in those texts might affect their lives, their children's lives, and the public good. Teaching the rhetorics of literary public spheres and encouraging students to practice rhetoric in local literary public spheres offer promise as a post–English studies pedagogy because these practices allow literary and other cultural texts to matter—to become inventional prompts not to mere contemplation but to public rhetorical exchanges and action.

What is rhetoric's role in literary public spheres? Though *The Structural Transformation of the Public Sphere* is Habermas at his most rhetoric-friendly (his later work—with the exception of *Between Facts and Norms*— arguably relegates rhetoric to manipulation and systematically distorted communication), he is not concerned with rhetoric as a historical praxis of thinking and acting and thus did not dwell explicitly on rhetoric's central role in literary and other kinds of public spheres. Rhetoric's role in literary public spheres is to help readers become rhetors. The process of forming public-oriented subjectivities helps students make arguments about literary and cultural texts as well as choose whether to form and then enter literary public spheres wherein other citizen critics can form judgments, not only of the literary text, but also of the *topoi* it raises. Rhetoric's role as a productive and a practical art as well as an analytical and a theoretical art puts it at the center of the activities of literary public spheres; without the ability to produce discourses, readers would never become rhetors; individual readers would never have to leave the consolation of the *vita contemplativa* and come out into the realm of rhetoric. Further, the practice of rhetoric in literary public spheres allows students a *locus* for inventing public-oriented subjectivities, something increasingly difficult to understand and do as public life is continually eroded.

Before examining the discourses of citizen critics themselves, however, I will first critique interpretive strategies that posit how "the reader" has read or should respond to literary discourses. Then I situate my discussion among various theorizations of publics and public spheres and review the work of critics who have tried to examine the relationship between literature and society. Finally, I close the chapter with a discussion of the benefits of an explicitly rhetorical approach to publics and suggest that a rhetorical study of public discourses written in response to controversial literary texts can help critics describe the process through which literary texts affect and perhaps enable democratic society. To put this another way, my enterprise here is an attempt to use rhetorical theory to change the focus of literary history and criticism in much the same way that social theory changed the focus of historiography (Thelen "Round Table"). That is, instead of focusing on "great man" renderings of literature or criticism—histories that posit novelistic or critical geniuses whose individual discursive acts changed society single-handedly—*Citizen Critics* attempts to move the focus of the critical act away from individual texts and individual readings and toward a more collective sense of interpretive rhetorical practice. That one consequence of this change of focus results in viewing institutional literary critics as marginal rather than central figures is not accidental. In that way, this project also serves as an alternative cultural history of criticism—but public criticism—in the twentieth century.

## "The Reader" and "The Audience"

Institutionalized literary criticism in the twentieth century, specifically since the effects of various formalisms translated themselves into the new criticism, has explicitly or implicitly relied for support of its arguments on appeals to what "the reader" would think of the text in question. Even as

criticism becomes more concerned with context—focusing on the psychology of the writer or of the reader or on the historical situation in which
the text was produced or is consumed—most criticism still relies on what
"the reader" or "we" will see during the process of reading. While such
abstractions present problems for any interpretation, they are especially
problematic for the controversial novels studied here. I must be clear that
my interest is not to explain or account for differences among interpretations; rather, I want to use those differences to show how a work of fiction
can lead to deliberation about public issues—political as well as aesthetic—
in literary public spheres. As the samples of discourse in successive chapters of this project will show, assumptions about how readers will read are
rarely absolutely textually "correct"; more importantly, the hegemonic
quality of such assumptions potentially limits the range of actual readings;
and, most serious for my enterprise, assumptions about "the reader" posit
reading as a private rather than as a public or even a social experience,
neither informed by nor informing other interpretations of the text.

Early in the twentieth century, I. A. Richards sought to ward off the effects of aestheticism and the critical whims of a burgeoning reading public by setting forth, as one of his titles suggests, *Principles of Literary Criticism*. Richards's aim was to educate readers, and while he insisted that he
was "not writing for specialists alone" (3), he explained that his purpose
was "to bring the level of popular appreciation nearer to the consensus of
best qualified opinion" (36). Indeed, it is clear that—even though he
worked with actual readers, some of whom wrote "protocols" for him
(*Practical* 4)—Richards was looking for the "right" kind of reader: when
he reports on two readers who disagreed about a Wordsworth sonnet to
the point that they "produced two different poems," he adds that "neither would be uncharacteristic of Wordsworth, although doubtless the first
reading is the one to be accepted" (*Principles* 208). The judge Richards
seeks is, ultimately, himself; the codified principles, his own: "no one in a
position to judge, who has, for example, some experience of teaching
English" (212) would mistake a false reading for "the true view" (63). Thus
Richards's move from aestheticism into the text, a move that advanced
literary criticism as a profession in many ways, nonetheless shifted the focus
of criticism away from actual readers and toward another kind of aesthete:
the "qualified" reader whose qualifications were delineated nowhere but
were merely suggested by the tastes of or actually embodied by the critic.

Yet as criticism started to become more rhetorically oriented, most markedly in the work of Wayne C. Booth, considerations of "the reader" did
not change significantly. Booth's *Rhetoric of Fiction* focuses on "the

author's means of controlling his reader" (xiii); while claiming to be concerned with the effects of narratives, Booth assumes those effects are the same for all readers. To wit, he uses the first person plural throughout *The Rhetoric of Fiction,* starting on the opening page: "'There was a man in the land of Uz, whose name was Job; and that man was perfect and upright, one that feared God, and eschewed evil.' With one stroke the unknown author has given *us* a kind of information never obtained about real people, even about *our* most intimate friends. Yet it is information that *we* must accept without question if *we* are to grasp the story that is to follow" (3; my emphasis). In the afterword to the second edition, however, Booth—characteristically and to his credit—confronts his own rhetoric: "I am shocked at the confidence my younger self sometimes shows in reporting how 'we' respond. Who are we, here? 'We' flesh-and-blood readers are unpredictable, and no one can speak with high reliability about us" (420). Nonetheless, Booth sticks to an abstraction—because his text-based methodology requires it, I need to add—that focuses on "the relatively stable audience postulated by the implied author" (421). Booth's *The Company We Keep,* for all its virtues as an ethics of fiction, suffers from a similar myopia; my enterprise here, again, is to understand acts of reading as public and rhetorical rather than private: the company kept by various literary works is more voluminous and polyphonic than Booth allows. Indeed, there are many different ways for audiences to make sense of texts within the constraints laid out by their implied authors, an issue raised but not engaged by other rhetoricians, among them Walter J. Ong in "A Writer's Audience Is Always a Fiction."[13]

Given its name, reader-response criticism offers what would sound like the most promising alternative for studying real readers. In her introduction to the collection of essays entitled *Reader-Response Criticism,* Jane P. Tompkins explains that

> reader-response criticism is not a conceptually unified critical position, but a term that has come to be associated with the work of critics who use the words *reader, the reading process,* and *response* to mark out an area for investigation. . . . Reader-response critics would argue that a poem cannot be understood apart from its results. Its "effects," psychological and otherwise, are essential to any accurate description of its meaning, since that meaning has no effective existence outside of its realization in the mind of a reader. (ix)

Yet reader-response criticism—from such text-based studies as Walker Gibson's and Booth's to the work of the phenomenologist Georges Poulet to the more interactional but still essentially formalist approaches of

Wolfgang Iser through its manifestation in such nomenclature as *narratee* (Prince) and *superreader* (Riffaterre)—only very rarely confronts the reality of real readers reading.

Similar to Iser's work in the way it makes inferences about readers from various formal aspects of literary texts, the work of Hans Robert Jauss is more sensitive to history than reader-response criticism is. Jauss, who influenced both reader-response and new historicist criticisms in the eighties, argued for an aesthetics of reception that enabled critics to generalize about readers' differing "horizons of expectations" (3–13; Machor vii–xi; Holub 16–19). Jauss's work encouraged critics to write "reception histories" of particular literary texts and to trace how readers might have read the same text differently at different historical moments. Yet because his reception aesthetic does not focus on individual readers or particular groups of readers, Jauss's work, too, fails to move criticism toward a serious engagement with the processes through which actual readers come to terms with literary texts—particularly in ways that are other than aesthetic.

When reader-response criticism does concern itself with actual readers, as in the work of Norman Holland, it often insists on an isolated individual reader instead of conceiving of reading and interpretation as social processes. Holland, a psychoanalytic reader-response critic who uses the responses of actual readers in *Five Readers Reading,* insists on ascribing all differences among readings to differences among individual personalities: "At the Center for the Psychological Study of the Arts, we have found that we can explain such differences in interpretation by examining differences in the personalities of the interpreters. More precisely, *interpretation is a function of identity*" ("Unity" 123). Holland defines identity as "an unchanging inner form or core of continuity" that each individual receives from her or his "mother-person" ("Unity" 121). Holland leaves no room for the social in the individual's psychology, and, along with David Bleich, sees reading as valuable only insofar as it teaches individual readers about their individual identities.

While he differs somewhat from Holland on the nature of interpretation, Bleich also advocates an interpretive practice that has at its core a concern with individual identities. In *Subjective Criticism,* Bleich hopes to restore the subjective nature of interpretation as against the "objective" and scientist urges of new criticism and generative linguistics. While Bleich's view of interpretation at first seems promising—he provides a way of seeing subjective criticism as socially constructed and as producing new knowledge—his ultimate focus on the psychodynamics of the classroom makes his work, at best, of little value for those concerned with the social effects of literature and, at worst, worrisome in terms of power and pedagogy.

Though the literature classroom is a priori a community of shared concerns for Bleich, there is no outside to this community; ultimately, the matter at hand is the psyche of each student. Bleich teaches subjective criticism by having his students submit "response statements" (132) that are then shared with the class in one form or another. Bleich describes a response statement as "a symbolic presentation of self, a contribution to a pedagogical community, and an articulation of that part of our reading experience we think we can negotiate into knowledge" (167). What is most troubling about Bleich's pedagogy is how he, first, evaluates response statements and, second, interprets them. Response statements are rewarded to the extent that they reflect "serious self-examination" (139), Bleich writes; in one example Bleich assesses a response statement as "psychologically authentic" (141) because the student answered all the questions. Bleich's interpretation of students' response statements points to the danger of viewing the classroom as concerned ultimately with individuals and their subjectivities and as a place in which a teacher can peer into students' "real" selves. As does Holland, Bleich reads interpretive practices as representations of individual psyches only; there is no room for an examination of the social—either in terms of the rhetorical nature of competing interpretations or in terms of the social nature of how fictional texts and interpretations of them affect social practices.

Decades before the term *reader-response* was coined, however, Louise Rosenblatt wrote her landmark *Literature as Exploration,* one of the earliest examples of criticism that considered the role individual readers play in making meaning of texts. In her preface to the first edition (1938), she posits the necessity of viewing the reader and the act of reading as active rather than passive; it is the transactional nature of Rosenblatt's approach to literature, expanded in her 1978 book, *The Reader, the Text, the Poem,* that makes her work most attractive for reader-response theorists and, indeed, any kind of criticism or theory focusing on actual readers as active participants in the social process of meaning-making. Like Bleich, Rosenblatt focuses on actual readers only through anecdotes; but the great strength of her work is her emphasis on the active and social nature of interpretation. "I have attempted to keep in the center of attention certain human pictures," Rosenblatt writes of her project in *Literature as Exploration:* "the student reading a book, immersed in the world it conjures up, or the student, his classmates, and the teacher interchanging ideas about it" (xii). Rosenblatt's theorization of reading as a historically specific social act sets her apart from other critics of all stripes and provides a ground for further theorizations of the social process of interpretation outside as well as inside the classroom.

Rosenblatt wrote in opposition to the pedagogical focus on literary history as well as to new critical formalism, which she described as "the current, almost hypnotically repeated, emphasis on 'the work itself' as distinct from author and reader" (277). She proposes a pedagogy to reflect her view of the dual social and aesthetic dimensions of interpretation. Briefly, she recommends that, first, teachers must create a setting in which students feel free to respond personally to literature; second, teachers must lead students in the process of "critically reevaluating" their assumptions and preoccupations through discussing interpretations with fellow students and teachers. Rosenblatt envisions a classroom that allows for "a free exchange of ideas" (110) and in which students will learn to compare and contrast their own personal views with socially established interpretive agreements. Finally, students and teachers should return to the text and to literary history—what Rosenblatt calls "background information" (123). This kind of information will have value "only when the student feels the need of it and when it is assimilated into the student's experience of particular literary works" (123).

Through following these three pedagogical steps, Rosenblatt maintains, students and teachers will arrive together at "a sound vision of the work" (79). Though she is infinitely kinder than Richards to readers' personal interpretations, she, too, sees certain interpretations as incorrect and literature as a means of gaining "critical consciousness of the strength or weaknesses of the emotional and intellectual equipment with which [the student] approaches literature (and life)" (107). In fact, reading and interpreting literature is for Rosenblatt a means of dialectical purification for students in which the personal is seen as limited and limiting and as needing to be replaced by the more universal: "Out of this (transaction among text, reader, and other readers) will arise a wider perspective and a readjustment of the framework of values with which to meet further experiences in literature and life" (108). Students exchange their personal reactions to literature for "fuller and sounder" interpretations (108) that conform to "universal human" concerns:

> If each author were completely different from every other human being, and if each reader were totally unique, there could, of course, be no communication. There are many experiences that we all have in common—birth, growth, love, death. We can communicate because of a common core of experience, even though there may be infinite personal variations. Human beings participate in

particular social systems and fall into groups such as age, sex, occupation, nation. These, too, offer general patterns upon which individual variations can be played. (27–28)

For Rosenblatt, as for Holland and Bleich, individual students are the ultimate concern. What sets Rosenblatt apart from these other critics, however, is her understanding of the social nature of interpretation. Bracketing her historically explicable focus on what is "universal" in literature, Rosenblatt's articulation of the social and interactive nature of interpretive practice makes her a valuable precursor to publics theory. In Rosenblatt's transactional conception of the reading process I have found the only example of self-described reader-response criticism not to let assumptions about "the reader" stand in the way of a social conception of interpretation.

Sometimes grouped with Rosenblatt in surveys of reader-response criticism for emphasizing the social nature of interpretation, Stanley Fish argued in 1980 for the the authority of interpretive communities (*Is There a Text in This Class?*). Though he uses the term *communities,* Fish's interpretive groups are social only insofar as individual interpreters happen to share interpretive assumptions with other individual interpreters; how they come to share those assumptions is not Fish's concern. In "Interpreting the *Variorum*" Fish begins by arguing that especially indeterminate passages, what he calls interpretive cruxes, "are not *meant* to be solved but to be experienced (they signify), and that consequently any procedure that attempts to determine which of a number of readings is correct will necessarily fail" (149). Fish argues that critics should make textual problems signify and that criticism should focus on "the reader's experience" of working through those cruxes: "It is the structure of the reader's experience rather than any structures available on the page that should be the object of description" (152). While most of "Interpreting the *Variorum*" focuses on individual readers, in the last few pages of the essay Fish uses the concept of interpretive communities as a means of arguing that "the notions of the 'same' or 'different' texts are fictions" (169). Interpretive communities, because they share certain interpretive assumptions and critical strategies, agree on what constitutes a certain text: "the notion 'same text' is the product of the possession by two or more readers of similar interpretive strategies. . . . These strategies exist prior to the act of reading and therefore determine the shape of what is read rather than, as is usually assumed, the other way around" (171). Perhaps because Fish's conception of interpretive communities functions as a means to another, larger end—his attempt to destabilize the formalist conception of "text"—

he seems to have no interest in the process through which different individual readers acquire, grapple with, accept, or reject interpretive assumptions and conventions.

Janice Radway's enterprise in *Reading the Romance* was to complicate critical responses to romance fiction and its cultural effects by using theories of reader response—she cites Fish's *Is There a Text in This Class?* in particular—as well as surveys of and interviews with real readers of romance novels. Though years earlier than other work in English studies focused on "reading publics," Radway uses *public* in *Reading the Romance* without any concern for the character and consequences of public discourse more generally or of the connection between public discourse and other practices of democracy (50–59). Ultimately, Radway's project makes inferences about the beliefs, needs, and values of "regular readers," as she calls them (9): "In the end, what I intend to offer here is a comprehensive explanation of why the women I interviewed find romance reading not only practically feasible and generally enjoyable but also emotionally necessary" (10). Like Bleich and Rosenblatt, Radway is ultimately concerned in *Reading the Romance* with individual motives for reading, not with the consequences of reading and writing for larger social and political structures. More damaging to the credibility of her study as an alternative critical method, she relies ultimately on a generalized if not idealized reader, one she calls "the composite reader" (14).

Like *Reading the Romance,* Radway's *A Feeling for Books* focuses on institutions and their effects on U.S. culture as reflected through the reading practices of middle America. While Radway's vast study of the Book-of-the-Month Club and its effects on middlebrow taste across the twentieth century complicates the means and pluralizes the sites of criticism, she addresses only the differences among different classes of reader, not those among different individual readers. Further, while she mentions Habermas and some of his literary commentators (Warner, Berlant, and Schudson), Radway is not concerned with the connection between the reading of literary texts and the formation of publics—or the possibility of democracy. Speaking from her "personal" or "private" history as well as from the vantages of literary criticism and ideology critique, Radway uses *private* and *public* unproblematically, as when she claims: "I was intensely aware of the intricate nature of the connection between my private past and my effort to make sense of the public history of the Book-of-the-Month Club" (12). "The public" is thus for Radway no more complicated than it was for the editors and marketers of the Book-of-the-Month Club catalogs, her cultural heroes.

Literary criticism, like traditional historiography, has tended to see literature and interpretation as individual acts of highly idealized or "great" actors. Even when critics championed focusing solely on texts or theorizing how "the reader" reads they have, with the partial exceptions of Rosenblatt and Radway, seen literature and interpretation not in terms of social phenomena carried on by real readers and concerning real-life effects but in terms of ideal readers, ideal authors, ideal texts, and ahistorical human concerns. The mass communications scholar Martin Allor has critiqued assumptions about "audience" in a somewhat similar fashion to what I am here suggesting about arguments that center on "the reader." He concludes that generalizations about audiences or readers tend to "bracket out analysis of the mediations between the practices of individuals and social rules, codes, and ideologies" (217). Allor suggests an interpretive practice that, instead of "propping up" its claims with an abstraction, would "realize that behind the abstraction there are different (at times incommensurate) questions concerning the relations of individuals, texts, practices, social organization, and social power" and would not "seek to subsume differences under the rubric of a single conceptualization" (217). This project is an attempt to argue for and demonstrate one such possible alternative critical practice. By studying the divergent and interacting interpretations of actual readers writing about fictional texts in rhetorically constructed literary public spheres, I want to suggest that public criticism may provide a better means than literary criticism does of studying the process through which literature has affected society.

## Publics Theories and Their Problems

*Ulysses, Tropic of Cancer, American Psycho,* and *Mercy* are more than literary artifacts; these books and the questions they have raised have been public issues discussed in conversation, written about in print, and—in some cases—addressed in broadcast media. In *The Function of Criticism,* Terry Eagleton articulates a need for the kind of change in critical focus I want to suggest through *Citizen Critics:* "criticism today lacks all substantive social function"; his enterprise is to raise "the question of what substantive social functions criticism might once again fulfill in our own time" (8). Eagleton's call is echoed by an increasing number of voices in criticism, cultural studies, and pedagogy. Stanley Aronowitz and Henry A. Giroux lament "the disappearance of political intellectuals" and argue that such a disappearance "corresponds to the passing of politics from 'public' life" (31). And Giroux argues that social criticism and pedagogy (and both of these as forms of the other) should lead to "critical citizenship," in which "critical educators" become "public intellectuals" in order to revitalize public life (*Border Crossings* 4, 242). Many scholars in cultural studies, too, argue that criticism and theory should play a wider social and political role (Lentricchia 7–8; Hall 280). But whereas these writers bemoan a lost public life or argue for a renewed one, they rarely either define what they mean by "public life" or, by engaging with those who have written about it, offer any accounts of how public life might be renewed. Given the growing sense that criticism should have a social function—and as a theoretical framework for the four case studies in this book that suggest public criticism has had social functions—I here examine theories of publics, how they form, what their purposes are, and how, while publics theory solves interpretive problems that conceptions of readers and audiences cannot, it is not without problems of its own.[14]

Since James Madison published what would become *The Federalist No. 10* in a New York newspaper, tension between factional interests and "the public good" has been a central issue in American democracy. In *Federalist No. 10,* Madison examined the causes of faction, delineated the consequences of tyrannies of the majority, and decided that "we behold a republican remedy for the diseases most incident to republican government" (23), a conclusion still argued today—most notably among civil libertarians and antipornography feminists. Madison's call for "a republican remedy" is echoed by John Dewey in *The Public and Its Problems:* how to cure the ills of democracy? More democracy. But Madison's and Dewey's conclusions do not explain how democracy can heal itself. While focusing on other primary characteristics of publics—e.g., the political (Dewey), the theatrical (Sennett), or the economic (Habermas and his commentators)—theorists have implicitly yet consistently suggested the rhetorical nature of publics and their formation. I will here focus on what these theorists of publics and public spheres can add to contemporary understanding of the nature and function of public discussion of any kind; of course in this project my ultimate interest is in public discussions about texts usually considered literary. Then I will discuss the benefits of an explicitly rhetorical approach to publics and what distinguishes interpretive practices situated in discussions of publics from those situated in discussions of audiences or readers.

While arguing for a representative form of democracy, Madison implicitly supported a rhetorical conception of faction and the public good. Admitting that curtailing the causes of faction would be unwise and unpracticable, as faction is an expected consequence of democracy—"The latent causes of faction are sown in the nature of man" (18)—Madison argues that a representative government of enlightened legislators is the best cure for the consequences of faction. Because of their capacity for disinterestedness among their common interest, enlightened legislators would be able to prevent the ills of faction, Madison reasons. How would these legislators achieve this disinterestedness? Through shared discourse, or "communication" (22)—the same means they would use to recognize their constituents' common interest. While foreshadowing many of the problems inherent in a liberal-democratic conception of the public, *Federalist No. 10* is an early recognition of the role of discourse and debate in solving the problems of faction versus the public good.

Drawing on many of Madison's conclusions yet fueled by post–World War I disillusionment with the democratic process, John Dewey's *The Public and Its Problems* begins by setting out a theory of publics and their formation that is primarily political, focusing on the relationship between the people and the state. According to Dewey, what distinguishes public from private transactions are the indirect consequences that accrue from public actions (12, 15–16). As Dewey builds his theory of publics, he moves away from the political as primary and becomes more explicit about the role of communication—especially literary or artistic—in the process whereby publics identify themselves.

Using Walter Lippmann's phrase, Dewey maintains that "the public is bewildered" (116) because the country is held together not by genuine common interests but by technological means: "Railways, travel and transportation, commerce, the mails, telegraph and telephone, newspapers create enough similarity of ideas and sentiments to keep the thing going as a whole, for they create interaction and interdependence" (114). Modern technologies make the nation appear to be unified; but the appearance is formal rather than substantive, Dewey argues. In spite of attained integration, or perhaps because of its nature, "the Public seems to be lost; it is certainly bewildered" (116); "the public is so bewildered that it cannot find itself" (122–23). Additionally, he suggests, individuals are isolated from each other and unaware not only of their social natures—"While singular beings in their singularity think, want, and decide, *what* they think and strive for, the content of their beliefs and intentions is a subject-matter provided by association" (25)—but also that their actions affect others. Dewey believes individuals share the consequences of individual actions because individuals are associated: "Singular things act, but they act together. Nothing has been discovered which acts in entire isolation. The action of everything is along with the action of other things. The 'along with' is of such a kind that the behavior of each is modified by its connection with the other" (22). One cause of the public's bewilderment is people's lack of awareness of their social natures and that they can change the state and themselves through what he calls "conjoint behavior" (23):

> Indirect, extensive, enduring and serious consequences of conjoint and interacting behavior call a public into existence having a common interest in controlling these consequences. But the machine age has so enormously expanded, multiplied, intensified and complicated the scope of the indirect consequences, have [*sic*] formed such immense and consolidated unions in action, on an impersonal rather than a community basis, that the resultant public cannot identify and distinguish itself. And this discovery is obviously an antecedent condition of any effective organization on its part. (126)

Unaware that they share the consequences not only of their actions but also of the policies of the state in which they live, citizens cannot find and identify common interest as the basis for conjoint action.

What remedy can there be for a public that does not recognize itself? Near the end of *The Public and Its Problems,* Dewey makes his solution explicit, declaring that improving the means and methods of communication is the only way citizens can recognize their common interest: "The essential need, in other words, is the improvement of the methods and conditions of debate, discussion and persuasion. That is *the* problem of the public. We have asserted that this improvement depends essentially upon freeing and perfecting the processes of inquiry and of dissemination of their conclusions" (208). Necessary for improved communication is absolute noncensorship, Dewey argues, but noncensorship alone is not enough: "The belief that thought and communication are now free simply because legal restrictions which once obtained have been done away with is absurd. . . . No man and no mind was ever emancipated merely by being left alone. Removal of formal limitations is but a negative condition; positive freedom is not a state but an act which involves methods and instrumentalities for control of conditions" (168). Indeed, for a public to recognize itself, action is required; a public in Dewey's terms requires that people not only consume communications that convince them of their common interest but also produce communications—speak or write in common—about that interest.

Dewey has in mind a specific kind of public medium. First of all, common interest and shared consequences cannot be communicated through the specialized discourses of highbrow experts. In addition, "the news" will not do as a means of recognizing common interest because business interests control publishers. Rather, Dewey says, "the inquiry which alone can furnish knowledge as a precondition of public judgments must be contemporary and quotidian" (180). Unlike the news media and academic journals, Dewey reasons, literature—when artists are free to write what they please—is less constrained and more likely to address and get responses from the quotidian:

> The freeing of the artist in literary presentation, in other words, is as much a precondition of the desirable creation of adequate opinion on public matters as is the freeing of social inquiry. Men's conscious life of opinion and judgment often proceeds on a superficial and trivial plane. But their lives reach a deeper level. The function of art has always been to break through the crust of conventionalized and routine consciousness. Common things, a flower, a gleam of moonlight, the song of a bird, not things rare and remote, are means with which the deeper levels of life are touched so that they spring up as desire and thought. This process is art. Poetry, the drama, the novel, are proofs that the problem of presentation is not insoluble. Artists have always been the real purveyors of news, for it is not the outward happening in itself which is new, but the kindling by it of emotion, perception, and appreciation. (182–84)

Dewey sees literary artists, "the real purveyors of news," as one primary means through which publics can recognize their common interests and shared consequences and work toward engaging in conjoint action. In this way, he invites analysis of how literary production elicits responses from the quotidian and encourages publics to recognize themselves.

The stakes of this multiplicity of publics are so high for Dewey because he sees the consequences of community—people sharing through reading, writing, speaking, and listening their recognition of common interests and consequences—as imperative for the continued political health not only of the United States but also of the world. "To learn to be human is to develop through the give-and-take of communication an effective sense of being an individually distinctive member of a community," he writes, "one who understands and appreciates its beliefs, desires and methods, and who contributes to a further conversion of organic powers into human resources and values" (154). Dewey's view of communitarianism as part of human education makes him tend toward the Great Community as his telos. At his best, he is aware of how unlikely his ideal is: "The Great Community, in the sense of free and full intercommunication, is conceivable," he insists. Yet he hedges his bet in a way that makes his theory of publics ultimately useful for contemporary scholars of publics: "But it can never possess all the qualities which mark a local community" (211).

Indeed, Dewey's constant move from "it" to "they," from "the public"

to "publics" and from "the Great Community" to "communities"—
though not what he wanted to stress—shows that he can be read as
emphasizing the local and the situated rather than the unified and the transcendent. He often uses "public" preceded by the indefinite article, pre-
figuring a move Nancy Fraser would make in one of her responses to
Habermas. And from time to time he sees the positive consequences of one
great, common public manifest themselves in more local, partial publics:
"Wherever there is conjoint activity whose consequences are appreciated
as good by all singular persons who take part in it, and where the realiza-
tion of the good is such as to effect an energetic desire and effort to sustain it in being just because it is a good shared by all, there is in so far a
community. The clear consciousness of a communal life, in all its implications, constitutes the idea of democracy" (149). This is the Dewey who
allows for the positive effects of local communities to pertain, even though
a particular public does not include every member of the nation. And in
addition to allowing for the local, Dewey at times leaves room for the tran-
sient nature of publics, though quite grudgingly: "What is the public? Is
the public a myth? Or does it come into being only in periods of marked
social transition when crucial alternative issues stand out, such as that
between throwing one's lot in with the conservation of established institutions or with forwarding new tendencies?" (123). Dewey's emphases on
literary texts as "news" and on private people recognizing common interests through reading and writing suggest that, while his reason for writing was his concern about a bewildered public writ large, he allows hope
for the reemergence of local and temporal publics, groups of private people
connected through common concerns and conjoint action and energized
by common texts.

While Richard Sennett would agree with Dewey that public life is in
eclipse, Sennett, in *The Fall of Public Man,* is more explicit about the role
of rhetoric—a rhetoric of display, anyway—in the *theatrum mundi,* the
stage on which eighteenth-century "public man" played out his publicness.
According to Sennett, the fall of public man came about when public codes
and means of coexisting and discoursing as equals[15] were replaced by an
obsession with an "authentic" self, which has culminated in the culture
of narcissism. The emergence of the intimate society, Sennett argues, has
prevented twentieth-century humanity from being able to coexist peace-
fully and productively in public, using agreed-upon codes of believability.
Besides codes of believability, Sennett's emphasis on a presentational rather
than a representational view of speech and dress make his theory of public behavior useful in reading public discourses about literary texts.

Sennett articulates his enterprise in *The Fall of Public Man* as creating "a theory of expression in public" (6). In this light, the book opens with a critique of contemporary public life centering on a Christopher Lasch–inspired view of narcissism, the end point of the fall of public man: narcissism "has arisen because a new kind of society encourages the growth of its psychic components and erases a sense of meaningful social encounter outside its terms, outside the boundaries of the single self, in public" (8). This new kind of society is void of public spaces where people can linger and interact. Instead, public spaces are meant to be moved through by isolated individuals rather than used for communication and, of secondary importance to Sennett, joint action by groups.

Sennett's historical metaphor of a fall depends, of course, upon a prelapsarian state, in this case, the *theatrum mundi* of eighteenth-century coffeehouses, salons, theaters, and opera houses in Paris and London. In these public places, "places where strangers might regularly meet" (17), people were "determined to remain strangers to each other" (23) instead of becoming intimates. Sennett studied "visual and verbal appearances in public," styles of dress, distinctions between public and private, and the material conditions of the two eighteenth-century capitals. During the eighteenth century, the emergence of the bourgeoisie created "a milieu of strangers in which many people [were] increasingly like each other but [did not] know it" (49). Sennett uses Daniel Defoe's descriptions of London and Pierre Marivaux's of Paris to exemplify the eighteenth-century capital, "a place where people of unknown origins can 'pass' because the whole city has grown through the migration of 'unknown quantities'" (52). Because no one is sure where his or her fellow city-dwellers come from, it is unclear what kind of behavior will gain the attention and belief of others in public, a realm of experience separate from private or intimate life.

It is in the *theatrum mundi* that codes of believability were tested and accepted by city-dwellers unsure of how to appear believable. Again, Sennett uses literary examples—Henry Fielding and Jean-Jacques Rousseau—to describe the *theatrum mundi,* a place where a "bridge was built between what was believable on the stage and what was believable on the street. . . . This bridge, in turn, gave men the means to be sociable, on impersonal grounds" (64). One characteristic of communication within the *theatrum mundi* was that speech was treated as a sign rather than as a symbol, that is, it was presentational rather than representational. Unlike in today's intimate society, in which "people speak of doing something 'unconsciously' or making an 'unconscious' slip which reveals their true feel-

ings to someone else" (24), in public life, "social *expression* will be con-
ceived of *as presentation* to other people of feelings which signify in and
of themselves, *rather than as representation* to other people of feeling
present and real to each self" (39). As such, public life shared much with
acting; the *theatrum mundi* existed before nineteenth-century ideas of the
authentic self came on the scene. The collapse of separate public and private spheres, Sennett argues, has deprived human beings of a realm in
which to present selves different from their private, perhaps "authentic"
selves. In this way, the intimate society prevents people from expressing
different selves to one another; "we are artists without an art" (28), Sennett
claims, and the art we have lost is playacting: "With an emphasis on psychological authenticity, people become inartistic in daily life because they
are unable to tap the fundamental creative strength of the actor, the ability to play with and invest feeling in external images of self. Thus we arrive at the hypothesis that theatricality has a special, hostile relation to
intimacy; theatricality has an equally special, friendly relation to a strong
public life" (37). Sennett's work allows for a presentational rather than
(as in Bleich and Holland) a psychological representational mode of reading acts of interpretation and thus assists in theorizing about public spaces
or spheres in which private people write publicly about works of literature in order to do more than solely get to know themselves better.

   While Sennett's critique of narcissism holds out little hope for any reemergence of publicness from the intimate society, Habermas's discussion
of literary public spheres suggests at least a glimmer. My use of Habermas
in this book seconds Thomas McCarthy's view of an "early" and a "later"
Habermas in his introduction to Habermas's *Communication and the Evolution of Society*. Though McCarthy's introduction does not mention *The
Structural Transformation of the Public Sphere* (it had not yet been translated into English[16]), that book, with its emphasis on the preeminence of
language in actual social practices, reflects Habermas's thought before he
encountered speech-act theory and began formulating his totalizing theories of human social action and universal pragmatics. In addition, the
Habermas of *The Structural Transformation of the Public Sphere* allows
a wider role for literature and argument in society; by the late seventies,
rhetoric for Habermas was merely strategic, its only end being control, and
literature was merely symbolic (not in a Burkean sense), its only end being self-expression. Habermas's analysis in *The Structural Transformation
of the Public Sphere* offers rhetorical and literary critics an opportunity
to test through their critical practices a historical conjecture that suggests

literary texts and the arguments of actual people in response to those texts played a primary role in creating the subjectivities that enabled enormous social changes.

In *The Structural Transformation of the Public Sphere,* Habermas not only chronicles the emergence and degeneration of the bourgeois public sphere but also stresses the importance of what he calls the "public sphere in the world of letters" of the eighteenth century. That literary public sphere, Habermas argues, was the structural predecessor to the bourgeois public sphere: "The public sphere in the political realm evolved from the public sphere in the world of letters; through the vehicle of public opinion it put the state in touch with the needs of society" (30–31). The public sphere, for Habermas, consisted of "public discussion among private individuals" (55), or "private people engaged in public rational-critical debate" (160). Habermas explains the "public" quality of the public sphere by distinguishing between "the affairs that private people pursued individually each in the interests of the reproduction of his own life and . . . the sort of interaction that united private people into a public" (160). Private people debating about issues that interest and concern them all constitutes for Habermas a public sphere; it does not preexist either spatially or temporally but rather comes into being as individuals engage in rational-critical debate.

Again, while not focusing explicitly on the rhetorical nature of the public sphere, Habermas nonetheless notes the importance of discussion among equals in a common space as the major criterion for the bourgeois public sphere. Indeed, what allowed that sphere to exist in the first place were the structures put in place by the literary public spheres of eighteenth-century Europe, in which reading publics became aware of themselves—much in Dewey's sense of recognizing common interests and shared consequences. Given that it was public discourse in speech and writing that fostered public spheres—a point seconded by Eagleton in *The Function of Criticism*—there is hope that a similar though historically and economically distinct literary public sphere could again create the structures for a robust extraliterary public sphere. This conclusion is, however, somewhat different from Habermas's own: he sees intraorganizational public spheres as the key to any future public sphere in the social welfare state of mass society. It is important to note, however, that for Habermas any reinvigoration of the public sphere would occur through intensive and reflective discourse and debate, what he calls "critical publicity" (248), and that each of the novels on which *Citizen Critics* focuses has fostered exceptional discourse and debate—often, because of the censorship issues involved, over the very question of publicity.

Habermas's conception of the public sphere has been addressed by several scholars who, regardless of their critiques, find the notion a rich starting point for analyzing discourse.[17] Nancy Fraser, for example, in "Rethinking the Public Sphere," critiques Habermas's contention that in the public sphere "discussion was to be open and accessible to all; merely private interests were to be inadmissible; inequalities of status were to be bracketed; and discussants were to deliberate as peers" (59). Fraser has argued that such idyllic conditions never actually existed,[18] that society has always consisted of competing interest groups, most of whom were silenced by the way "debate about the common good" was perceived. Social inequalities were not eliminated but only bracketed, Fraser argues, and "discursive interaction within the bourgeois public sphere was governed by protocols of style and decorum that were themselves correlates and markers of status inequality. These functioned informally to marginalize women and members of the plebian classes and to prevent them from participating as peers" (63).

Thus, Fraser has theorized the existence of what she calls subaltern counterpublics, which she defines as "parallel discursive arenas where members of subordinated social groups invent and circulate counterdiscourses, which in turn permit them to formulate oppositional interpretations of their identities, interests, and needs" (67). These counterpublics serve two roles: first, to support the subordinated groups among themselves; and, second, to train members of these groups to engage in "activities directed toward wider publics" (69). Although publics theory has advanced greatly because of Fraser's critique of Habermas, my enterprise is to analyze the different voices *within different public spheres* rather than to look at the counterdiscourses *within the groups themselves*. In other words, instead of studying the discourses of the New York Society for the Suppression of Vice by reading its internal newsletter or of professional writers by reading the *Authors Guild Monthly,* I chose instead to focus on how the arguments of and within these groups entered the public sphere through the more general print media.[19] "All told, then," Fraser writes, "there do not seem to be any conceptual (as opposed to empirical) barriers to the possibility of a socially egalitarian, multi-cultural society that is also a participatory democracy. But this will necessarily be a society with many different publics, including at least one public in which participants can deliberate as peers across lines of difference about policy that concerns them all" (127). Those are the kinds of literary public spheres, I would argue, that arose to greater and lesser degrees in the wake of the controversies over *Ulysses, Tropic of Cancer, American Psycho,* and *Mercy:* publics in which many different groups and many different counterpublics entered discursively formed public spheres to argue for their perception of the common good in the context of a troubling and controversial fictional text.

Another criterion the discourses about these novels meet as to their publicness involves their mass-mediated nature. Writing again on the social welfare state—and in what could be seen as a seconding of Dewey's concern with the "means of communication"—Habermas stresses the kind of media required to forge a public sphere in a mass culture: "In a large public body this kind of communication requires specific means for transmitting information and influencing those who receive it. Today newspapers and magazines, radio and television are the media of the public sphere" ("Public Sphere" 49). The discourses about these four novels are disseminated into and through a mass-mediated public sphere in which private people—precisely because the medium was writing rather than speech—were, in Sennett's terms, forced to operate as strangers in language that could be read (at least potentially) as presentational rather than as representational. Yet the issue of representation—albeit in a somewhat different sense—raises another potential problem for conceptions of publics and public spheres. In her article "Can the Subaltern Speak?" in *Marxism and the Interpretation of Culture,* Gayatri Chakravorty Spivak argues that many leftist intellectuals prevent under- or unrepresented groups from having voices precisely because the intellectuals think their work gives these others a voice. To make her case, Spivak distinguishes between two senses of *representation:* "representation as 'speaking for,' as in politics, and representation as 're-presentation,' as in art or philosophy" (275). This distinction enables Spivak to critique work that talks about "women" or "the post-colonial subject" or any "other" as a homogeneous collective and as representing not the subalterns but the views of intellectuals. "One must nevertheless insist that the colonized subaltern *subject* is irretrievably heterogeneous," Spivak writes (284); "to ignore the subaltern today is, willy-nilly, to continue the imperialist project" (298). She concludes: "The subaltern cannot speak. There is no virtue in global laundry lists with 'woman' as a pious item. Representation has not withered away. The female intellectual as intellectual has a circumscribed task which she must not disown with a flourish" (308).

While Spivak's work has been an important step toward articulating how critics often silence the voices of the very people about whom they are trying to write, her distinction between the two meanings of *representation* elides the difference between Sennett's senses of *presentation* and *representation* in public discourse. Again, I would argue that public interpretations are read most profitably when they are read as presentational. That interpretations can be read as representational is obvious in the work of Holland and Bleich and many others in composition and literary criticism. But writing in the public sphere—writing among strangers—by its nature allows people to playact, to re-present themselves, though of course others must interpret those re-presentations.[20]

Oddly, Spivak implicitly supports Sennett's view of presentation versus representation twice in her essay. In a note to the paragraph critiquing the work of leftist intellectuals, she writes, "My remarks concluding this paragraph, criticizing intellectuals' representations of subaltern groups, should be rigorously distinguished from a coalition politics that takes into account its framing within socialized capital and unites people not because they are oppressed but because they are exploited. This model works best within a parliamentary democracy, *where representation is not only not banished but elaborately staged*" (309; my emphasis). Representation here allows for action as divorced from the authenticity of the subject, as does Spivak's repeated critique of the developments in nineteenth-century European philosophy that led to the rise of the authentic subject. Perhaps more importantly, Spivak's account of the systematic silencing of subaltern groups by the intellectuals who would represent them raises the issue of how subaltern groups can be heard in public, an issue to which I will return in chapters 5 and 6. For now, I will reiterate: instead of reading public discourses as the representations of individual and "authentic" psyches, I read these discourses as inherently presentational and thus public. Indeed, while interpretation of any kind is social by nature because it happens through reading and writing in company, the discourses of citizen critics are public as well as social because of writers' presented concerns for a shared future.

Of the growing number of investigations of different kinds of publics and public spheres, one that not only subverts the assumption that all theories and studies of publics are de facto enlightenment-besotted and exclusionary but also offers strong empirical evidence that different kinds of publics may emerge through different processes in even the most oppressive circumstances is Elsa Barkley Brown's study of African American women in the First African Baptist Church in 1880s Norfolk, Virginia. Brown studied the process these women went through to regain traditional discursive and political power first in their church and then in the mainstream of Republican politics. Her work challenges the assumption that certain people are always silenced in and by certain kinds of publics because of who they are: "Scholars' assumptions of an unbroken line of exclusion of African American women from formal political associations in the late nineteenth century has obscured fundamental changes in the political understandings within African American communities in the transition from slavery to freedom" (112). In fact, Brown argues, African American women were not fighting to enter public discourse for the first time in the 1880s but rather to reenter it, "to retain space they traditionally held in the immediate post-emancipation period" (112). Brown's account of the women at the First African Baptist Church allows teachers and students a point of departure for not only reimagining but also re-realizing citizenship. Again, in Brown's words, "by the very nature of their participation—the inclusion of women and children, the engagement through prayer, the disregard of formal rules for speakers and audience, the engagement from the galleries in the formal legislative sessions—Afro-Richmonders challenged liberal bourgeois notions of rational discourse" (114). Brown's study and others like it are widening the ground on which accounts of publics and public spheres can be constructed and revised, thus allowing our students and us a warrant for expanding our definitions and practices of civic discourse and civic life.

Finally, for a public to recognize itself, action is required; a public in Dewey's terms requires that people not only consume communications that convince them of their common interest but also produce communications about that interest. Further, Habermas notes that any public sphere must itself be subjected to publicity: "The public sphere . . . can perform functions of political critique and control, beyond mere participation in political compromises, *only to the extent that it is itself radically subjected to the requirements of publicity,* that is to say, that it again becomes a public sphere in the strict sense" (208; my emphasis). The environment of publicity around the very question of whether each of the four novels discussed in this book should have been published, sold, or bought is itself one of the major issues surrounding these four books.

Indeed, it is partly Habermas's emphasis on publicity that led me to focus on novels that generated a great deal of public outcry. Books censored or recommended for censorship are more likely to have some potential effect on society—whether in the form of specific court cases or more general discourses about and changes in values. Further, the literature on censorship cases tends to be polemical, participating in a master narrative of free speech over censorship (see especially Ernst; Hutchison; and Rembar).

*Citizen Critics* is not intended to be a de facto celebration of free speech; rather, through the detailed study of the public discourses surrounding *Ulysses, Tropic of Cancer, American Psycho,* and *Mercy,* first, it is intended to serve as an empirical base from which to observe how people argue in public about literary texts and censorship issues. Second, it is intended to provide the groundwork for a more serviceable account of what literary public spheres are, how they form, what kinds of argumentative strategies go on in them, and how literary works and public arguments about them affect society. Third, it is intended to improve, through its critical method and its pedagogical implications, the quality of our democracy. It thus provides a rhetorical alternative to such books as Earl Shorris's *The New American Blues,* in which he argues for a return to a great books pedagogy as a means of teaching the "basic tools of citizenship" (341).

By accounting for the discursive processes through which publics form, publics theory allows the critical lens to focus on discourse in actually existing political systems; thus, it is more likely to result in theory and criticism that can build a basis for studying and effecting social change. In addition, by adding an explicitly rhetorical and processual conception of publics and public spheres to the work of Habermas, Sennett, and Dewey, rhetoricians create a space in which Habermas and others can be used more directly to interpret, in the case of *Citizen Critics,* how literary publics and other kinds of publics come into being. Once at that point, the discussion can turn to rhetorical analysis of the public discourses of the citizen critics themselves, a kind of analysis that, because it focuses on recurring *topoi,* understands rhetoric as an inventional and productive art as well as a way of reading.

## Citizen Critics in Four Literary Public Spheres

*Citizen Critics* both confirms and critiques Habermas's account of structural transformation and the structural role of literary public spheres, particularly since he underestimated the extent to which publicity would become a *topos* for critical publicity. At least where highly publicized novels are concerned, institutional critics in literary public spheres seem more able to question the sources of publicity than Habermas imagined. Yet few citizens feel willing or able to join the fray anymore, and thus most novels do not become public issues, at least not in the sense that their publicity leads to democratic participation and public judgment. Just as importantly, *Citizen Critics* enacts definitional claims about the different forms literary public spheres have taken in the twentieth century and might take in the future, thus further complicating Habermas's master narrative of structural transformation. Chapter 2 focuses on a literary public sphere institution-alized through a particular publication, the *Little Review,* and composed of relative cultural elites. Chapter 3 shows that a literary public sphere can be limited geographically and that geography can help describe the shared interests of the varied participants. Of the four case studies in this book, nonexpert citizen critics were most active in the literary public sphere that grew around *Tropic of Cancer,* in part because the novel was a local con-cern. Chapter 4 suggests that a literary public sphere can be a national phenomenon, though it is less clear in the case of *American Psycho* what caused the silence among citizen critics about the book: has literature be-come so much a discourse of aesthetic experts and the media so controlled by monied elites that citizens assume their views will not be heard? Finally, chapter 5 suggests that certain metaphors, when used to describe literary public spheres, systematically exclude so many voices that it is unclear whether a literary public sphere can be said to exist at all. In fact, it was the 1991 publication of *American Psycho* and *Mercy* and their very dif-ferent public receptions that first sparked the project that became *Citizen Critics.* I consider the four case studies in this book not a history of public debate over censorship in the twentieth century but rather, following Rich-ard Sennett's method in *The Fall of Public Man,* "postholes" (xx) that together form a line from which I can make inferences about the shape of discourses over the century. Ultimately, these case studies suggest that the process through which texts usually considered literary affect social prac-tices can be studied empirically by analyzing the contours of public debate as reflected in the rhetorical strategies as well as the effects of the discourses of citizen critics.

## NOTES

1. Though she would retain the phrase *public intellectual,* Ellen Cushman made a similar point in her opinion piece "The Public Intellectual, Service Learning, and Activist Research" in *College English.*

2. *The Good Citizen,* a collection of essays by nine academic critics, is an inter-esting case in point. The collection is sobering in its contributors' diagnoses of contemporary public life. Yet while its editors, David Batstone and Eduardo Mendieta, see their collection as "demand[ing] that we engage in a deliberation about the values that give direction to our political community" (3), the book of-fers little other than maxims ("Declare a war on ignorance," 39) by way of prac-tical or productive means for change. I discuss another, very different book by the same title, *The Good Citizen* by Michael Schudson, in chapter 6.

3. This normative sense of participatory democratic practice is reiterated in Jürgen Habermas's discussion of civil privatism in *Between Facts and Norms* (see especially 77–81, 118–31, 504–7).

4. The late U.S. Supreme Court Justice William J. Brennan used the phrase *citizen-critic* in the landmark 1964 *New York Times Co. v. Sullivan* decision (376 U.S. 254). The case, which in the words of the decision "determine[d] for the first time the extent to which the constitutional protections for speech and press limit a state's power to award damages in a libel action brought by a public official against critics of his official conduct," was originally brought by an elected commissioner of public affairs in Montgomery, Alabama, against four black ministers and the *New York Times* for publishing an advertisement on its editorial page. An Alabama jury awarded the commissioner, L. B. Sullivan, $500,000 in damages for libel. But the Supreme Court reversed the decision:

> We consider this case against the background of a profound national commitment to the principle that debate on public issues should be uninhibited, robust, and wide-open, and that it may well include vehement, caustic, and sometimes unpleasantly sharp attacks on government and public officials. . . . Such a privilege for criticism of official conduct is appropriately analogous to the protection afforded a public official when he is sued for libel by a private citizen. . . . Analogous considerations support the privilege for the citizen-critic of government. It is as much his duty to criticize as it is the official's duty to administer. . . . As Madison said, "The censorial power is in the people over the government, and not in the government over the people." It would give public servants an unjustified preference over the public they serve, if critics of official conduct did not have a fair equivalent of the immunity granted to the officials themselves. We conclude that such a privilege is required by the First and Fourteenth Amendments.

5. By *empirical* I mean a kind of reasoning based on records but also on the judgments of the teller: empirical as opposed to positivist and as opposed to theoretical. I am not using this term in the way compositionists do but rather in the way I understand Carroll Arnold to have used it. For a discussion of Arnold's use of the term in his critical and pedagogical practice, see Gerard A. Hauser's "Conversations with Carroll Arnold about the Empirical Attitude." It is important to note that my sense of empirical predates the modernist "empiricism" of Locke; rather, it is resonant with ancient rhetoricians' acceptance of the necessity of both evidence and human judgment. Empiricism-become-positivism has resulted in such monstrosities as "evidence-based medicine" in managed care, in which the judgment of individual physicians meeting with individual patients to decide the best course is discounted because of statistical predictive models of what pharmaceutical remedies or surgical procedures are deemed most economical.

6. My conclusions about literary public spheres in this country during the twentieth century are deeply informed by Habermas's account of structural transformation, which I discuss at some length below. In addition, Ralph Engelman's *Public*

*Radio and Television in America* and Robert McChesney's accounts of corporate control of U.S. media and the effects of that control on the possibility of participatory democracy in *Corporate Media and the Threat to Democracy* and *Telecommunications, Mass Media, and Democracy* have helped me enormously. My conclusions are also informed by my vocation as a teacher of rhetoric, a productive and practical art whose end is judgment (*krisis*).

7. The *topoi* of this particular debate over and between cultural English studies and rhetorical criticism were instantiated in the early nineties by Steven Mailloux and Michael C. Leff in books, articles, and conference papers on, respectively, rhetorical hermeneutics and hermeneutical rhetoric. Though *Citizen Critics* shares some interpretive assumptions with Mailloux's rhetorical hermeneutics, my insistence on rhetoric as a productive art suggests my enterprise here is in concert with Leff's hermeneutical rhetoric as well. Ultimately, instead of using hermeneutical rhetoric to study already-written discourses, however, I am most passionate about rhetoric's power as an art productive of discourses and subjectivities for the present and future.

8. Though my critique of reader-response criticism later in this chapter originates from a concern different from Mailloux's, his rhetorical hermeneutics is similar to what I have in mind as a critical method, based as it is on rhetorical practices in historical context. With Mailloux, I want to situate the foundations of meaning within rhetorical exchanges; in addition, however, my "thick rhetorical analysis of interpretation" (17), as Mailloux refers to the fruits of rhetorical hermeneutics, depends upon a view of citizen critics as active participants in the inventions and judgments of literary public spheres and, again, on rhetoric as a productive (rather than merely an analytical or a hermeneutic) art.

9. Hauser's theory is articulated and his case studies contextualized in *Vernacular Voices*.

10. The structural development of the bourgeois public sphere required a split in subjectivity between *homme* and *bourgeois,* a split that was and is not necessary for public subjectivity-formation in literary public spheres. I expand on this distinction and its consequences in chapter 6. For Habermas's distinctions between the literary public sphere and the bourgeois public sphere, see *Structural Transformation of the Public Sphere* (27, 30–40, 141), a point he echoes in *Between Facts and Norms* (504–7).

11. For a tale of how a *topos* can be architectonically productive while inventing sustainable communities and technologies, see Weisman.

12. Dreyfus and Rabinow make a much more thorough argument about Foucault's method, which they call "interpretive analytics" (xxii, 118).

13. Ong and other rhetorical theorists whose work has had its greatest reception among writing teachers (Booth "Rhetorical Stance"; Bitzer, "Rhetoric and Public Knowledge"; Park "The Meanings of 'Audience'"; Elbow) share a purpose quite different from what I am after here: these theorists want to use *audience* to get writers to think more productively about the kinds of readers who might read

their writing and to use that conception as a device for invention. Douglas Park's critique of audience analysis as not sufficiently social shows that this kind of theory, while important in the history of writing instruction and of immense value to students who have learned to put it into practice, involves at some level the kinds of generalizations that this project—though in a very different context—is working against ("Analyzing Audiences"). Jack Selzer sorts through different terms for— and meanings of—*audience* and *reader* for writing teachers in "More Meanings of *Audience*."

14. Commentary on Habermas's notion of structural transformation has produced several special editions of journals and at least two anthologies, *Habermas and the Public Sphere*, edited by Craig Calhoun, and *The Black Public Sphere*, edited by the Black Public Sphere Collective. I focus here instead on earlier discussions of publics because I understand most of them among literary critics as not primarily concerned with the problems of democracy.

15. While Sennett's notion of the *theatrum mundi* is open to the same criticisms as Habermas's notion of the bourgeois public sphere (see note 17), Sennett nowhere says the *theatrum mundi* is counterfactual (see note 18).

16. A revision of his work as a graduate student, Habermas's *The Structural Transformation of the Public Sphere*, published in German in 1962, was not translated into English until 1989.

17. Much of the voluminous criticism of Habermas focuses on his theories of human social action and universal pragmatics, which are not of concern to me here. I have thus focused on critiques of Habermas that respond to his analysis of publics and implicit questions of representation.

18. Habermas himself views the bourgeois public sphere as counterfactual, thus combining empirical investigation and theorizing in a way that makes *The Structural Transformation of the Public Sphere* methodologically hybrid. See McCarthy on Habermas's view that critical social theory should be situated between philosophy and science (vii–xvi).

19. This intention was complicated by response to Dworkin's *Mercy*, in which case substantive discussion of the book occurred among book reviewers and within what Fraser would call subaltern counterpublics (see chapter 5).

20. I connect this to the rhetorical concept of ethos and discuss it and its relation to public subjectivity-formation in chapter 6.

# 2

## From "Improper Novel" to "Contemporary Classic": Joyce's *Ulysses*, 1918–30

"Ulysses" is a curious production, not wholly uninteresting, especially to psychopathologists. ("Taste, Not Morals")

Finally, I venture a prophecy: Not ten men or women out of a hundred can read "Ulysses" through, and of the ten who succeed in doing so, five of them will do it as a tour de force. I am probably the only person, aside from the author, that has ever read it twice from beginning to end. I have learned more psychology and psychiatry from it than I did in ten years at the Neurological Institute. (Collins 17)

These were the first impressions of James Joyce's *Ulysses* that the *New York Times,* the nation's paper of record, presented to its readers. Though Margaret Anderson and Jane Heap had published the novel serially in the *Little Review* until they were stopped by court order in 1921,[1] press coverage of the trial of the *Little Review* was spotty and unsympathetic to the novel (Anderson, *Thirty Years' War* 226). Indeed, two *New York Times* news stories and two editorials devoted to the trial and conviction of Anderson and Heap on charges of obscenity brought by John R. Sumner, Anthony Comstock's successor as secretary of the New York Society for the Prevention of Vice, focused on the court's opinion that the book was "unintelligible" and the product of "a disordered mind." And though Djuna Barnes's feature story in the April 1922 issue of *Vanity Fair* portrayed Joyce as an unequivocal genius—much as the *Little Review* had—the *New York Times Book Review and Magazine* was read by more people than all the other publications combined that carried stories on Joyce. In fact, Joseph Collins's review of the Shakespeare and Company edition of *Ulysses* is representative of early public discourses about the novel in that, while

Collins finds *Ulysses* unintelligible, he suspects Joyce of literary genius and, as will become clear, associates that genius with psychopathology.

Yet little more than a decade after Anderson and Heap were fined one hundred dollars for printing in the *Little Review* what would later come to be called the "Nausicaa" episode of *Ulysses*—"Improper Novel Costs Women $100," the 22 February 1921 *New York Times* headline read—Judge John M. Woolsey, declaring that "'Ulysses' is a sincere and honest book," ruled that Random House could admit Joyce's novel into the United States (*United States v. One Book Called "Ulysses" by James Joyce* 5 F. Supp. 1182 [S.D.N.Y. 1933]). Indeed, the three U.S. trials of *Ulysses*—the first in 1921, over publication of the "Nausicaa" episode in the *Little Review*, and the second and third, in 1933 and 1934, over Random House's attempt to distribute the book in the United States—changed U.S. censorship law significantly.[2] Morris L. Ernst, who defended *Ulysses* for Random House in 1933, has argued that "the *Ulysses* case set a precedent not so much because of any rule it enunciated as because it represented a psychological breakthrough in the censorship field. After the *Ulysses* case the general community notion of what was 'dirty' became just a little more sophisticated" (*Censorship* 94). In a more comprehensive attempt to account for the complicated vortex of psychology, sociology, and the law involved in the process of social and legal change, Felice Flanery Lewis recounts the interaction between "the obscenity issue" and the history of literature in the United States. Explaining the relative dearth of obscenity cases in the United States before 1890, Lewis argues that "judges seem to have tacitly assumed that the nature of obscenity needed no explanation—that obscenity was readily recognizable beyond doubt or question. They also appear not to have questioned their authority under common law to ban material considered obscene" (6). Lewis cites a decision by Judge Curtis Bok of Pennsylvania in *Commonwealth v. Gordon* that suggests "prevailing social consciousness" determines obscenity decisions as much as codified law does. Before 1890, Bok wrote, "'the formulation of the common-law proscription of obscene publication did not amount to very much. It is a good example of a social restriction that became law and was allowed to slumber until a change of social consciousness should animate it. It is the prevailing social consciousness that matters quite as much as the law'" (qtd. in Lewis 6).

In her history of obscenity and literature in the United States Lewis argues implicitly that changes in social consciousness foster changes in legal codes.[3] I expand and refine that position by arguing that public discourse—in this case, the discourses of actual readers of *Ulysses* writing in a literary public sphere about issues raised by the publication of excerpts of the novel—can reveal for study the processes through which literary texts and the discourses of citizen critics in response to them and to each other may effect changes in social practices. I argue in this chapter that between 1918, when the *Little Review* began its serial publication of *Ulysses,* and 1930, when Stuart Gilbert published *James Joyce's "Ulysses"* and pushed the novel toward its status as "classic" that would eventually gain it legally sanctioned publication in the United States in 1934,[4] public discourses helped set the discursive stage for the "psychological breakthrough" instantiated in Woolsey's decision. By the time of that decision, 1933, and the ruling that upheld it, 1934, judgments about the merit of *Ulysses* hinged on the view of it as "a contemporary classic" (*United States v. One Book Entitled Ulysses by James Joyce* 72 F.2d 705 [2d Cir. 1934]). Woolsey defined Joyce as "one of the most powerful and innovative writers in the English language" (*United States v. One Book Called "Ulysses"*); and Judge Augustus Hand, in the ruling upholding the Woolsey decision, declared that Joyce "may be regarded as a pioneer among those writers who have adopted the 'stream-of-consciousness' method of presenting fiction. . . . Ulysses is rated as a book of considerable power by persons whose opinions are entitled to weight" (*United States v. One Book Entitled Ulysses by James Joyce*). The word *classic,* especially when employed by critics cited as "expert witnesses" in obscenity trials, can squelch public discussion of literary merit or social value. Thus, to analyze which arguments succeeded in transforming an "improper novel" into a "contemporary classic," I will focus here on the first furor over *Ulysses*—its serial publication in the *Little Review,* the confiscation and burning of the issues of the *Little Review* containing the "Lestrygonians," "Scylla and Charybdis," and "Cyclops" episodes, and the trial of the *Little Review* over publication of part of the "Nausicaa" episode; I will also include public discourses in the United States in response to Shakespeare and Company's decision to publish *Ulysses* in Paris in 1922. Though the *topoi* of the discourses of citizen critics may not have won the day, the arguments actual readers raised about *Ulysses* are strikingly similar to those raised about *Tropic of Cancer, American Psycho, Mercy,* and other controversial books across the century. In the wake of the initial publication of *Ulysses,* readers wrote publicly in the *Little Review* and in other periodicals not only to come to terms with the novel's complexity but also to persuade other people how to think about it and the *topoi* its publication raised. *Ulysses* was, then, a public issue early in its history, a fact that is overshadowed by its rich and more widely known history as an aesthetic object.

The first trial of *Ulysses* and the public discourses that surrounded it are also worth study in light of an issue that Joyce scholarship in particular and literary criticism in general have consistently avoided. While focusing on biographical criticism and theories that posit how "the reader" should read *Ulysses,* scholars have given little attention to how actual readers have read and responded to it. Charles Duff's *James Joyce and the Plain Reader* (1932) and William Powell Jones's *James Joyce and the Common Reader* (1955) are interpretive works that provide, in Jones's telling phrase, "the simple approach to Joyce" (ix) in an attempt to help untrained readers understand the book. Unlike Jones, however, my intent here is not to simplify *Ulysses* but rather, in part, to acknowledge its complexity by focusing on a few of the ways early readers wrote in public about how they read and understood it. I will not focus on what Joyce said about his book or, ultimately, argue for an interpretation that conjectures about how "the reader" will read or should react to *Ulysses.* Rather, I examine the public discourses written in response to Joyce's novel—and in response to one another—to affect public opinion about *Ulysses* as well as about the *topoi* its publication raised. In other words, I will study how the publication of Joyce's novel functioned to encourage deliberation about literature, obscenity, censorship, and democracy in the literary public sphere that grew up around it as readers attempted to come to terms publicly with the complexity of the novel. Ultimately, I argue that the *topoi* of these discourses helped to generate *topoi* for the Woolsey decision in particular and, therefore, were productive of changes in censorship law in general.

The discourses responding to *Ulysses* are not postulations about theoretical readers reading a classic text. Many of the discourses appear in no bibliography of writings about the novel presumably because they are considered public rather than scholarly discourses, written by untrained readers rather than expert critics. These discourses were written by people engaged in rational-critical debate about social issues raised by writing that intrigued and threatened them: actual readers—the *Little Review* refers to them as "Reader Critics"—who wrote about their readings of and responses to *Ulysses* and the issues it raised in order to affect what their readers, in turn, might think about the book and the issues it raised. In the preface to *The Function of Criticism,* Terry Eagleton argues that "criticism today lacks all substantive social function" (7); his enterprise is to raise "the question of what substantive social functions criticism might once again fulfil in our own time" (8). *Ulysses* received so much attention in part because it raised issues with implications beyond the aesthetic; it tied aesthetic issues to such social questions as the role of the artist in society as well as a culture's definitions of obscenity and indecency. "It is arguable that criticism was only ever significant when it engaged with more than literary issues," Eagleton writes, "when, for whatever historical reason, the 'literary' was suddenly foregrounded as the medium of vital concerns deeply rooted in the general intellectual, cultural and political life of an epoch. . . . It has only been when criticism, in the act of speaking of literature, emits a lateral message about the shape and destiny of a whole culture that its voice has compelled widespread attention" (107). The furor over *Ulysses* energized what Eagleton would call "a kind of shadowy public sphere" (*Ideology* 402) and what Habermas has called "a public sphere in the world of letters" (*Structural Transformation* 50). Habermas argues that eighteenth-century literary public spheres allowed people to discuss cultural products—he puts special emphasis on the novel—as private people come together publicly to discuss common interests. These discussions, which fostered a consciousness that encouraged people to be critical of the state, were the direct structural predecessors of the bourgeois public sphere; hence, Habermas's historical argument suggests the primary role of fictional texts in effecting social change as well as the promise of literary public spheres and the kinds of subjectivity formation they foster as a means of reclaiming public space and participatory democracy. Informed by critiques by Nancy Fraser and others, Habermas's conception of literary public spheres offers critics an opportunity to test, through critical practices, the historical conjecture that literary texts and the arguments of actual readers in response to those texts play a role in effecting social changes through the discourses they produce. What rhetoricians can add to Habermas's observation is an empirical sense of how that process of change unfolds.

Concomitant with what Habermas's historical conjecture can offer rhetoricians as a starting point to studying how fictional texts effect social changes, rhetoric offers those who use such contemporary theorists as Habermas a rich and diverse inventory of theories and lexicons[5] about how thought and language are produced and operate in society. To study the discursive process through which Joyce's novel and public arguments about it fostered deliberation that led to changes in social consciousness and law, I here analyze the *topoi* of the public discourses about *Ulysses*. Until 1930 these public discourses in the United States clustered around four major interrelated *topoi*: publicity and the public—Who is "the reading public"? Who may judge art? Who are the elite or experts? Who are laypersons?; intelligibility—Why would the *Little Review* publish *Ulysses* if its readers were baffled by it? If a work is unintelligible, how can it be obscene or dangerous or even offensive?; obscenity—What is obscene? Can "true art" be obscene? Is art or literature different from other language?; and psychopathology—Is to write about psychosis to be psychotic? Is to read about vice to become vicious? Are great artists psychopathic? Structured by these four *topoi,* this chapter recounts the public discourses about *Ulysses* in the literary public sphere that formed around it, and I argue that public discourses about the first trial of *Ulysses*—in particular, Margaret Anderson's and Jane Heap's insistence on turning all questions about *Ulysses* into questions of "true art" or "the true artist"—set the discursive stage for the Woolsey decision. Finally, to end the chapter, I will elaborate on the implications of specific rhetorical strategies employed by those writing publicly about *Ulysses.*

## *Ulysses* in Public

Whether *Ulysses* should be published, for whom it should be published, and why it should be published were among the most frequently recurring *topoi* in early public discourses about the novel. That portions of the novel first appeared in the *Little Review* was a consequence of Margaret Anderson's views of art and the public, which were reflected in the slogan she and Jane Heap added to the journal in its fourth year of publication, the same year it began to publish *Ulysses*—"The Little Review: MAKING NO COMPROMISE WITH THE PUBLIC TASTE." Anderson explained that this slogan was a response to *Poetry*'s, which declared, a la Whitman, "To have great poets we must have great audiences too" (*Thirty Years' War* 60); but Heap maintained that Ezra Pound suggested their slogan, and she and Anderson accepted it ("Reply to Mary Widney"). In any case, Heap's and Anderson's essays and responses to letters to the editor in the *Little Review* plainly state their view that "true" artists and those who appreciated "true" art were—sometimes, it seems, almost literally—a breed apart from the rest of "the reading public."

In one of the clearest indications of how she and Heap viewed "the reading public," Anderson wrote "To the Book Publishers of America" in the December 1919 issue of the *Little Review.* After discussing the advertising problems caused by publishing *Ulysses,* Anderson concluded by reiterating her views of the public and by associating those views with her magazine's recurring need for money:

> For nearly six years we have published, in America, a magazine of highly specialized thinking. Financially unsupported (except by donations amounting to a few hundred dollars), representing no vested interests, no publishers' interests, no aged magazines and reviews nor staffs of the same, we have managed to keep

alive in spite of an unsympathetic and ignorant public, a jeering press, and a censor that suspects the worst of any effort dedicated to the best.

... I ask whether you can give your support, at least once a year, to the one magazine in America in which the man of letters may obtain a hearing among his peers, ungarbled in editorial rooms to suit the public taste. (167)

Anderson here uses several strategies of dissociation—the *Little Review* as superior to other little magazines, *Little Review* subscribers as superior to the "ignorant public," "highly specialized thinking" as superior to "the public taste" (what Perelman and Olbrechts-Tyteca call "transivity," 227)—as well as antithesis. Her rhetorical strategies make clear that it was her view of *Ulysses* as "true" art, rather than a concern for the reading public, that made her eager to publish excerpts of Joyce's novel-in-progress for the first time.

Heap was clear on what the *Little Review*'s public was *not*. In "Art and the Law," originally published in the September–December 1920 issue of the *Little Review*, Heap derided the definition of "society" or "public" held by the New York Society for the Prevention of Vice: "The society for which Mr. Sumner is agent, I am told, was founded to protect the public from corruption. When asked *what public?* its defenders spring to the rock on which America was founded: the cream-puff of sentimentality, and answer chivalrously 'Our young girls.' So the mind of the young girl rules this country?" (5). Both Anderson and Heap stressed that their sense of whom Joyce was writing to and being published for was not this public; indeed, any question of "the public" was moot: they published Joyce because he was Joyce. One unsigned letter, in the May–June 1920 issue, raised the question of Joyce's public: "Can you tell me when James Joyce's 'Ulysses' will appear in book form? Do you think the public will ever be ready for such a book?" Again, Heap's reply consisted of her own mix of distaste for the public and stubborn certainty about Joyce's genius: "'Ulysses' will probably appear in book form in America if there is a publisher for it who will have sense enough to avoid the public. Joyce has perfected a technique that has enabled him to avoid almost all but those rabid for literature" (Reply to Letter, "'Ulysses'"). Heap's oxymoronical desire for a publisher who would "avoid the public" manifests the paradoxical views she and Anderson held of their readers.

In fact, no matter how firm a definition—and how firmly negative an evaluation—of "the public" Heap and Anderson held, the *Little Review*'s publication of *Ulysses* fostered repeated discussion of those definitional and evaluative questions. Most of the letters that followed were published under the heading "The Reader Critic," a label suggesting that Anderson's and

Heap's views of their readers and "the reading public" were more complicated than they admitted. In one of the first letters in response to *Ulysses,*
T. D. O'B. of Philadelphia wrote in the July 1918 issue, "If the artist 'has
no concern with audiences' why publish his work?—and why do the magazines that publish this transcendent art push as hard as 'the vulgar sort'
for sales? There is an inconsistency here that my mind—a fairly elastic
one—cannot away with." In response to this reader's reasoned—and so-
phisticatedly syntaxed—criticism, Heap, who replied to correspondence
when she chose, had the last word:

> Sometimes I grow a bit weary of these kindergarten questions by people who
> have failed to read before asking. . . . All I can say to people insisting on the great
> audience idea is to try this "to-have-great-poets-we-must-have-great-audiences"
> test on other forms of creation,—physical creation, for instance.
> To have great audiences an art magazine must have a great sales department.
> The *Little Review* has no sales department—yet?—*jh* (58)

Heap's reliance on *ad personam* attacks (see chapter 5 and Perelman and
Olbrechts-Tyteca 110–12) suggests on the one hand that she viewed readers in much the same way that she viewed artists—as born rather than
made. On the other hand, her move to *ad personam* suggests she sensed
the paradoxes lurking within her writing. Tautly tangled around Heap and
Anderson's distaste for "the reading public" was their need for increased
subscriptions and sales to stay alive. Among the paradoxes of the *Little
Review* was Anderson and Heap's desire to produce a publication that
could "avoid the public" and still afford to publish. Complicating this was
that while they wanted to publish "great art" and needed revenue to do
that, if too many people liked or could appreciate or even understand something and support it, it must be neither "true" art nor very valuable by their
own criteria.[6]
Another letter in the same issue, headlined "The Layman Speaks—!!"
seems to agree with the *Little Review*'s sense of the public on some accounts—but not all. Written by Rex Hunter of Chicago, the letter began,
"The June number of the *Little Review* seems to me to be the best yet. It
makes a wider appeal. Of course I don't mean that it will reach the multitude—no good stuff does that—but that it will please people who are tired
of the commercialized hokum in the average magazine and are honestly
desirous of getting something better, yet who are dismayed by the printing of almost an entire number in French" (61–62). Here, Hunter attempts
to draw a line between "good stuff" and "commercialized hokum" by
commenting on one of Heap and Anderson's prior strategies for gaining

subscriptions and bolstering sales: The *Little Review* had, indeed, published an issue entirely in French, about which some readers wrote in praise. While agreeing that the *Little Review* should not try to reach the multitude, Hunter's letter ended by suggesting that Joyce did not represent the kind of material that had a "wider appeal": "The impressionistic prose of James Joyce begins to be a bit bewildering, even to those who believe that he is on the right track" (62). Anderson and Heap, as would become clearer and clearer in their discourses about *Ulysses,* believed that anyone who would dare to question Joyce's style would automatically consign herself or himself to the status of layperson rather than critic.

Many *Little Review* readers were confounded by the excerpts of Joyce's novel: confounded yet interested or, echoing Hunter's letter, bewildered yet believing Joyce "on the right track." One unsigned letter, in the May–June 1920 issue, manifested this combination of belief and confusion quite clearly: "I read him each month with eagerness, but I must confess that I am defeated in my intelligence. Now tell the truth,—do you yourselves know where the story is at the present moment, how much time has elapsed,—just where are we? Have you any clue as to when the story will end?" ("'Ulysses'"). For Anderson and Heap, faithful belief in Joyce's genius was a prerequisite to legitimation in the pages of the *Little Review*; on the whole, art and literature are issues more of belief than of judgment. Yet Heap's reply shows that even those who most ardently believed in Joyce's genius sometimes misread him: "We haven't any advance chapters in hand, but it would seem that we are drawing towards the Circe episode and the close of the story. The question of time seems simple and unobscured. The story is laid in perhaps the talk centre of the universe, but time is not affected; the time of the present chapter is about five thirty or six in the evening of the same day on which the story started,—I think Tuesday. Mr. Bloom has had a long day since he cooked his breakfast of kidney, but he has lost no time.—*jh*" (Reply to "'Ulysses'" 72).

The final letter in the *Little Review* concerning *Ulysses* and publicity came in the July–August 1920 issue. Again, Anderson and Heap's view of the public is the issue, and Mary Widney is the writer: "If you are sincerely regardless of the public taste why be so blatant about it? . . . The small boy whistling in the grave yard—and the *Little Review* slapping the face of public taste. Some way it lacks dignity, and, what is more serious, casts aspersions on the worthiness of the movement it espouses. I may be misunderstanding grossly, but as I have said, I am puzzled. Won't you explain?" (32–33). Of course Heap explained, writing a reply that, as mentioned above, offered her explanation of the journal's slogan. Yet Heap ended her letter by reaffirming her view of the public: "I believe in peace and silence for and from the 'masses'—a happy undisturbed people." Indeed, Widney's self-questioning philophronesis (Lanham, *Handlist* 115)— "I may be misunderstanding grossly"—suggests she knew she was transgressing a tenet of the *Little Review*'s artistic dogma but still felt her point was important enough to risk public humiliation. And at the pens of Anderson and Heap, humiliation is often what "Reader Critics" received.

Anderson had another chance at the public in the issue of the *Little Review* that carried the final installment of *Ulysses*. In what she called a "defense of James Joyce" and headlined "An Obvious Statement (for the Millionth Time)," Anderson argued that the only question concerning *Ulysses* for the court "is the relation of the artist—the great writer—to the public" (8). She answered the question: "*First, the artist has no responsibility to the public whatever; but the public should be conscious of its responsibility to him, being mysteriously and eternally in his debt. . . . Second, the position of the great artist is impregnable.* You can no more destroy him than you can create him. You can no more limit his expression, patronizingly suggest that his genius present itself in channels personally pleasing to you, than you can eat the stars" (8).

Since for Anderson *Ulysses* was a question of "true art" rather than of values, consequences, or law, she argued that art should be judged not in court and not by the likes of John Sumner: "If Mr. Sumner were asked to judge pearls, for instance, he wouldn't dream of expressing an opinion unless he really knew how a good pearl must feel to the touch, how it must weigh, what color it must be. In short, unless he were a connoisseur he wouldn't be doing these things" (9). Anderson argued for a "caste system," "where the artist is protected from the assault of the philistine" (10). After all, she reasoned, "*Only certain kinds of people are capable of art emotion (aesthetic emotion). They are the artist himself and the critic whose capacity for appreciation proves itself by an equal capacity to create*" (10). Thus, above all, art should not be judged by the layperson. In her final statement in the *Little Review* about the American reading public and publication of *Ulysses,* she complained:

> In America, every human being, no matter what his training, his business, his qualifications, *makes some mysterious identification of himself with the artist.* He says, . . . "I don't know anything about Art, I couldn't write a poem or compose a piece of music to save my life, but I know what I like, I have a very good critical sense, and I *feel* the way the artist does." They mean they eat Art, live on it,—go to hear good music in order to drown in the emotions it gives them. . . . You can tell a man who knows a great deal about insurance, for instance, that

he doesn't know enough mechanical engineering to build a bridge, and he doesn't feel insulted. But if you tell a plumber, or an engineer, a business man, a lawyer, a scholar, a club woman, a debutante, that they are not artists, not creators in this special sense, they take it as the deepest insult. (11–12)

Anderson and Heap believed strongly in the line that dissociated the artists from the nonartists, the creative geniuses from the rest of the world. According to them, the majority of the world certainly could not be trusted to respond to the works of the artistic minority, hence their continual use of dissociative arguments and arguments that rested on definitions and implicit evaluations of the "true" artist. Anderson and Heap—in the way they talked about *Ulysses* and argued for Joyce's artistic immunity from the curious public—perhaps confirm what Max Eastman would write in *Harper's* nearly a decade later: Joyce "speaks a private language" (635). And the private person Joyce was speaking to had to be one of the believers, his or her aesthetic soul already saved.

Of the discourses about *Ulysses* in the literary public sphere that formed around it from 1918 to 1930, the only article that contrasted this kind of distaste for the public with Joyce's own sentiments in *Ulysses* was published in a 1922 *New Republic* review of the novel by Edmund Wilson.[7] Though responding to Arnold Bennett rather than anyone in the *Little Review,* Wilson complained that *Ulysses* had been read as being "a colossal 'down' on humanity" (164). In fact, Wilson argued, *Ulysses* has as one of its main characters a more or less representative member of the bourgeoisie: "Poor Bloom, with his generous impulses and his attempts to understand and master life, is the epic symbol of reasoning man, humiliated and ridiculous, yet extricating himself by cunning from the spirits which seek to destroy him" (164). Wilson wrote that Joyce had great feeling for the common man and woman; Joyce, Wilson wrote, "makes his bourgeois figures command our sympathy and respect by letting us see in them the throes of the human mind straining always to perpetuate and perfect itself and of the body always laboring and throbbing to throw up some beauty from its darkness" (164). Wilson's inferences about Joyce's politics, a hermeneutical feat made possible through the character of Bloom, may be seen to reflect harshly on Anderson and Heap's distaste for any but the born genius. However questionable such distinctions may seem today, legal decisions resting on them were largely what enabled *Ulysses* to be published in the United States at all, a point I will return to in the conclusion of this chapter. A final paradox may be that only after it was published by Random House was it widely enough circulated to reach the majority of layreaders—Heap's plumbers and mechanical engineers—if it ever has reached them at all.

## Intelligibility

Very closely related to the *topos* of publicity—as suggested by some of the letters above—was the *topos* of intelligibility: why would the *Little Review* or Shakespeare and Company publish *Ulysses* if no one could understand it? While this issue centers on who is reading the book, Anderson and Heap again argued the issue by shifting all questions of intelligibility to questions about the nature of the "true artist" and his or her lack of responsibility to anything except inner compulsions.

The first responses to *Ulysses* in the *Little Review* consistently raised the issue of intelligibility. The very first, published in the May 1918 issue and written by Israel Solon of New York, suggested that the difficulty of Joyce's work might ultimately sabotage the novel. Responding to an essay that ran with the first installment of *Ulysses,* Solon wrote:

> James Joyce has plunged deep into himself, to be sure; but not before he had erected about himself an almost insurmountable wall. He has developed a technique that none but the most disciplined, the most persistent and sympathetic are able to break through. For myself, I should never make use of any term nearly so precipitate as plunging when describing the art of James Joyce. I should say that James Joyce adventures slowly and painfully with a huge stone deliberately tied to his middle, that he might sink readily and stay under long and be all but unable to retreat. (63)

Heap made no reply to Solon's letter; other letters gave her better opportunities. One, headlined "What Joyce Is Up Against," was written by one S. S. B. of Chicago:

> Really now: Joyce! what does he think he's doing? What do you think he is doing? I swear I've read his "Ulysses" and haven't found out yet what it's about, who is who or where. Each month he's worse than the last. I consider myself fairly intelligent. I have read more than most. There are some few things I expect of a writer. One of them is coherence. Joyce will have to change his style if he wants to get on. Very few have the time or patience to struggle with his impressionistic stuff—to get nothing out of it even then. (54)

Heap's reply was direct and reflected her contempt for anyone admitting difficulty with Joyce's style or narrative strategies. In addition, however, Heap again stressed that writers had no responsibility to be intelligible to anyone:

> You consider yourself an intelligent, "well-read" person. Did it ever occur to you to read anything on the nature of writers? If it should you might help to remove from the mind of the reading public—Whitman's great audience—some

of the superstition of its importance to the writer; some of its superstition of being able to put any compulsion upon an artist. All compulsion exists within the artist. It would take too long to discuss this fully here. The only concern of the artist is to try in one short lifetime to meet these inner compulsions. He has no concern with the audiences and their demands.—*jh* (54)

As with the issue of "the reading public," all discussion of intelligibility in the *Little Review* suggested that Anderson and Heap wanted no common ground with their critical readers. For Anderson and Heap even to admit that they understood the question of intelligibility would immediately exclude them from the only company they wished to keep—those who need not inquire about the intelligibility of outward manifestations of the true artist's inner compulsions.

Intelligibility and the related issue of obscenity were the most common *topoi* in press reports on the trial of the *Little Review*. The first newspaper article, an unsigned story in the 15 February 1921 *New York Tribune*, reported that John Cowper Powys, serving as a witness for the defense, testified that "Joyce's style was too 'obscure' to 'deprave and corrupt the public,' comparing it to a cubist painting in the sense that the latter was a departure from the orthodox methods of painting" ("Court Puzzled"). And in a 22 February 1921 *New York Times* story covering the decision, one of the justices summed up the sentiments of the court: "I think this novel is unintelligible" ("Improper Novel").

Indeed, press coverage of the trial showed that intelligibility was a problem not just for readers of *Ulysses:* as the following excerpt from the same *Tribune* article shows, the court had intelligibility problems with the entire proceedings. This was the first general-circulation article on the *Little Review*'s publication of *Ulysses;* as such it served as an introduction to the novel at least for New York City readers, who were potential contributors to the forming literary public sphere:

> When Mr. [Philip] Moeller [president of the Theater Guild and witness for the defense] said that Joyce employed the "Freudian method of psychoanalysis" in "Ulysses," and added that the book "most emphatically was not aphrodisiac," Justice Kernochan called a halt.
>
> "What's this!" he exploded. "What's that?"
>
> Mr. [John] Quinn [Anderson and Heap's attorney and a friend of Pound and patron to Joyce] rushed forward with an explanation. "Well, if I may explain to your honor," he said, "aphrodisiac is an adjective derived from the noun Aphrodite, supposed to be the goddess of beauty or love"—
>
> "I understand that," broke in Justice Kernochan, "but I don't understand what this man is talking about. He might as well be talking in Russian."

Public discomfort aside, the question of the intelligibility of *Ulysses* went far beyond its initial serial publication in the *Little Review* and far beyond the first trial; the question of intelligibility was the first issue presented in most popular accounts of the novel, even after its private publication by Shakespeare and Company. Joseph Collins's review of *Ulysses* in the 28 May 1922 *New York Times Book Review and Magazine* began by focusing on that issue and by again suggesting dissociations: "A few intuitive, sensitive visionaries may understand and comprehend 'Ulysses,' James Joyce's new and mammoth volume, without going through a course of training or instruction, but the average intelligent reader will glean little or nothing from it" (6). A few lines later, however, Collins made a move that became a commonplace in reviews that led to the Woolsey decision. After commenting on the book's unintelligibility, Collins wrote: "'Ulysses' is the most important contribution that has been made to fictional literature in the twentieth century" (6). Writing in 1922, Collins was one of the first to move toward an explicit association of the unintelligible with the important in literature,[8] an argument of association that continues to be employed today. Similarly, Edmund Wilson, whose review of *Ulysses* for the *New Republic* was generally quite enthusiastic, associated Joyce's difficult style with his literary importance. While Wilson questioned Joyce's stylistic choices in certain episodes—he wrote, for instance, that "Mr. Joyce has done ill in attempting to graft burlesque upon realism; he has written some of the most unreadable chapters in the whole history of fiction" (165)—just one paragraph later he exclaimed, "Yet, for all its appalling longueurs, *Ulysses* is a work of high genius" (165).

The chorus of "unintelligible but brilliant" or "unreadable but genius" judgments was attacked by N. P. Dawson in his article "The Cuttlefish School of Writers" in the January 1923 issue of *Forum* magazine. Dawson began with this observation: "How true it is that one-half of the world does not know what the other half reads; how true and perhaps how fortunate" (1174). Dawson went on to argue that *Ulysses* and other difficult works by modern writers have hoodwinked "the young captains of literature" into thinking that they are art rather than "interesting abnormalit[ies]" (1175). When Dawson wrote his essay, *Ulysses* was still so relatively obscure that he could get away with publishing a description of the "Penelope" episode as "the topsy-turvy, horrible ravings of a woman in child birth" (1176). Dawson made fun of Joyce, T. S. Eliot, and Waldo Frank for publishing work so unintelligible that typographical errors went undetected for months or years. Near the end of the article, explaining his title, Dawson wrote: "For a given degree of talent, there is an increasing school of writers who imitate the cuttlefish, and conceal their shortcomings by 'ejecting an inky fluid,' which is the definition the dictionary gives of a cuttlefish. The Cuttlefish School would not be a bad name for these writers who perhaps not being as great geniuses as they would like to be, eject their inky fluid, splash about and make a great fuss, so that it is difficult to tell what it is all about, and it might as well be genius as anything else" (1182). Dawson at one point reassured his audience: "A comforting thought for the bewildered reader is that he is not expected to understand books like 'Ulysses' and its inevitable spawn" (1179). In fact, Dawson explained, "if an author of this new school should find that he was understood, it is said that he would consider he had failed. He writes for himself alone. Why should the books of such an author be published and sold, or even be 'privately printed, for distribution among charitable friends,' a bewildered reader may ask. Why should the innermost thoughts of such an author not be kept for himself alone? But these, of course, are stupid questions" (1179). Like "Reader Critic" Mary Widney on the issue of "the reading public," Dawson had a clear sense that his questions and criticisms transgressed unspoken tenets of artistic taste even as he argued that *Ulysses* was an "abnormality" rather than art. Yet unlike Widney, Dawson was one of the very few institutional critics by 1923 willing to go public with doubts about Joyce's work, despite its difficulty. Dawson concluded his essay this way: "There is no great cause to worry" about *Ulysses*. "Not more than five or ten people will be able to read the new novel. Its proper place will be under glass in a museum, instead of on the open shelves of a circulating library" (1184). Other than Dawson and one or two of the *Little Review*'s "Reader Critics," few were willing to pursue the issue. To do so was to mark oneself as clearly out of the fold—not one of the elect. To subject Joyce's novel to reasonable scrutiny was to show oneself as not understanding that "true" art was above such questioning. Either you understood or you did not. Thus reading texts was as much a question of inborn genius as writing them was.

Yet even more complicated than the question of the intelligibility of *Ulysses* was the relationship between intelligibility and obscenity in the episodes published in the *Little Review,* especially "Nausicaa." What exactly the relationship was and what consequences it had for which publics was much discussed—along with definitions of obscenity—in the literary public sphere.

## Obscenity

"Margaret C. Anderson and Jane Heap, publisher and editor respectively of the Little Review, at 27 West Eighth Street, each paid a fine of $50 imposed by Justices McInerney, Kernochan and Moss in Special Sessions yesterday, for publishing an improper novel," reported the *New York Times* in a 22 February 1921 edition. "The court held that parts of the story seemed to be harmful to the morals of the community" ("Improper Novel"). Thus concluded the only direct coverage of the *Little Review* decision in general-circulation newspapers. Yet the *Times*'s editorial the day after the news story ran took a slightly different tack: "In strict fact, however, 'Ulysses' is not immoral—not so, at least, in the sense of tendency or capacity for leading any reader, young or old, into vicious courses. . . . That most people would find the story incomprehensible and therefore dull is, perhaps, its complete vindication from the charge of immorality. Perhaps that, too, is a reason for letting anybody who wants to print such stuff do it" ("Taste, Not Morals"). "Incomprehensible but dull," a phrase the *Times* repeated in its editorial after the 1933 Woolsey decision, raises the thorny question of whether an incomprehensible or unintelligible text can be obscene or indecent. Even more to the point is the issue of who gets to decide what is obscene and how possible negative effects of literary texts might be described or measured.

Anderson, in her essay "To the Book Publishers of America," seized upon the issue of obscenity and made it a constant theme in the rest of her writings about *Ulysses*. When she traveled around the Northeast to encourage publishers to advertise in the *Little Review,* she met strong opposition from many based on her decision to publish the novel: "One of the things that amused and angered me the most was the attitude toward James Joyce and other of our contributors who are considered obscene. Joyce is incomprehensible, yes, but nevertheless violently obscene" (66). Anderson then makes what would become her and Heap's characteristic response to questions about the obscenity of Ulysses: they continually moved questions that centered on the obscenity of "the act"—*Ulysses*—to questions that centered on "the person"—Joyce's genius.[9] Anderson first focused on the definition of obscenity. After reminding the publishers that they regularly cut "objectionable" material from their novelists' works, she continued, "I should have remembered not to ask a naive question. The subject matter chosen by the men who write today may be objectionable. The war was objectionable, but it occurred to me that I couldn't stop it. And I haven't yet attempted to control the mind of the times" (66–67).

Definitional arguments about the nature of obscenity were common in public discourses about *Ulysses,* both in the pages of the *Little Review* and, later, in the more popular press. In the *Little Review,* R. McM. of Los Angeles requested in a letter published in the June 1918 issue that the editors justify publishing Joyce on grounds other than the "mere statement that 'his work is art.' Justify some of Joyce's obscene commonplaces taken from life neither for power nor beauty nor for any reason but to arrest attention, cheap Bowery vileness." Heap replied, defending Joyce in what would become characteristic fashion: "It is impossible for Joyce to be obscene. He is too concentrated on his work. He is too religious about life." Again, Heap and Anderson insisted on changing questions of obscenity— as they had done with questions of intelligibility and readership—into unarguable absolutes about the nature of art and genius.

Heap reiterated this view of Joyce and his work many times, but her most forceful statement came in her most often anthologized essay, "Art and the Law," which she begins by renouncing any authority on the subject of obscenity, again moving the argument to questions of art: "I do not understand Obscenity; I have never studied it nor had it, but I know that it must be a terrible and peculiar menace to the United States. I know that there is an expensive department maintained in Washington with a chief and fifty assistants to prevent its spread—and in and for New York we have the Sumner vigilanti" (6). In one of only four examples of *Little Review* editors explicating the excerpted text of *Ulysses,* Heap explained—first textually and then philosophically—why she did not define the "Nausicaa" episode as obscene:

> To a mind somewhat used to life Mr. Joyce's chapter seems to be a record of the simplest, most unpreventable, most unfocused sex thoughts possible in a rightly-constructed, unashamed human being. Mr. Joyce is not teaching early Egyptian perversions nor inventing new ones. Girls lean back everywhere, showing lace and silk stockings; wear low cut sleeveless gowns, breathless bathing suits; men think thoughts and have emotions about these things everywhere— seldom as delicately and imaginatively as Mr. Bloom—and no one is corrupted. Can merely reading about the thoughts he thinks corrupt a man when his thoughts do not? All power to the artist, but this is not his function.
>
> It was the poet, the artist, who discovered love, created the lover, made sex everything that it is beyond a function. It is the Mr. Sumners who have made it an obscenity. (6)

In addition to increasing her veneration of the artist by claiming no one but the poet or artist has saved sex from being mere "function," Heap asserts that the function of art is precisely *not* to "corrupt a man," not to be aphrodisiac. Joyce is merely representing life as it is. And, Heap argues, merely reading about representations of Bloom's response to Gerty MacDowell will not cause readers to reenact the scene.

Finally, to conclude her essay, Heap once again moves the *locus* of the argument from questions of obscenity to questions of aesthetics: "The only question relevant at all to 'Ulysses' is—Is it a work of Art? The men best capable of judging have pronounced it a work of the first rank. Anyone with a brain would hesitate to question the necessity in an artist to create, or his ability to choose the right subject matter. Anyone who has read 'Exiles,' 'The Portrait,' and 'Ulysses' from the beginning, could not rush in with talk of obscenity. No man has been more crucified on his sensibilities than James Joyce" (7). Heap's reliance on the authority of the "men best capable of judging" again raises the issues of authority and, ultimately, canonicity. Her use of the word *crucified* finally makes explicit the associations between art as a question of belief and Joyce as a martyr that colored many of her and Anderson's public discourses about *Ulysses*. Instead of judging for herself, Heap suggests, she believes in Joyce as a true artist because certain authorities have suggested that she do so.

Associations other than religious prompted another "Reader Critic" to raise a slightly different issue, wondering why modern art needed to be obscene to be art. Headlined "The Good Old Days" and published in the March 1920 issue, the letter reflected concern for changing standards of morality during the second decade of the twentieth century: "Great artists of other times have conveyed beautiful ideas, simply, and reached even the most naive minds. Why not now? Only because modern artists are mad, writhing and grotesquely posturing, drugged with neurotic and oblique feeling" (60). The unsigned letter concluded: "To read and see and feel such art leaves one with the same sick nausea and distaste as when one has become a party to some shameful orgy" (61). (This reader would not be the last to consider *Ulysses* nauseating; Woolsey declared, "whilst in many places the effect of 'Ulysses' on the reader is undoubtedly somewhat emetic, nowhere does it tend to be an aphrodisiac" [*United States v. One Book Called "Ulysses"*].) In response, Heap used yet another rhetorical strategy to change questions of obscenity to questions of art—this time to questions of the artist himself. Heap offered a pithy reply making, in Perelman and Olbrechts-Tyteca's terms (293–96), the person coexistent with the act: "Can you imagine James Joyce ashamed of what he writes?" (62).

Finally, the last letter in the *Little Review* discussing the question of obscenity in *Ulysses* manifested a sense of impatience. F. E. R. wrote in the April 1920 issue: "And what caused the suppression of the January issue?

The Joyce, I suppose. I have been through the whole number very care-
fully and the 'Ulysses' is the only offender I can find. But why cavil about
Joyce at this late day?—it would seem to me that after all these months he
could be accepted, obscenity and all, for surely the post-office authorities
should recognize that only a few read him, and those few not just the kind
to have their whole moral natures overthrown by frankness about natural functions." Like Heap, this writer sees Joyce as merely representing
"natural functions"; resting assured that only a few will read Joyce—and
that those few would be of a certain "moral nature"—this writer concludes
that the fuss should be over. This writer suggests a *topos* that would also
be part of the grounds for the Woolsey decision: when the issue is obscenity, the focus should be on the reader rather than merely on the text—a
very different coexistence of the person with the act than the one Heap
and Anderson argued for.

## Psychopathology

Not an explicit part of the discourse in the *Little Review* but certainly part
of the trial—indeed, the focus of the decision—was the question of Joyce's
mental health, his "disordered mind," as the court decision was quoted
in the 23 February 1921 *New York Tribune* editorial ("Mr. Sumner's Glorious Victory"). That Joyce might have been a psychopath—indeed, that
any author who could describe the thoughts of the likes of Bloom, Stephen,
Molly, and Gerty had to be in some way mentally ill—was hinted at by
many, and not just when the book was first serialized. Eight years later,
Max Eastman would make the same implication: "Communication is here
reduced to a minimum. The values are private—as private as the emotional
life of the insane. . . . This literary form also finds its involuntary parallel
in the madhouse" (634–35).

The most blatant and continuous examples of the connection between
Joyce's writing and his mental health came from the *New York Times*. From
its coverage of the *Little Review* trial and its review of *Ulysses* in 1922 to
a feature article as late as 1927, writers at the newspaper talked about
Joyce's work in terms of mental illness. The first suggestion was in the *Little
Review* trial editorial that opened this chapter: "'Ulysses' is a curious production, not wholly uninteresting, especially to psychopathologists." Even
more remarkable—and much more explicit—is Joseph Collins's 28 May
1922 review of *Ulysses*. In addition to claiming that the novel taught him
"more psychology and psychiatry" than "ten years at the Neurological
Institute," Dr. Collins, as his byline reads, constructed a biography of Joyce/

Dedalus that purported to explain how Joyce came to write both *A Portrait of the Artist as a Young Man* and *Ulysses:* "In early life Mr. Joyce had definitely identified himself as Dedalus, the Athenian architect, sculptor, and magician. This probably took place about the time that he became convinced he was not the child of his parents but a person of distinction and they his foster parents. A very common occurrence in potential psychopaths and budding geniuses" (6). Collins insisted on conflating author and character, at one point declaring that "'Ulysses' comes nearer to being the perfect revelation of a personality than any book in existence" (6). Yet Collins also made the explicit move to discussions of madness. Joyce, Collins wrote, was the only person "outside of a madhouse who has let flow from his pen random and purposeful thoughts just as they are produced. He does not seek to give them orderliness, sequence, or interdependence" (6). Collins suggested that because Joyce revealed about his characters—or, rather, according to Collins, about himself—things that most people would never reveal, Joyce was not well. Collins singled out Joyce's treatment of Bloom for special attention: "When a master technician of words and phrases sets himself the unconscious mind of a moral monster, a pervert and an invert, an apostate to his race and his religion, the simulacrum of a man who has neither cultural background nor personal self-respect, who can neither be taught by experience nor lessoned by example, as Mr. Joyce has done in drawing the picture of Leopold Bloom . . . he undoubtedly knew full well what he was undertaking" (6). Collins continued, disheartened that were it not for Joyce, such intimate data on the perversions of modern man would no longer be available: "Heretofore our only avenues of information of such personalities led through the asylums for the insane, for it was there that such revelations as those of Mr. Joyce were made without reserve" (6).

Simeon Strunsky took a slightly different tack in his 1927 *New York Times Book Review* feature entitled "About Books, *More or Less.*" In it, he argued that Joyce's attention to the minutiae of life is not normal and requires "a rediscovery of the word 'accept.'" Strunsky explained to readers that "among the data of knowledge which 'Ulysses' finds it necessary to assemble . . . are a number of rediscoveries which have attracted the attention of the censor both in this country and in England." He continued,

Mr. Joyce has rediscovered certain physiological processes which are stressed by the authors of books on the care of children in a separate chapter dealing with the importance of forming regular habits at as early an age as possible. He has rediscovered interests and occupations which badly brought-up little boys discovered before him and are in the habit of scribbling on walls and fences. Mr.

Joyce has rediscovered—well—everything about life; and only then, it would appear, has it become possible for him to accept life. Before accepting life he has insisted on a detailed statement, black on white, omitting nothing.

Strunsky concludes that, for Joyce, to accept life is "to make much ado about everything."

After diagnosing the acceptance of everything about life as a particularly modern disease, Strunsky suggests that some things about life should not be accepted—or at least not discussed: "Our reticences are not always hypocrisy or denial. They are rather things accepted so completely as to be forgotten." Then, again focusing on Joyce, Strunsky concluded his essay: "When grown-up men develop a passionate interest in . . . physical and physiological exercises that the child puts out of his mind at 3 years and at 5, they not infrequently end up in the insane asylum."

Besides moving the *locus* of argument from Joyce's book to Joyce himself—as manifested through his characters—discourses about Joyce's mental state commented on the credentials necessary for judging works of literature. While applauding the court's decision in the trial of the *Little Review,* the *New York Tribune* editorial questioned Sumner's knowledge about literature and psychopathology. The editorial ended by proposing that the Society for the Prevention of Vice "secure an advisory board of representative writers and publishers, with a psychiatrist or two, and submit questions of obscenity in literature to their preliminary judgment" ("Mr. Sumner's Glorious Victory").

## The Incomprehensible Genius

*Ulysses*—before becoming the classic canonical text that later readers and scholars have generally agreed it is, at least in the academy—fostered considerable deliberation about issues of publicity, intelligibility, obscenity, and the relationship between psychopathic characters and the writers who create them. Well before its canonicity was settled, Joyce's book got people arguing with each other, deliberating by writing in public about issues of common concern. Should such a book be published? If so, how and for whom? Who is qualified to decide? What if readers are offended? Or what if they cannot "understand" the book? What is obscenity? What is the relationship between it and intelligibility? Does writing about a psychopath imply that one is a psychopath? Does reading about vice persuade readers to be vicious? While "Reader Critics" continued to question—to the extent that they were given an opportunity to do so—blind belief in Joyce's genius, Heap and Anderson moved all questions about *Ulysses* to questions about Joyce. And their answer to any question about Joyce was that he was a true artist. Nothing else needed to be said.

Whatever the writers of these discourses disagreed on—and it is clear that they disagreed on much—they were genuinely and deeply concerned for the future of a world that could produce *Ulysses*. Yet many of them were even more concerned that some would seek to suppress a work not only so powerful but also so revealing about the very conditions that gave it substance. The "Reader Critics" whose public discourses I have studied—even Margaret Anderson and Jane Heap, who argued that the artist and the art should give no consideration to the public—seemed to assert through the practice of writing that their criticism had a public purpose: to make the real people to whom they were writing reconsider how they felt about a complex and compelling book and, through that book, how they felt about their shared world. Indeed, the discourses of Anderson and Heap may be seen to have had great effect; the *topoi* upon which Woolsey and Hand constructed their decisions are precisely the *topoi* about which Anderson and Heap were most insistent.

In his decision in *United States v. One Book Called "Ulysses,"* for example, Woolsey offered two reasons for allowing the novel into the United States. First, Woolsey had to judge Joyce's intent—censorship law at the time located the definitional question of "pornography" in its maker's intent (Lewis 5, 41, 47, 127)—and Woolsey argued that *Ulysses* was a "sincere and honest" book. In what is probably the most often quoted part of his decision, Woolsey ruled that "in spite of its unusual frankness, I do not detect anywhere the leer of the sensualist. I hold, therefore, that it is not pornographic." His warrant for the claim that Joyce was not leering seems to rest largely on his view that Joyce is a "true artist," a literary genius. In what makes for odd legal prose, Woolsey writes: "Joyce has attempted—it seems to me, with astonishing success—to show how the screen of consciousness with its ever-shifting kaleidoscopic impressions carries, as it were on a plastic palimpsest, not only what is in the focus of each man's observation of the actual things about him, but also in a penumbral zone residua of past impressions, some recent and some drawn up by association from the domain of the subconscious." Yet Woolsey bolsters his argument about intent with another claim: "If Joyce did not attempt to be honest in developing the technique which he has adopted in 'Ulysses,' the result would be psychologically misleading and unfaithful to his chosen technique. Such an attitude would be artistically inexcusable." As with issues of publicity, intelligibility, and obscenity in the *Little Review,* the issue of intent here becomes an issue of artistic integrity. Ultimately, the argument that got *Ulysses* into the United States was that the book was "true art" no matter its difficulty, no matter its possible obscenity.

Why Woolsey is known for his decision on *Ulysses*—and why the decision is often interpreted as a turning point in censorship law—involves something other than his relocation of the question of intent to a question of artistic merit. In addition to the question of intent, Woolsey raised the question of effect: "I must endeavor to apply a more objective standard to his book in order to determine its effect in the result, irrespective of the intent with which it was written." Since both sides agreed to forego their right to a jury trial—no great surprise—Woolsey needed to come up with some other standard of "objectivity." Woolsey used this as his carpenter's rule: "Whether a particular book would tend to excite such impulses and thoughts must be tested by the court's opinion as to its effect on a person with average sex instincts—what the French would call *l'homme moyen sensuel*." To determine whether *Ulysses* was obscene, Woolsey gave two friends the legal definition of obscenity and asked them whether the novel fit that definition. Woolsey explains:

> These literary assessors—as I might properly describe them—were called on separately, and neither knew that I was consulting the other. They are men whose opinion on literature and on life I value most highly. They had both read "Ulysses" and, of course, were wholly unconnected with this cause. . . . I was interested to find that they both agreed with my opinion: That reading "Ulysses" in its entirety, as a book must be read on such a test as this, did not tend to excite sexual impulses or lustful thoughts, but that its net effect on them was only that of a somewhat tragic and very powerful commentary on the inner lives of men and women.

In place of a jury of citizen critics, Woolsey called on "literary assessors" to provide an "objective" standard to which he could compare his own judgment of the book. He concludes: "It is only with the normal person that the law is concerned. Such a test as I have described, therefore, is the only proper test of obscenity in the case of a book like 'Ulysses' which is a sincere and serious attempt to devise a new literary method for the observation and description of mankind." Woolsey left wide open the space between "literary assessor" and "normal person," and thus turned the question of effect into a question of literary value as well.

Upholding Woolsey's decision, Judge Hand, in *United States v. One Book Entitled Ulysses by James Joyce,* reiterated Woolsey's arguments, beginning with Joyce's status as literary genius as conferred by "persons whose opinions are entitled to weight." He then, again, moves all issues of obscenity and intelligibility to questions of aesthetics: "That numerous long passages in Ulysses contain matter that is obscene under any fair definition of the word cannot be gainsaid. . . . Page after page of the book is, or seems to be, incomprehensible. But many passages show the trained hand of an artist."

Heap and Anderson's dismissal of those who questioned *Ulysses* or doubted Joyce's genius on any grounds supports Habermas's view of the place of literary periodicals at the beginning of the twentieth century. Habermas stresses that these periodicals never wanted to address "the reading public" insofar as that public represented the majority of the middle class: "The literary periodicals which since the end of the nineteenth century have functioned as the polemical platforms for an avant-garde that changes with the fashions have never had, nor even sought, links with the stratum of a culturally interested bourgeoisie" (*Structural Transformation* 162). This observation fits into Habermas's theory of structural transformation: by refusing to address seriously any public questions about *Ulysses,* Heap and Anderson showed their *Little Review* to be part of a depoliticized social sphere as much as it was part of any literary public sphere. Yet the resonance of Woolsey's and Hand's reasoning with Anderson and Heap's public writings seems to belie Habermas's observation—as well as Anderson and Heap's claims that "true" artists and critics should have no concern for their public. This observation twists Eagleton's claim at the end of *The Function of Criticism* that criticism can have cultural effects only when it "re-connect[s] the symbolic to the political" (123), that it must have an intended social function to be socially important.

Indeed, Anderson and Heap's rhetorical strategies, which consistently pulled *Ulysses* away from questions of publicity and obscenity, as well as Woolsey's and Hand's relocation of legal issues to the realm of aesthetics, are precisely what finally got *Ulysses* legally into the country. *Ulysses* entered the United States not because of the *topoi* of citizen critics but because of the *topoi* of elites, most of which were repeated in legal decisions. Perhaps a larger conclusion from the first trial of *Ulysses* is that all criticism has social consequences, even when the fact of such consequences is anathema to the critic. In any case, questions that Anderson, Heap, and others tried consistently to move into questions of "true art" are with us still, in realms political, critical, and rhetorical. In the next three chapters of this book I study how similar issues were argued publicly in three other twentieth-century literary public spheres.

NOTES

1. To review the early publication history of *Ulysses*, see Ellmann (434–570) and Anderson (*Thirty Years' War* 174–227) as well as the *Little Review* (volumes 4–7).

Whereas excerpts of three of the four novels I focus on in *Citizen Critics* appeared in the literary public spheres that they fostered (no one in Chicago excerpted *Tropic of Cancer* except in private letters sent to "concerned citizens"), I do not include an excerpt of *Ulysses* in this chapter because, unlike *American Psycho* and *Mercy*, it is a canonical text; in addition, it was published serially in the *Little Review*.

2. One recent work recounting some of these conflicts is Jeffrey Segall's *Joyce in America*. Concentrating on controversies about *Ulysses* after Woolsey, Segall has studied *Ulysses* as "a cultural nexus over which critics with opposed ideological perspectives did battle" (3). Bruce Arnold's 1991 book *The Scandal of Ulysses* also includes a recounting of the trials in the United States (4–5, 8–11) and Europe. As Arnold explains in his foreword and manifests throughout the book, however, *The Scandal of Ulysses* is more an attempt to delineate the issues in the contemporary battle of editions between John Kidd and Hans Walter Gabler than it is a work of historical scholarship. For more recent work on the question of the textual authority of different editions of *Ulysses*, see Charles Rossman's introduction and bibliography to a special issue of *Studies in the Novel*.

3. While her historical scholarship is thorough and her project unique, Lewis's book ultimately suffers from the kind of absolutist First Amendment bias that affects many books on literature and obscenity (see, for example, Ernst [with whom Lewis collaborated]; Hutchison; and Rembar). For a critique of the absolutist and consequentialist positions, see Stanley Fish, *There's No Such Thing as Free Speech . . . and It's a Good Thing, Too*.

4. Segall attributes Joyce's canonicity in part to Gilbert's book (3).

5. By *lexicon* I do not mean to suggest a "Lexicon Rhetoricae" in the sense that Burke said he meant it in *Counter-Statement*. I mean that the history and theory of rhetoric offers several more or less codified vocabularies or lexicons that allow rhetoricians to talk about how language works, *topoi* and *stases* in particular (see chapter 1).

6. What I am calling here "paradoxes" could also be discussed as "incompatibilities." While not systematically discussing paradoxes (443–44) and incompatibilities (195–97) together, Perelman and Olbrechts-Tyteca do discuss paradoxes as incompatibilities (443). The point for this study is that interpreting Anderson and Heap's paradoxes can illuminate their choice of rhetorical strategies.

7. Segall argues that this review and Wilson's writing about Joyce in the thirties founded one of the "dual trajectories of Joyce criticism" about Joyce's political consciousness (9, 183). Segall reads Wilson as one of "those independent-minded Marxists who, gravitating toward the more liberal cultural perspective of Trotsky during the 1930s, read with fascination and general sympathy the work of Joyce and other modernists" (9).

8. See chapter 4 of Jeffrey Walker's *Bardic Ethos and the American Epic Poem* for an account of the modernist appropriation and revision of the conventions of bardic poetry and its distinguishing characteristics—one of which was unintelligibility: "The primitivistic and non-rational, or even the antirational, continued to be a conventional sign among the modernists of the poet's virtue as a man allied, like Emerson's wise man and orphic poet, with truth and God—or with the exalted psychic modes of the biological elite" (78). For these writers, endlessness, inconclusion, and unintelligibility became "signs of the poet's *authority*" (81).

9. Perelman and Olbrechts-Tyteca see the argumentative strategy of making the person coextensive with the act (293–305) as a substitution of the essential (the person) with the transitory (the act): "Considering a phenomenon as part of the person's structure endows it with a higher status" (294). Anderson used this strategy to move, once more, questions about *Ulysses* to questions about Joyce, self-evident because Joyce was a genius.

# 3

# "A Slut in the Neighborhood": Tropic of Cancer in Chicago

Twenty-five thousand copies of the pornographic novel, "Tropic of Cancer," have been shipped into Chicago, and tens of thousands more are on their way.

Before publicizing these facts, deep consideration must be given to whether this attention serves to increase the demand for the book.

The alternative is to ignore it. "Tropic of Cancer" cannot be ignored. Its circulation is an insult to the community.

It is like a slut walking down a neighborhood street, half undressed and spewing filth to those near her.

The slut has a legal right to be on the street. "Tropic of Cancer" has literary merit, in the opinion of competent critics, and because of this the justice department has given the opinion it has a legal right to circulate.

Police in Chicago and suburbs are outraged by the book. They consider it obscene and potentially harmful to youngsters who will provide the major market. . . . Police officials who deal with juvenile sex criminals believe the book will corrupt young people and stimulate them toward sexual offenses. (Mabley "Paperback Insult")

The following letters appeared on the editorial page of the *Chicago Sun-Times* on 13 March 1962:

I would like to express my complete disgust after reading Hoke Norris' column in the Sun-Times March 7. The 10,000 letters sent out by the Citizens for Decent Literature were to make the people addressed aware of the immoral contents of "Tropic of Cancer," which is so freely sold to juveniles upon request. We are not trying to censor literature, but trying to keep out of reach of children indecent literature and filth. . . . You have failed to uphold the moral standards of all the communities which you serve. (Lazarz)

The above letter is representative of many received in criticism of Norris's position, restated in the following letter. Editor.

Apparently the facts, though endlessly repeated, are never grasped by some people. The chief justice of the Cook County Superior Court has ruled that "Tropic of Cancer," in its entirety, is not pornographic. The "Citizens for Decent Literature," by extracting certain passages, probably created a pornographic book and sent it through the U.S. mails. Judge Epstein based his judgment on the often repeated U.S. Supreme Court rule that books must be considered in their entirety, not in fragments. If Mrs. Lazarz doesn't want to buy "Tropic of Cancer," she has a right not to buy it. If I want to buy it, I have a right to buy it. I have a right to buy it, without interference from her or anybody else. The case is as simple as that. (Norris)

Permit me to introduce myself—I am a regular reader of your paper. I am a Roman Catholic and was for three years a monk-seminarian. . . . I want to congratulate Hoke Norris for his forthright columns on censorship and his outstanding part in the struggle for civil liberties. They are a breath of fresh air in a nation being lulled far too much into sleep in matters of civil liberties and censorship. You respect the intelligence of people to make use of their God-given sense to decide for themselves what they wish to read or not. Not a group or an individual who assumes some special talent and divine inspiration to decide for all others what is good. (Kennedy)

Scholars of literature and obscenity often credit the Woolsey and Hand decisions, on the heels of the Smoot-Hawley Tariff Act of 1930, with clearing the way for legal publication and sale in America of not only Joyce's *Ulysses* but also many other controversial works of literature (see Lockhart and McClure; Gertz and Lewis; Rembar; F. Lewis). In her book *Literature, Obscenity, and Law,* for instance, Felice Flanery Lewis concludes a chapter with the observation that the definition of *Ulysses* as "a modern classic" "made *Ulysses* a bridge between standard classics and the eventual clearing of novels such as Miller's *Tropic of Cancer*" (133). While the importance of individual court decisions as legal precedents cannot be gainsaid, the emphasis by Lewis and other scholars on them can obscure the incremental discursive and rhetorical processes through which social changes occur. In other words, while passage of the Smoot-Hawley Tariff Act undoubtedly aided in the fight to get *Ulysses* into the country, discussions in literary public spheres about definitions of "true art" and the nature of the literary artist set the discursive stage for such legal arguments.

Henry Miller's *Tropic of Cancer* provides an even more complicated instance of the relationship among public discourse, legal discourse, and social change. Ultimately, I argue that public discourses about *Tropic of Cancer* in Chicago affected not only court decisions about that particular book but also later public discussions of the relationships among obscenity, censorship, and social change. Written in the early thirties while Miller was living in Paris, *Tropic of Cancer* was published in Paris in 1934 by Obelisk Press and promptly banned by U.S. Customs.[1] Given the legal and extralegal censorship efforts in the United States,[2] no legal attempt was made to bring *Tropic of Cancer* into the United States until 1948. Ernest J. Besig, director of the Northern California American Civil Liberties Union, tried to bring *Tropic of Cancer* and *Tropic of Capricorn* through U.S. Customs in San Francisco, but five years later the U.S. Customs ban was upheld by the U.S. District Court, Northern District of California (*Besig v. United States,* 208 F.2d 142 [9th Cir. 1953]). Judge Lewis E. Godman's decision in *Besig* suggests that, even twenty years after Woolsey's decision, attitudes toward censorship and the social purpose of literature had not changed. In the few paragraphs she devotes to recounting the thirty-year *Tropic of Cancer* censorship tale, Lewis stresses that Besig's attempt to use depositions from literary critics, among whom Miller's work was widely known and appreciated, was denied. Lewis also notes that the decision reiterated "the familiar concepts that a book should be uplifting, and may be all the more dangerous because it is well written" (208). E. R. Hutchison, quoting the decision, stressed Godman's conservative criteria: the judge perceived his ruling against the books as protecting "the dignity of the human person and the stability of the family unit, which are the cornerstone of our system of society" (34). As Charles Rembar points out, the *Besig* decision was used in an attempt to keep *Lady Chatterley's Lover* out of the United States in 1959 on the grounds that it violated contemporary community standards (117). Clearly, as of the midfifties, no one had made an argument that forcefully enough countered attitudes about the purpose of literature, the role of literary "experts" in society, the definitions of "obscenity" or "community standards," or whether literature or obscenity were entitled to First Amendment protection.

Indeed, in the two decades since the Woolsey and Hand decisions, change had come slowly to censorship law and social attitudes about what was then sometimes called "problem fiction" (see Moon). The closest analog to Smoot-Hawley for the *Tropic of Cancer* case would be the 1959 U.S. Supreme Court ruling in *Roth v. United States,* in which Justice William J. Brennan Jr., writing the majority decision, ruled that obscenity was not constitutionally protected speech or press (*Roth v. United States,* 354 U.S. 476 [1957]). Interpretations of Brennan's five criteria for obscenity in *Roth* would become integral in the more than sixty court cases involving *Tropic of Cancer* and the public discourses surrounding them. Brennan's now famous guideline was as follows: to pronounce a work obscene involved determining "whether to [1] the average person, applying [2] contemporary community standards, [3] the dominant theme of the material taken as a whole appeals to [4] the prurient interest." Brennan added what came to be known as the "social value" test: "All ideas having even the slightest redeeming social importance . . . have the full protection of the guaranties [of the Bill of Rights], unless excludable because they encroach upon the limited area of more important interests [5]." Thus, in *Roth,* the U.S. Supreme Court for the first time articulated specific—if highly interpretable—criteria for determining whether a work was obscene. According to Lewis, *Roth* had direct and powerful effects in literary history. "The concepts expressed in [*Roth*], especially that of redeeming social importance, became the key to the eventual clearing of controversial novels such as *Lady Chatterley's Lover, Tropic of Cancer,* and *Fanny Hill*" (188). In the wake of *Roth* and publication of *Lady Chatterley's Lover* in the United States,[3] proponents of Miller and his novels readied to try once again to get the books published legally in the United States (for details, see Hutchison 40–50 and Gertz and Lewis xix).

Between June 1961, when Grove Press published *Tropic of Cancer,* and June 1964, when the U.S. Supreme Court summarily affirmed the book's right to circulate legally in the United States, roughly sixty court cases involving the novel had been heard at different judicial levels, making Miller, according to his lawyer, Elmer Gertz, "the most litigated author in history" (Gertz and Lewis 228) and *Tropic of Cancer,* according to E. R. Hutchison, "the most censored novel in American history" (2). That Grove Press owner Barney Rosset anticipated some litigation but perhaps not the deluge that ensued is suggested by his offer to pay to defend all booksellers prosecuted for selling *Tropic of Cancer* (Hutchison 53–54; Gertz and Lewis xix–xx; Rembar 169). Though both the U.S. Justice Department and the U.S. Post Office had cleared the book for distribution and sale, only days after Grove Press published *Tropic of Cancer* on 24 June 1961— twenty-seven years after the book was first published in Paris—legal troubles began.[4] Police officers threatening booksellers with arrest was the most common form of censorship; when booksellers persisted by not pulling *Tropic of Cancer* off their shelves, arrests were made (see, among many others, Hutchison 1–2, 74, 80–95, 98, 119; Norris "'Cancer' in Chicago"; "Dealer Charged in Smut Case"; "Suburb Police Act to Bar Miller Book"; "Police Chiefs Sued for Ban on Book Sales"; "Police Censorship"; Kellough; "Kings, Councilors"). A 17 October 1961 *Chicago Sun-Times* story, "Civil Liberties Unit Sues to Halt Ban on 'Tropic,'" reported that Evanston Police Chief Hubert G. Kelsh "is accused of entering Kroch's & Brentano's

Evanston store and threatening employees with arrest unless they withdrew from sale not only the paperback but the hard-cover version." This action resulted in one of the first countersuits over *Tropic of Cancer* in the country; in the suit, the Illinois ACLU charged several suburban Chicago police chiefs with unconstitutionally preventing the sale of the novel.[5] Despite the number of arrests, suits, and countersuits filed specifically about the legality of selling *Tropic of Cancer,* testimony about the book itself was never heard by the U.S. Supreme Court. In what should have ended the history of litigation over Miller's first novel,[6] the high court summarily reversed the conviction of a Florida bookseller for selling *Tropic of Cancer,* ruling that Miller's novel was not obscene and, as such, was constitutionally protected, but offered no written opinion on the issue (*Grove Press v. Gerstein,* 378 U.S. 577 [1964], rev'g 156 So. 2d 537 [Fla. App. 1963]).[7]

While the 1957 *Roth* decision and *topoi* from related cases, then, were in some ways vehicles for the U.S. Supreme Court's anticlimactic clearing of *Tropic of Cancer,* the sheer quantity as well as the particular argumentative strategies of public discourses between 1961 and 1964 also affected judgments about the book at local, state, and national levels. In addition to being the most litigated book, *Tropic of Cancer* was also one of the most widely and intensely discussed books in newspapers and magazines in the twentieth century. Without endorsing polling data as a mark of the quality of knowledge or opinion of Miller, I find the opening paragraph of Hutchison's *Tropic of Cancer on Trial* revealing in that it manifests the quantity of public attention Miller and *Tropic of Cancer* received between 1961 and 1964:

> If in the early part of 1961 Elmo Roper had polled the best possible cross section of Americans on their knowledge of Henry Miller and a book called *Tropic of Cancer,* fewer than one out of a hundred would have been able to answer him intelligently. Less than a year later, however, probably two out of three Americans could have filled in his questionnaire. By 1964, Roper would have had to climb the hills to discover a citizen who hadn't heard about the one man and the one book that had ignited the censorship holocaust searing the whole United States. (1)

In the three years that passed between initial U.S. publication of *Tropic of Cancer* and the U.S. Supreme Court's ultimate—if not resounding—clearing of it, public discourses in response to the many "police actions" and contradictory court decisions about the book produced for public scrutiny literally thousands of arguments for and against a wide range of issues. As with the case of *Ulysses,* the vast majority of these initial public discourses go unrecorded in bibliographies because they are not considered "critical" responses to a canonical "literary" text. More than with *Ulysses,* however, Miller bibliographers have made localized attempts to document newspaper and magazine writings about the book—perhaps because of Miller's less canonical status or because the book attracted so many censors and litigants.[8] Nonetheless, the majority of news stories, columns, and letters to the editor discussed in this chapter are included in no bibliography.

This chapter studies the public discourses in response to *Tropic of Cancer* in Chicago as published in four major metropolitan daily newspapers—the morning *Chicago Tribune* and *Chicago Sun-Times* and the afternoon *Chicago Daily News* and *Chicago's American.* I discuss events from the publication of the novel in June 1961 to the trial before Judge Samuel B. Epstein in Cook County Superior Court in January 1962 of several suburban police officers for suppressing the book to the announcement of Epstein's decision in late February 1962 that *Tropic of Cancer* was not obscene to the twenty-eight-month appeal of Epstein's decision to the Illinois Supreme Court and to that court's decision in June 1964 that the book was, after all, obscene.[9] The Illinois Supreme Court withdrew its obscenity ruling on 7 July 1964, after it reasoned that the U.S. Supreme Court's 22 June *per curiam* ruling made its decision moot.

I was drawn to the Chicago literary public sphere for several reasons. First, competing major metropolitan daily newspapers of diametrically opposed political persuasions offered a chance to study the ways different newspapers covered and editorialized the issues.[10] Early on in the fray, the *Tribune* changed the name of its Sunday best-seller list from "Best Selling Books in the Midwest" to "Among the Best Selling Books in the Midwest" so that it would not have to "draw attention to gutter literature" ("Best Selling Books in the Midwest"; "A Change Is Made"; "Among the Best Selling Books in the Midwest"). In its 13 August 1961 editorial, "Sent to the Cleaner," the paper explained, "We have come to the conclusion that we can no longer publish this list raw. Recently and tardily, we have become aware that some of the best sellers that have appeared on our lists were sewer-written by dirty-fingered authors for dirty-minded readers. We aren't going to further this game by giving publicity to such authors and their titles. . . . We will not knowingly include in it any book that is intended to make money for its author and publisher by being nastier than the next." The *Tribune*'s action was met with a flurry of letters to the editor—most of which are discussed below—but no comment from the city's other newspapers. *Chicago's American* banned all mention of the book, referring to Miller's novel as "that book" in copy and "THAT Book" in headlines ("Trial Opens Tomorrow on 'THAT Book'"; "Author and Publisher of THAT Book File Suit"); the *Tribune* would not mention the book by name, referring in news stories to "a controversial book" ("Eight Suburbs Dismissed in Book Ban Suit").

The *Tribune* and *Chicago's American* firmly fought against *Tropic of Cancer*. In classic Robert McCormick style, the *Tribune* did not report on Epstein's February 1962 ruling that the book was not obscene; instead, two days later, the *Tribune* ran a wire story about a Los Angeles jury finding the novel obscene and added, "The trial could set a precedent here for suppression of the book" ("Novel Ruled Obscene; Book Seller Guilty"). Conversely, the *Sun-Times* and the *Daily News* just as firmly supported their readers' right to read *Tropic of Cancer*—if any of those readers so desired. Columnists Hoke Norris of the *Sun-Times* and Jack Mabley of *Chicago's American* wrote consistently about the book; both Norris and Mabley were called as witnesses in the Cook County Superior Court trial over *Tropic of Cancer*—Norris for the prosecution (of the police chiefs) and Mabley for the defense.[11]

Another reason the *Tropic of Cancer* situation in Chicago is worth study is the role extralegal censorship played. As suggested above, the number and ferocity of "police actions" was incredible; at one point, Elmer Gertz, Miller's attorney, was handling sixteen different suits against police chiefs in the city and suburbs. Citizen groups were also active in Chicago after Epstein announced his decision. Citizens for Decent Literature, a local protest group, excerpted nineteen passages from the novel and mailed them to ten thousand people in and around Chicago. While Mabley supported this action ("'That Book' to Get Shock Treatment"), Norris commented that in doing so the citizens' group demonstrated a lack of understanding of U.S. Supreme Court rulings on literature and obscenity, which consistently required works to be considered in their entirety. "The extracts, within the book, are not pornographic," Norris wrote; "separated, they become something else" ("Flood of Filth"). Finally, both the month-long delay before Epstein's decision and the nearly two-and-one-half-year delay between his decision and the Illinois Supreme Court's reversal of it allowed time for the volume of public discourses in the four Chicago newspapers to have some effect. Indeed, Epstein was publicly lauded by some (see, for example, "Statement of Support") and lambasted by many more (see, for example, "Judge Keeps Ban on 'Tropic' Sale").[12]

In sum, the public discourses in Chicago in the wake of publication of *Tropic of Cancer* offer a unique opportunity to study an intensely active literary public sphere with definite geographical limitations in which appeared and were argued the *topoi* upon which the *Roth* and *Jacobellis* decisions were made and on which many later obscenity decisions and debates focus (see note 7). First, writers used publicity as a *locus* of quantity argument. In Perelman and Olbrechts-Tyteca's terms, *loci* of quantity assert "the superiority of that which is accepted by the greater number of people" (86). While publicity was in some senses feared, those who argued against the book believed wholeheartedly that the more people who knew about the book's evil, the less threatening the book would be.

Even more striking is the clash of *loci* of quantity versus *loci* of quality over the question of standards in discussions about *Tropic of Cancer*: as expressed by a *Chicago Daily News* columnist, "What are contemporary community standards? And who is to determine them?" (Lind). Many arguments about the effect of a book so salacious as *Tropic of Cancer*— what *Chicago's American* columnist Jack Mabley consistently figured as "a slut in the neighborhood"—centered on definitions of "community" and whose authority answered such questions. Arguments about community standards depended on claims about the majority (a *locus* of quantity); the other side of that argument was the protection of individual rights and responsibilities (a *locus* of quality). Indeed, the whole issue can be seen in terms of *loci* of quantity—the rights of "the community," "the people," or "the public interest"—versus *loci* of quality—the rights of a "unique" book, author, or individual. In Perelman and Olbrechts-Tyteca's terms, *loci* of quality pertain "when the strength of numbers is challenged" and when "the unique is linked to a concrete value" (89), in this case literary merit and freedom of speech.

In addition to questions of "community standards" and authority, debates about *Tropic of Cancer* centered on the social effects of "problem" literature and obscenity, interestingly so since this debate occurred while academic new criticism was at its apex in the same city. These arguments depended on what Perelman and Olbrechts-Tyteca call argument by unlimited development (287–92), a structure also used by those who claimed that *Tropic of Cancer* should be not suppressed because censorship of one book or film would lead to censorship of infinitely more. While those who read and wrote publicly in the Chicago literary public sphere often reasoned about definitions of obscenity and the scope of First Amendment protection, discourses about the social value of literature seem to have most affected further deliberations and actions about *Tropic of Cancer* and other literature— including debates about such novels as *American Psycho* and *Mercy*.

In this chapter, then, I analyze public arguments about publicity, "community standards," authority, and the social effects of literature as discussed in the literary public sphere that grew in response to publication and sale of *Tropic of Cancer* in and around Chicago and argue that those discourses helped shape legal decisions and further debates on issues of censorship and social change. Given the polarity of opinion among the newspapers and the sharply divided pro- and anticensorship forces in Chicago, is it valid to claim these are all participants in one literary public sphere? Though opinions were deeply divided, it is clear that—as in the case of *Ulysses*—those who read and wrote publicly about *Tropic of Cancer* held a concern for their shared world, often expressed as a concern for the rights and well-being of their children. Though not everyone agreed on their specific responsibility, all agreed—partly through the act of writing itself and partly through the arguments they made—that they shared some responsibility for the situation and its outcome. As expressed in a letter written by Mrs. Paul A. McHugh to the *Tribune,* "We all share the responsibility to stem this 'dirty deluge.'" Partly because of their geographical proximity, those who wrote would share the consequences of any ultimate judgment about *Tropic of Cancer.* As such, they constituted a public; even those who wrote on behalf of what might be called special interest groups were participating in a wider public because they agreed "on the formation of this intellectual community, and, after that, on the fact of debating a specific question together" (Perelman and Olbrechts-Tyteca 14; see also chapter 1).

The following public discourses on and about *Tropic of Cancer* in Chicago reveal for scrutiny the rhetorical processes through which a controversial work of fiction played a part in changing social values and practices during a time when courts around the country—from municipal courts to the highest court in the land—were deeply divided at even the definitional *stasis* on nearly every obscenity case that came before them.

## Publicity, Public Opinion, and the Public Interest

A tiny four-column-inch review in the *Chicago Daily News* in July 1961 marks the first mention of *Tropic of Cancer*'s entry into Chicago (Bradley). But it was the *Tribune's* 13 August editorial, "Sent to the Cleaner," that gave the book its first extended publicity—ironic since the editorial and the change of policy it attempted to justify were prompted by fears of the possible negative consequences of giving the book publicity. As mentioned above, the editorial explained the newspaper's decision to change the title of its best-seller list to avoid publicizing "stinkers." The editors reasoned that there is a difference between "news" and "publicity" and that such a definitional distinction—in addition to conjectures about the intentions of authors and publishers—would enable them to decide which books did not belong on their best-seller list: "Otherwise respectable bookmen have comforted themselves after publishing the stinkers by telling themselves that the fault lies with the readers who crave this kind of thing. We, too, have been deceiving ourselves with the notion that what the publishers publish and what the booksellers sell in largest volume are facts to be recorded by us, like changes in the stock market and batting averages, because people are interested in them." But, the editorial continued, given that the best-seller list helped sell "gutter literature," the newspaper would no longer publicize any book "intended to make money for its author and publisher by being nastier than the next. . . . We aren't going to further this game by giving publicity to such authors and their titles." From the first mention of *Tropic of Cancer* in the *Tribune* and *Chicago's American,* publicity was seen in some senses as an evil to be avoided—avoided, anyway, when it would sell dangerous books and make money for a few unscrupulous authors and publishers.

A week later, the day the *Tribune* removed *Tropic of Cancer* from the best-seller list and changed the list's title, the newspaper ran a second explanatory column, "A Change Is Made," beside the renamed list. In it, the editors reiterated that, although the best-seller list was not meant to recommend books, "a feeling has developed that such a listing carries implied approval." Much more strongly than the editorial, this statement tied the *Tribune*'s actions to "the public interest" and definitions of a newspaper's responsibility to its readers:

> We will continue to review such books, as a means of informing our readers, when we feel they are by an author of sufficient reputation or will be publicized to such an extent that critical attention should be offered. But if they then become best sellers you will have to get the news elsewhere. Too many book buyers, it was felt, were using the best seller lists as an indiscriminate guide and found themselves with books they didn't want around the house, or were sorry they had sent as gifts. . . . Some of those [books] left on [the list] will offend some readers. But it has been decided that it is not in the public interest to continue to offer the best seller list unchecked.

The editors argue that it is sometimes in "the public interest" to keep information from the public, especially when that information can have what the newspaper came to regard as negative consequences. When a controversial book has received a certain amount of publicity already, however, the *Tribune* would risk further publicity by offering "critical attention" in what the newspaper claimed was the public interest. The policy and the argumentative strategies combined *loci* of quantity (what is best for the most people—what is in "the public interest") with the appearance/reality pair (it would appear that it would be in the public interest for our readers to be as fully informed as possible; but—"We have been deceiving ourselves," as the editorial states—in reality, our readers are better off if we keep this information from them). In so arguing, the newspaper put itself in the role of an authority on obscenity, a point I will return to.

The *Tribune* published more than thirty letters in response to its decision to rename the best-seller list, most of them in favor of the change; letters were initially grouped under two headlines, "For Us" and "Against Us." Writers supporting the *Tribune* generally hoped that publicity over the change would work in the interests of what one letter writer described as "the finer impulses and desires of a thinking man" (Berthold). They also tended to stress the press's responsibility to fight moral decline and to act in what the writers saw as the public interest; thus they also depended on *loci* of quantity arguments about the most good for the most people. Conversely, letters criticizing the *Tribune* tended to attack the definitional distinction between publicity and news and, as discussed later in this chapter, questioned the possibility of judging a writer's or publisher's intent or asked who should have the authority to judge whether a book has social value or whether it is obscene.

Writers who supported the *Tribune*'s new policy articulated a hope that publicity would work in their favor—a clear use of a *locus* of quantity. Rosalie M. Gordon, identifying herself as "Editor, 'America's Future,'" encouraged the *Tribune* and its readers to feel they were part of a burgeoning bandwagon: "Let's hope you have started something that will spread widely." Mrs. Paul A. McHugh expressed a similar sentiment: "We . . . trust that other publications will soon follow your lead." John T. Pirie, president of Carson Pirie Scott and prime competitor of Marshall Field IV, who also owned the *Sun-Times,* entered the fray when he supported the *Tribune*'s position: "Because of your Sunday editorial about the character of books and other literature that are being printed, I have asked our people to write to the publishers and tell them we will not handle filthy, immoral books, and we are returning those that we have." While publicity was sometimes seen as an agent that worked against moral good—witness the *Tribune*'s initial editorial and columns by Jack Mabley of *Chicago's American*—it was also seen as a tool that could assist in the fight against obscene books and moral decline in general—in addition to selling department store wares.

Those writing in support of the *Tribune*'s policy also responded to arguments about the responsibility of the press to act in the public interest. Again, how that interest was defined depended on whether writers used *loci* of quantity or *loci* of quality. Many people simply lauded the *Tribune* for its editorial and change of policy: K. C. Day's statement—"'Sent to the Cleaner' is one of the finest examples of journalistic responsibility and integrity that I have seen in recent years. Congratulations and stick to it"— is a clear example of that kind of response. Yet other writers associated the editorial with more philosophical comments about the role of the press in society. C. R. Billimack wrote, "It seems high time that responsible newspapers reflect standards of morality and decency as honestly seen by their editors, as opposed to simply 'reporting' with emphasis on the sensational." This distinction between "reflecting" and "simply 'reporting'" is articulated differently by Jack D. Parker, identified as "Rector, St. Gregory's Episcopal Church": "A newspaper has the responsibility to lead in some areas, rather than merely to follow [and thereby encourage] trends that are an expression of some of the sickness of our age." Again, publicity can be seen either as a positive or a negative force, depending on the writer's view of its consequences.

Some readers wholly accepted the *Tribune*'s definitional distinction between what is news and what is not, sometimes conflating editorial policy with reporting, as this writer did: "This is responsible newspaper reporting" (Spoor). Several letter writers saw the *Tribune*'s policy as having real social effects. Mrs. Fred J. Tooze, president of the National Women's Christian Temperance Union, wrote that the *Tribune*'s "fine public service" of changing the best-seller list "will prove a real help to Chicago, and we believe to the nation also"; another writer added, "Decisions like yours will allay, to some extent, the shallowness of today's thinking among our readers" (Lipuma). Many readers seem to express a genuine appreciation for what the *Tribune* had done. As Casper Apeland wrote, "How easily you could have hidden behind the cloak of 'giving your readers what they want.'" Of course, in some senses, that is exactly what the *Tribune* did.

Many others were not nearly so appreciative. The *Tribune* editorial's definitional argument about what is and is not news came in for heavy fire. After asking what criteria the *Tribune* would use to bar books from the best-seller list, A. Kolben extended the *Tribune*'s definitional claim about what deserves to be regarded as news and responded directly to the editorial's argument by comparison: "This form of pseudo-moralistic selectivity could also be applied to the stock market. Why not omit stocks of companies that have been convicted of price fixing or antitrust violations? Furthermore, surely no upstanding citizen would wish to know the batting average of a ball player who has run afoul of the law." While Kolben made more explicit the moral nature of the *Tribune's* definitional claim, Joseph M. Faulkner of the "Main Street Book Store" stressed that the *Tribune* should run news regardless of its morality: "A list of best sellers is a news item just the same as obituaries and crime reports. It tells what is happening and not what we think should happen." Finally, some readers connected the *Tribune's* best-seller policy with its reputation for slanted news coverage: "From now on when you report the election of 23 Republican Congressmen, we'll all wonder whether there were only seven Democrats elected—or 107" (Nelson).

Indeed, the tie between news coverage and public opinion was discussed again and again in the pages of the *Tribune* during the three years that *Tropic of Cancer* was on trial in Illinois. Writing on a different matter, Richard M. Selleg coined a phrase that applies to the *Tribune's* best-seller policy as well as to its coverage of the trial of *Tropic of Cancer.* Reflecting on public opinion as manufactured and institutions' responsibilities in that light, Selleg writes:

> While in Spain recently I had an opportunity to talk informally with a state department official and his wife. During the course of the conversation the question arose of the effect that public opinion has upon the formation of foreign policy emanating from the state department.
>
> I was astounded to hear this burocrat assert that the state department forms public opinion, and thereby is not influenced by it.
>
> The recent episode in which the state department has denied Moise Tshombe a visa to come to this supposed great land of free speech smacks of an attempt to form public opinion by omission—omission of the opportunity for Tshombe to state his case before a free audience in this country and not just in the Congo.

"Public opinion by omission" is a charge readers made against the *Tribune* in connection with its coverage of different judicial decisions on *Tropic of Cancer.* Fred Jordan wrote to complain that the *Tribune* neglected to mention Epstein's comments about the perils of censorship and people's right to read: "I protest your slanted report on the hearing on the injunction against 'Tropic of Cancer,' particularly Judge Epstein's ruling that cleared it of obscenity charges. Your report said in the lead paragraph that the judge had found passages which were 'lewd, vile, vulgar, and [containing] revolting language.' Nowhere did you say the judge had found the book to be 'a literary work of substantial merit.'" In closing, Jordan made a distinction between news and editorials that not all readers would be willing or able to make: "You surely didn't like the ruling, but the place to show such dislike would have been in your editorial page." Yet just as publicity was argued as a warrant on both sides of the question, slanted news coverage was a charge heard on both sides of the *Tropic of Cancer* debate. Writing to the *Chicago Daily News,* Herbert D. Toenies complains that the newspaper argued for freedom only on issues it was in favor of. "Your editorial of Feb. 23 on Judge Epstein's ruling is typical of your paper's biased opinions," Toenies wrote. "Using the guise of a freedom fighter, you condone—yea even endorse—the printing and selling of 'lewd, coarse, and disgusting literature'. . . . Where were you with your great crusade for freedom when flouridationists invaded our country, yea even conquered our fair city?" Toenies's argument resonates again with the conflict between *loci* of quantity and *loci* of quality: he asks that the *Daily News* stay on one side consistently, arguing for individual freedom in the case of choosing the ingredients in tap water as well as the books in one's living room.

Significantly, publicity and definitional claims about what is and is not news did not become an issue in the *Sun-Times,* the newspaper that most consistently provided news coverage of the trials of *Tropic of Cancer,* most vociferously argued for individual rights over community standards, and published the largest number of letters about the novel. As in the *Tribune,* however, publicity was an issue in *Chicago's American* from the first mention of the book in Jack Mabley's 13 October 1961 column. Unlike the *Tribune,* the *American* never made an explicit statement about why it would not, after Mabley's column, refer to the book or its author by name.

Mabley's column opens by reporting that twenty-five thousand copies of *Tropic of Cancer* had been shipped to Chicago, "and tens of thousands more are on their way." Then Mabley adds: "Before publicizing these facts, deep consideration must be given to whether this attention serves to increase the demand for the book" ("Paperback Insult"). Mabley stresses the negative effects of publicity in such cases, much as the *Tribune* did in its editorial and much as Anne Bartlett does in a letter to the *Chicago Daily News:* "I hope the boys in City Hall are aware that what the prohibition era did for whisky, the censorship era will do for sex. When they hold up the newsstands and confiscate such books as 'Tropic of Cancer' and the girlie magazines, they only whet the public's appetite for more of the same." Publicity is bad because it sells more pornographic novels. Yet Mabley's alarmist tone and his repeated use of the slut metaphor to discuss the book suggest he did not see publicity as the ultimate evil in and of itself.[13] The alternative to publicizing the book, Mabley writes,

> is to ignore it. "Tropic of Cancer" cannot be ignored. Its circulation is an insult to the community. . . .
> The book deals heavily with carnal experiences, with perversion, with human

filth and excrement. To the unsophisticated reader it is nauseating and repulsive.

Police officials who deal with juvenile sex criminals believe the book will corrupt young people and stimulate them toward sexual offenses.

Mayor Daley turned purple at his press conference yesterday when a Chicago's American reporter read him a passage.

Mabley is sufficiently worried about the effects of the book on young people that he foregoes his concern with publicizing the book; as such, he displays his and reflects others' ambivalence about publicity. In the *Tribune* publicity is a phenomenon to be feared when it has negative consequences but used when it might have positive consequences. For readers publicity is most often a tool for "the public interest." Mabley's rhetoric manifests both views of publicity and, as such, suggests how *loci* of quality and quantity conflict; those tensions are even clearer when community standards are discussed in the Chicago literary public sphere that formed after *Tropic of Cancer* came to town.

## Which Community's Standards?

The conflict between *loci* of quantity and quality in arguments about *Tropic of Cancer* often hinged on arguments about community standards, attempts to define what was meant by "community," and the relationship between group and individual rights. As Gertz and Rembar point out in their accounts of litigation over the novel, Justice Brennan was unclear about definitions of community in his *Roth* decision; as a result Rembar used the Massachusetts *Tropic of Cancer* case—the first ban in the country—to attempt to clarify the definition of "community" as a "national community" rather than a "local community" (see Gertz and Lewis 158; Rembar 190). That a community of literary critics—"highbrow" or "sophisticated readers," as they are often called in courtroom and newspaper discourse—might find the book acceptable did little to convince opposed citizens that it was not obscene; literary merit as a *locus* of quality issue was often meant to undercut the judgments of the majority. Conversely, that certain suburbanites found Miller either not to their taste or dangerous did not convince other readers that the book should be banned. Further, arguments over whom the book would harm—those needing protection from the book or from the "Peeping Toms" who would read it—depended on questions about community and dissociations between "us" and "them."

In yet another of his statements on *Tropic of Cancer*, a *Chicago's American* news story reported that the columnist Jack Mabley testified in

Epstein's court that "90 to 95 per cent of the purchasers of the book would be juveniles 'or persons with juvenile minds. People would buy the book because they have heard it was dirty.' In cross-examination, Mabley testified that he read the book 'because it was news'" ("Book Damaging, Mabley Testifies"). Many definitional arguments about "community standards" attempted to dissociate those who would desire to read *Tropic of Cancer* from those who would not—"the people" or "the community." In its editorial "Sent to the Cleaner," the *Tribune* removed from its best-seller list literature meant "for dirty-minded readers." In a letter supporting that editorial, Rev. Louis Stumpf claimed that "gutter literature is not the demand of the people," a dissociation echoed by Vangie R. Morrisey in another letter: "Congratulations! Decent people have hesitated to purchase for home use or as gifts, books which are rated as 'best sellers' but which, on being opened, may bring a blush of shame." E. R. Rekruceak echoed those sentiments in *Chicago's American:* "The material in this book certainly does not measure up to the standards of decent people." "The people," that is, "those who are not dirty-minded," or "decent people," will have no desire to buy *Tropic of Cancer*—or even to know that it is a best-seller.

Such arguments about who constituted "the community" and just what "standards" prevailed were a part of the *Tropic of Cancer* debate from its beginnings in Chicago. In one of the first news stories on the novel's arrival in Chicago, "Book Shocks Daley, He Orders Probe," an unidentified *Chicago's American* reporter quoted one of Mayor Daley's lawyers, who stressed that different communities have different standards: "The Chicago and Illinois laws against obscenity were amended recently to conform with the latest ruling on the matter by a United States Supreme court. This ruling indicates that local court decisions must hinge on contemporary reading standards in various communities. Since this book has been riding high on best seller lists all over the country, the question arises: 'Can this book be banned legally here if it was accepted under our standards?' I believe it should be, but can it?" Yet dissociations about what "the community" would and would not accept and what role the press played in manufacturing those judgments were clouded in the most "conservative" of the four newspapers each day under the caption "Girl-Watching Department." On the very day the *Tribune* changed the title of its best-seller list and removed *Tropic of Cancer* from that list, for example, *Chicago's American* ran a photo of a young woman spread eagle on her stomach and wearing a bikini. Under the photo was this caption: "DREAM IN A STREAM: Forming a most delightful 'X' with her shapely limbs, Dutch Film Actress Thea

Flammy strikes an unusual position in Tiber River in Rome." If "community standards" would accept that without question, why all the fuss about
*Tropic of Cancer?*

A possible answer to that question came through arguments about "the
average Chicagoan" or "the average reader," arguments closely associated
with "community standards." The "average reader" of *Chicago's American* saw no contradiction between banning smut and ogling photos of
young women. In one of several letters he wrote to Chicago newspapers
during the *Tropic of Cancer* debate, Edward W. Rekruciak claimed in a
letter to the *Daily News* that Miller's book should not be sold because "the
material in the book does not represent the standards of the average Chicagoan." He continued: "The Municipal Code of Chicago plainly states
that obscenity is based on an average person applying contemporary community standards. I cannot agree with the judge that the average person
in Chicago accepts the material in this book as his or her standard." Arguments like Rekruciak's drew responses that hinged on individual rights,
again showing how *loci* of quantity and quality conflicted at many points
in this literary public sphere. Joseph M. Gabriel wrote in the *Daily News*
that while standards are one thing, behavior is another:

> Writers of letters to the editor have stated that "the standards of our commu-
> nity are set by the average adult citizen, not by the literary critic," etc, and that
> "these individuals are in a distinct minority and democracy has just suffered a
> setback when the minority determines the standards of the majority."
>
> Who in our area is *forcing* the majority to buy Mr. Miller's book? Under what
> guise of virtue or morality does the majority have the right to inflict its views of
> freedom, taste, etc., upon a minority?

This clash between majority and minority or group and individual rights,
a recurring point of conflict in discussions about censorship and questions
of literary merit, grew more complicated when the minority was represented as a sexual deviant or an innocent child. Jack McPhaul wrote in
the *Chicago Sun-Times* about the high cost of the hardcover edition of
*Tropic of Cancer:* "I can't think of any other recent novel with that high a
price tag. . . . It would be a pity if someone were out to make a killing from
among the Peeping Toms who will inevitably invest in the book for the sole
purpose of a scavenger hunt for the four-letter words." McPhaul's use of
the phrase "Peeping Toms" was more blatant than most writers' dissociations; nevertheless, many who argued that the book should be suppressed
did so in the guise of protecting others from the book or its consequences.
Mrs. Theodore T. Lazarz represented many of those writing letters when

she explained that she was fighting against *Tropic of Cancer* to protect children from the harm that the book would do: "The 10,000 letters sent out by the Citizens for Decent Literature were to make the people addressed aware of the immoral contents of 'Tropic of Cancer,' which is so freely sold to juveniles upon request. We are . . . trying to keep out of reach of children indecent literature and filth." Lazarz's letter depends on a certain view of the social impact of literature, a point I will return to below. Nonetheless, she clearly sees her role—and the role of the press—as protecting children from a harmful book.

Not all writers, however, dissociated themselves from those who read or desired to read what Charles M. Crowe, "President, Church Federation of Greater Chicago," described as "books of trashy content." Perhaps basing his argument on the depravity of humanity, Crowe argued that the newspaper, like governmental safety programs, could save people from themselves: "We have pure food and drug laws to prevent unscrupulous profiteers from poisoning our bodies, yet we actually encourage equally unscrupulous authors and publishers to poison our minds. We have laws against pornographic trash being peddled on the news stands, yet excuse equally pornographic materials in novels under the lame excuse of freedom of speech." More often, however, writers made arguments about community standards in an effort to argue that they and the newspapers could save others from the evil of books like *Tropic of Cancer*.

In an argument structured very much like dissociations of "dirty-minded readers" from "decent people"—an argument backed up by news coverage that stressed the provincial nature of Chicago's suburbs—Edward F. McElroy, "Commander, Department of Illinois Catholic War Veterans USA," responded to Epstein's admission that *Tropic of Cancer* shocked him upon first reading:

> The Illinois Department of Catholic War Veterans would like to go on record as opposing distribution of a book that shocks a judge the first time he reads it. Further, the department would like to state for its members living in Judge Epstein's jurisdiction that their standards of decency still do not accept the use of dirty words or the description of lewd and vulgar incidents into their homes. They have a right therefore to resent a book which brings these things into their community.
>
> They are confident that the average citizen in the community shares their indignation. If a judge is shocked by a book, think of the impact it will have on young people who read it—youth who may not be concerned with literary values.

McElroy's conflation in his first paragraph of "into their homes" and "into their community" manifests a lack of boundary between inside and outside, public and private that reflects the absence of a separate private sphere. In addition, McElroy dissociated Epstein's jurisdiction—all of Cook County—from municipal Chicago and stressed that "average citizens" do not accept the lowered standards of the urbanites.

A story by Jack Lind in the *Chicago Daily News* even more directly addressed the issue of "community standards" and differences between city and suburb. After explaining the criteria established in *Roth* and quoting Gertz on the number of communities across the country that had declared *Tropic of Cancer* not obscene, Lind quotes Gertz at greater length on the subject of Chicago, its suburbs, and the rest of the country:

> "I can't see the strange logic in Chicago being a world apart—especially since Chicago is one of the great educational and cultural centers in the nation."
>
> To make his point, Gertz has introduced a long statement listing the city's universities, professional schools, publishing houses and libraries.
>
> "We have more than 100 libraries of consequence," he said. "Yet Chicagoans, for all their literateness, supposedly can't decide for themselves whether they want to read the 'Tropic.'
>
> "The question in determining this case is not what the community standards are in Oak Park or Maywood," says Gertz.
>
> "The phrase refers to the wide community of the country. Why should Chicago's standards be any different from the rest of the country?"

Yet it was just that desire—to hold firm in the face of deteriorating moral standards—that prompted so many readers to write publicly in response to *Tropic of Cancer*. After the Illinois Supreme Court decision, columnist Jack Mabley could claim with pride, "Chicago is getting a reputation around the country as a very straight-laced town, as far as circulation of salacious books is concerned" ("Smut Sellers' Strange Views of the Law").

Not all readers, of course, were so pleased to have their "suburban jewels," as the columnist Hoke Norris described the outlying areas ("Police Censor Book"), determine their reputation or their reading matter. In a letter to the *Tribune* following its change of policy on the best-seller list, James R. Turner admonished the newspaper: "This new policy is something I would have expected from a country weekly, but not from one of the country's 10 best newspapers." And a few months later, Alvin Jasper Marks appealed directly to city-dwellers to dissociate themselves from suburban closed-mindedness: "I believe it is now time to speak concerning the banning of sales of the book 'Tropic of Cancer' in Chicago. I believe Chicago, the 'Second City,' can't afford to be petty and provincial over a book that is a landmark in literature. We as a city cannot afford to be biased by the myopic beliefs of suburbanites." News coverage of the long-awaited Illinois Supreme Court decision on *Tropic of Cancer* stressed that standards in the city might change at a pace different from that in the suburbs: "'Despite the trial court's observation that the coverall bathing suit appears to be being replaced by the bikini, and the ballroom dance by the twist, and that perhaps society today is more sophisticated than it was a generation ago, we do not feel that the contemporary community standards of Chicago or of this state are such that restriction upon the circulation of such books as "Tropic of Cancer" . . . is beyond the purview of police power'" (M. Jones 1).

While most writers would concede that Miller and Grove Press did not have the typical suburbanite in mind when they wrote and published *Tropic of Cancer,* others argued that the book was meant for a highbrow audience only. Articles covering the Illinois Supreme Court decision stressed the court's statement that Miller's novel was intended "'for the intellectually sophisticated'" (M. Jones 1) or "a highly literate, sophisticated audience" ("Court Rules on 'Tropic'"). Yet many readers were strongly opposed to any elite group having final say over their reading matter. Other readers were adamant that Miller and Grove Press published *Tropic of Cancer* to appeal to low- rather than highbrow audiences, the mass rather than the few. In any case, arguments supporting the Illinois Supreme Court ruling that the book was obscene and therefore could not be sold in the state pointed out that Miller and Grove Press should not have the question of audience both ways. While noting that Grove Press had argued for the book on the criterion of literary merit and that Epstein had used that criterion to make his decision, *Chicago's American* stressed in an editorial that the Illinois Supreme Court had remarked that the book featured a "suggestive appeal on its cover which was plainly aimed at promoting mass readership" ("Court Rules on 'Tropic'"). *Chicago's American* lauded the state court for seeing the hypocrisy of Grove Press's arguments and rejecting them: "The ruling amounts to saying, quite sensibly, that publishers can't have it both ways. If a shocking book is claimed to have subtle literary values that only the discriminating can enjoy, then it shouldn't be peddled as a mass-circulation scandal item. On the other hand, if publishers appeal frankly to prurient appetites, then they can't fall back on virtuous claims to 'literary merit'" ("Court Rules on 'Tropic'").

While impossible to determine absolutely, intent remained an issue in public, if not legal, discourses about *Tropic of Cancer.* The *Tribune* used intention as part of its rationale for changing its best-seller list—"Recently and tardily, we have become aware that some of the best sellers that have appeared on our lists were sewer-written by dirty-fingered authors" ("Sent to the Cleaner")—and was roundly criticized by readers. James R. Turner, for example, argued that decisions based on authorial intention would make the *Tribune* "look rather foolish":

> According to your editorial, it seems that not the vividness or frequency of sexual passages will keep a book off the list, but the intention of the author. How can you judge intention?
>
> Henry Miller's books may have more frequent and four-letter-word treatment of sex than most. Yet Miller's intention probably did not include making more money "by being nastier than the next." Will Hemingway, O'Hara, Mailer, and Nabokov, along with Miller, all be stricken from future lists, or are they acceptable? Or are some of these gentlemen artistic in intent and others simply mercenary? How will you look inside their minds to find out?

As the *Daily News* columnist Sydney J. Harris pointed out, "not since *Ulysses*" had legal decisions about literary obscenity cases hinged on authorial intent: "Admittedly, the intentions of an author are difficult to judge. This is why I think all literary censorship is dangerous and stupid. Bad books fall by the way; good ones, no matter how 'dirty' they seem, persist." Unable to know for sure about authors' and publishers' intentions, readers decided for themselves whom the author and publisher intended the book for—sexual deviants, innocent children, highbrow critics, juvenile delinquents. And in that way, public discussions of censorship paralleled changes in legal discourse: arguments based on intent moved to arguments based on community standards. But those arguments raised even more serious epistemological and practical problems.

In the wake of the U.S. Supreme Court's summary affirmation of Grove Press's right to sell *Tropic of Cancer* nationwide, Jack Mabley again assumed the voice of the majority: "I'd guess 95 percent of the American people favor more control of pornography than the Supreme court allows by its recent decisions. This does not make the Supreme court wrong, but it does cry that a means must be found to reconcile the extreme position of the court with the wishes of the vast majority of people" ("Court Ruling to Bring New Flood of Smut"). Mabley's argument implies that the rulings of the court are not authoritative because they contradict the will of the vast majority of Americans. Yet, as these discussions about "community standards" have shown, the opinion of no one segment of the population in itself was authoritative enough to be consistently accepted as the "community standard." In that way, "community standards" and questions of authority were very much connected, as a letter from Edward W. Rekruciak to the *Chicago Daily News* showed: "The standards of our community are set by the average adult citizen, not by the literary critic, author, professor, or even by the judge." Just as the divisive legacy of the U.S. Supreme Court's ambiguous "community standards" criterion has led to case after case and conflicting decision after conflicting decision, arguments in Chicago about "community standards"—that is, the authority of any particular group—did not provide a clear enough indication of what would and would not be acceptable to all. In that vacuum, many readers turned their attention to asking, If not "the people" or "the community," who was or should be the authority on matters of controversial books and their distribution—newspapers? police? judges? literary critics? or readers exercising their right to read or not as they desired?

## Authority

Whenever the issue of authority arose, definitional claims about the nature of censorship soon followed; no one—especially no one legitimating his or her own power—wanted to be associated with the word *censor*. Even the Citizens for Decent Literature dissociated their activities from censorship. Mrs. Theodore T. Lazarz wrote that those in her organization "are not trying to censor literature," just to protect children. Of all the parties in the Chicago literary public sphere that formed in the wake of publication and distribution of *Tropic of Cancer*, however, the two newspapers that set themselves up as authorities on the question of which books were and were not worthy of attention remained most adamant that, no matter how forcefully they favored suppression of *Tropic of Cancer*, they were in no way censoring it.

In the initial editorial explaining its change of policy on its best-seller list, the *Tribune* used authority as one of its points of departure. Its new list would not include "works which seem to have crossed the boundary line between good taste and bad. This is a thankless and unwelcome task which, we feel, better belongs to the publishers." But since the publishers either do not have the authority or will not take responsibility, the task falls to newspapers. "But it is not censorship," the *Tribune* insisted; the editorial added, "Obviously we will eliminate from the list as few books as possible." No matter how much the *Tribune*'s editors hedged, readers wrote in response to the newspaper's authority to make such decisions. J. J. S. wrote to exclaim: "You really have painted yourself into a corner! Imagine The Tribune coming out for censorship and, in fact, assuming the job itself! No, you are not going in for book burning or censorship; you are merely going to expunge from the list of best sellers the best sellers which you decide should not be best sellers! Who is going to be your authority?"

Chicago's newspaper columnists argued among themselves about definitions of censorship and just where their authority began and ended. In the aftermath of Epstein's decision that *Tropic of Cancer* was not obscene, Jack Mabley of *Chicago's American* lent his wholehearted support to the efforts of the Citizens for Decent Literature and their campaign to give "ten thousand prominent Chicagoans the shock of their lives Monday when they open their mail." Mabley explained the group's activities in a column entitled "'That Book' to Get Shock Treatment":

> A group of Chicago citizens, who are stunned at the court's ruling, have decided to try a shock treatment themselves to waken responsible Chicagoans to what has happened.
>
> They have reproduced 19 passages from the book and put them into a six page letter. The letter is being mailed today to priests, rabbis, ministers, civic leaders, educators, politicians—"to people who have something to say about the world we live in."

Mabley saw his authority as a "newspaperman" as a reasonable and ethical means to give support to a cause he obviously believed in; as he put it, "the First thing to do is make the community aware of the seriousness of the problem. Not thru boycotts or threats, but thru intelligent communication. This evil can be fought and it can be overcome, without jeopardizing freedom of the press." While he was arguing for the suppression of a book, he did not see his actions as threatening the First Amendment; and as a newspaper columnist, he saw nothing contradictory in his use of authority.

Criticizing Mabley's support of Citizens for Decent Literature, Hoke Norris made different definitional claims about a newspaper's authority and its responsibilities on issues of censorship. Norris begins his column headlined "Flood of Filth" by putting Mabley's authority squarely in conflict with the authority of the law: "Though a Superior Court judge here has ruled that 'Tropic of Cancer' is not pornographic, Jack Mabley of Chicago's American has returned to his assaults upon that novel." After arguing that what the organization compiled and mailed to ten thousand Chicagoans is more likely to be ruled pornographic than is Miller's novel taken in its entirety, Norris continues: "There's still another curious aspect of Mabley's attacks upon 'Tropic of Cancer.' It involves a newspaper's attitude toward censorship." Norris then recounts that four days after Mabley ran a column calling on booksellers to suppress *Tropic of Cancer,* Mabley and his newspaper ran a story objecting to 101 drugstores in and around Chicago that refused to sell the *American* because it had published a story many druggists found objectionable. Norris then quoted the *American*'s ensuing anticensorship editorial: "'This attempt to influence Chicago's American won't work. We will continue to print the news. . . . We will continue to give the druggists the right to be heard but we will not surrender to the druggists—nor any other group—the right to edit the American.'" Norris argued that Mabley and the editorial board of the *American*

> can't have it both ways. If Mabley is right, you are wrong; I think you are right. And I know that the editor of a book-publishing firm has the same rights as a newspaper—he should not feel that, sitting at his elbow, there's a Big Brother saying, "No, no, you cannot print that." If we urge druggists, and others, to remove a book from their shelves, how can we complain when, in the same spirit, they remove a newspaper from their shelves?
>
> In October, "Tropic of Cancer" had not been judicially considered. It was legal (as it still is) to sell it anywhere in Cook County. If we don't want our newspapers taken off sale at the petulant whim of special groups, we must not advocate the removal of a book because some people object to it. Gentlemen, our freedoms are indivisible. An attack on one of them is an attack on all of them.

Norris's absolutism and newspapers' concomitant responsibility were issues many others worried over, often using argument by unlimited development. Robert Cromie wrote in his column "The Bystander" that suppressing books or limiting individual freedoms in any way is wrong because "when you launch something of this sort it grows and grows until it becomes ridiculous." Even Epstein's ruling contained such an argument; as quoted in Hoke Norris's 2 March 1962 column, Epstein stated, "'censorship has no fixed boundaries.'"

These kinds of arguments made another possible authority—the police—most worrisome for many in and around Chicago. Norris, again, was most vociferous about the "police actions" involving *Tropic of Cancer*. In the first of his many columns on Miller's novel, Norris challenged the credentials of the police to judge literature. After reporting that suburban police had asked booksellers to remove *Tropic of Cancer* from their shelves, Norris added: "A survey of the stores and distributors indicated quick compliance with the wishes of the eminent literary critics in the various police departments. The word of these critics—thoroughly versed, as they no doubt are, in the art not only of making arrests but of judging books for literary merit—was evidently enough for most of the sellers of books" ("Police Censor Book"). More damaging than the actions of the police themselves, according to Norris, was the gutless compliance of the book-sellers and the consequent lack of freedom to read: "Evidently they've been making this decision [what is and is not obscene] for years; evidently, the booksellers have been going along with them." Norris severely criticizes the police chiefs and their officers for suppressing *Tropic of Cancer* on their own authority: "The point of the whole matter is that nobody in authority but the suburban police themselves have decided that this book should not be sold. They have not consulted judge or jury or even a literary critic on the subject. They have served as judge and jury—and literary critic—and then have gone about, lacking any court action whatever, and 'advised' the sellers of books that they ought not to sell 'Tropic of Cancer.'" The *Sun-Times* reiterated many of Norris's points two weeks later in an editorial entitled "Police Censorship." "No court in the United States has declared 'Tropic of Cancer' obscene," the editors argued. The suburban police "sought to accomplish censorship through police pressure rather than through legal action."

The *Daily News* columnist Sydney J. Harris had similar disrespect for the credentials of police officers to judge reading matter. While dissociating himself from the book—as many others, even Norris, had done at one time or another—Harris makes clear that the cops should not be calling the shots where literature is concerned: "'Ulysses,' by James Joyce, happens to be a great book; 'Tropic of Cancer,' by Henry Miller, happens not to be. But the illiterate policemen and hypocritical politicians who are frantically trying to ban the Miller book don't know the difference, and don't care." As though he had not made his point clearly enough earlier on, Harris ends his column by reiterating his disrespect and once again dissociating himself from *Tropic of Cancer:* "There would be no great loss to the world of letters if every copy of 'Tropic of Cancer' were dropped into the ocean. But there would be a tremendous loss to our cultural values if the Neanderthals in public offices and police stations were to decide what we should and should not read. Civilization is in greater danger from them than from the Henry Millers of the world." As in many other cases, the authority of the police to remove books at will is contrasted with the individual citizen's right to choose what to read. In addition, those supporting the right of *Tropic of Cancer* to be sold had to distance themselves from the book to remain credible to their readers.

In the only letter I found from a police officer, Lt. B. Kellough of the Maywood Police Department wrote to the *Sun-Times* to defend the practices of his colleagues—and to dissociate his activities from censorship. His letter, headlined "Duty of Police," began by claiming that suburban ordinances justify the arrests of booksellers for refusing to suppress *Tropic of Cancer:* "I do not believe that any of our freedoms should be abridged—and I do not think that they are. However, we cannot wait when a dangerous situation arises. Action has to be taken immediately or it will be to no avail." By stressing action over judgment, Kellough deemphasizes what Norris and Harris so vehemently opposed: that the police are telling others what they can and cannot read. Kellough sees the issue as commonsensical: "As far as being a critic is concerned—you do not have to be any kind of a literary critic to know that filth such as is contained in this book is obscene. One further thought, who is qualified to be a critic?" Kellough ends his letter by defending his actions in terms very similar to "the public interest": "I, myself, am very happy to see that so many police officers and police departments will 'stick their necks out' to act in behalf of the good of their community."

Whereas officers such as Kellough were proud to act to protect their communities, one official in a higher public office was a bit more reticent when it came to "the public interest" versus individual rights. In a *Sun-Times* news story, Malcolm Wise reported that while Mayor Daley was considering whether to revive a "long-dormant citizens advisory committee on indecent literature," he was not happy about having to make such a move. Wise wrote that "the mayor reportedly doesn't want to be put in the position of trying to tell people what they cannot read."

Though Mayor Daley could—and did—step aside from this act of judgment, justices at local, state, and national levels had no such luxury, though the length of time many of them took to announce their decisions suggests they wished they could have. Indeed, the length of time between trial and decision, compounded by the many, many conflicting decisions on *Tropic of Cancer,* caused people to challenge the authority of judges and obscenity law in the wake of the book's publication.

Columnists and editorial writers openly questioned Epstein's decision, especially in light of readers' overwhelming distaste for the book; one reader even argued that Epstein should be impeached for the ruling (Smith). A letter to the *Sun-Times* by Regina Rekruciak is more representative of the challenges Epstein's authority received publicly. The writer began by making appeals to "the people" and by arguing with the judge's reasoning: "Chief Justice Samuel B. Epstein's ruling Feb. 21, that 'Tropic of Cancer' isn't obscene and has literary merits is an insult to the intelligence of decent, God-fearing and educated people. His two comparisons that the 'tastes and customs change from generation to generation' won't be accepted as examples to excuse immorality. The bikini didn't replace the coverall bathing suit, and twist is a fad which will never be a replacement for the normal dance steps." The writer ended her letter by again attacking the judge's authority, questioning his sense of justice and social welfare: "Any court, critic, or organization who will defend such writings under the guise of freedom is abandoning justice and prudence and society will suffer from it."

Paul Molloy, the television critic for the *Sun-Times,* wrote that while he deplores "the idea of a policeman ordering a storekeeper to remove a book from his shelf, . . . I cannot agree with Judge Epstein that Henry Miller's putrefaction, which *Time* magazine called 'a very dirty book indeed,' is a literary work of substantial merit." *Chicago's American* editorialized against Epstein precisely on the basis of abdication of authority: the effect of his decision, the newspaper argued, "was to make all such rulings almost wholly dependent on personal opinion. A workable legal standard of obscenity is hard to establish; a legal standard of literary merit would be flatly impossible. Anyone can SAY that a book has literary merit; the claim is just not susceptible to proof or disproof" ("Court Rules on 'Tropic'"). Perhaps most damaging to Epstein's authority was a decision in a Los Angeles case two days after his decision was announced in which a jury ruled the novel obscene and banned its sale. Regardless, what kind of authority judges had in telling people what they could or could not read—and the justice of that authority—were central issues in public deliberations on *Tropic of Cancer.*

Just as judges' authority came into question, the authority of obscenity laws themselves was challenged time and time again between 1961 and 1964 in Chicago. Early "police actions" were clearly in conflict with *Roth;* even after Epstein's decision on *Tropic of Cancer,* however, suppression of the book continued. In one of the weirder instances of suppression, four actors reading passages of the novel were arrested by vice squad detectives at a Near North Side "night spot" three weeks after Epstein's decision was announced. According to the news story "'Tropic of Cancer' Reading Raided" in the *Sun-Times,* "The well-dressed audience of 60 persons had paid $1.50 each to hear the performance. A discussion period was to follow the reading." The newspaper quoted the actors as wondering why they had been arrested, given Epstein's decision: "The actors argued at the police station that in view of the judge's ruling, they couldn't possibly have violated any law by reading passages from the book in public."

Laws were questioned—and none too gently—all through the *Tropic of Cancer* debate. As soon as police arrests and intimidations began, some readers questioned the initial U.S. Justice Department ruling that the book could circulate. As Mrs. George Lewis wrote in *Chicago's American,* "Why can't local people suppress a book that reeks of filth? What senile member of the justice department had the audacity to pronounce this book mailable?" Then she called on a higher authority, one many readers alluded to but few mentioned by name: "If citizens remain silent in this outrageous situation, may God have mercy on us."

The authority of judges, laws, and literary critics intertwined through the many trials of *Tropic of Cancer,* as it has on nearly every literary obscenity case in the twentieth century. Whereas Godman in *Besig* would not allow the testimony of literary critics, Epstein used their arguments to inform his opinion of the novel's social and literary merit. And Norris stressed this criterion when he ran excerpts of Epstein's decision in a column entitled "Guest Columnist":

> "The plaintiffs [the publisher of the book, and others] have introduced the oral testimony of a professor of modern literature, a literary editor of a Chicago newspaper [the *Sun-Times*], and a mass of opinion of literary critics, authors, and reviewers who characterized 'Tropic of Cancer' as of substantial literary value.... The defense submitted the testimony of a minister, a psychiatrist, a social scientist, the head of a crime prevention agency and a columnist for a Chicago newspaper [*Chicago's American*], all eminent in their respective fields of endeavor, who condemned the book as obscene. None of them, however, laid claim to being literary experts and rendered no opinion on the literary value of the book."[14]

Overturning Epstein's decision, the Illinois Supreme Court justices refused to act as literary critics: "The high court's decision, written by Justice Harry B. Hershey of Taylorville, was unanimous. It said the members do not claim to be qualified as literary critics 'and will not in this opinion undertake to resolve any dispute as to whether "Tropic" has literary merit'" (M. Jones).

Like the judges, literary critics were less than unanimous on the topic of *Tropic of Cancer;* this difference of opinion among "experts"—along with a strong dose of anti-intellectualism—brought literary critics in for heavy fire, too. Jack Mabley was the first of many to point out that different literary critics saw different things in Miller's novel. A week after Epstein's decision and his revelation that he had weighed testimony from literary critics quite heavily, Mabley informed his readers that, in the Los Angeles trial resulting in a jury decision against the book, Leon Uris had called *Tropic of Cancer* "'Trash. Perverted, irrational babbling'" ("Court Ruling").

As though answering other newspapers' use of literary critics who spoke out against *Tropic of Cancer,* the *Sun-Times* ran a wire story that seems utterly nonsensical unless read in the context of the debate over Miller's novel. The Associated Press story, an interview with Louis Untermeyer, was edited to stress the sections on censorship and the *topos* of unlimited development:

> Asked about moves in various parts of the United States to ban sale of Henry Miller's book "Tropic of Cancer," Untermeyer said:
> "I can't believe in censorship because I don't know where you can draw the line, and I don't know who is to be elected to draw that line."
> He added, "My feeling is that books should not be burned and books never do hurt anybody. I think a book will find its proper reader, or even its improper reader, but I am not [and] I don't know who is fit or able to draw that line and say 'This should be read, this should not be printed.'"

Yet this characteristic move by some literary critics to question any authority on the issue of censorship was not beyond critique, either. One instance of readers' impatience with such arguments is a letter published in Mabley's 7 March 1962 column. Mrs. J. D. Ellis of Chicago, who identifies herself as a "former teacher," argues that professors and "the liberal establishment" have much to answer for: "'The publishers of pornographic material and the makers of obscene movies are fully aware of what they are doing, and because they coin money they do not care. They shrewdly count on the ever present, ever eager professor or authority to rush to defend their rights to circulate their wares. These same defenders of the right to poison children's minds would take to the ramparts if tainted foods or rotten meats were sold to their children.'"

Because the authority of literary critics was often perceived as highbrow—"Nobody should let the critics and the professors intimidate him," Norris wrote in an early 1962 column ("Literary Taste")—and because the authority of the masses was often perceived as tyrannous, many involved in the debate over *Tropic of Cancer* argued for the authority of the individual reader rather than the expert critic or the interest group in determining what should and should not be read by that person alone. Thomas E. Boyle declared in an early letter to the *Sun-Times:* "Let people themselves judge what is trash, and unsold copies returned to publishers will determine the quality of literature to come." Boyle associated those who would use their authority to stand in the way of individual taste with Adolf Hitler: "I don't think we can employ Hitler-like tactics in attempting to discern public taste. Censorship should be an individual family affair and not imposed on adults by hypocritical tin gods who set themselves up as omniscient authorities."

Many other readers resented the efforts of citizens' groups or police officers to impose their taste or morality on others. As James A. Kennedy wrote, praising Norris's stand on civil liberties, "You respect the intelligence of people to make use of their God-given sense to decide for themselves what they wish to read or not. Not a group or an individual who assumes some special talent and divine inspiration to decide for all others what is good." In one of the very few anticensorship letters that made it into *Chicago's American,* Oke G. Pamp wrote to inform readers that the Wisconsin Supreme Court had ruled *Tropic of Cancer* not obscene. In the ruling, Pamp wrote, the justices declared: "'Altho some of the words would not be tolerated in our society if inflicted on unwilling listeners, an offended reader need only to close the book in order to escape.' I wish every book censor would memorize those lines."

This assertion of individual rights was taken up, largely through the efforts of Grove Press and Elmer Gertz, as a right-to-read issue. In a *Sun-Times* news story on a pretrial motion, a reporter captured Epstein's acceptance of the definitional "right-to-read" argument and his consequent decision not to dismiss the case against the suburban police chiefs. The reporter continued, "Edward C. Hoffert, attorney for suburban Mount Prospect, 'contended that in bringing the suit on behalf of two citizens' "right to read" the American Civil Liberties Union had claimed a right that is not guaranteed by the Constitution.' The judge replied, 'I think we can infer that freedom of the press is freedom to read the press. What is the value of printing something if the reciprocal right of reading is not given?'" ("Trial Set Jan. 10 in ACLU Suit on 'Tropic of Cancer'").

Indeed, Epstein made individual readers' right to read one of his major arguments in his ruling. In the *Sun-Times* report on his verdict, Epstein was quoted as saying, "'Literature which has some social merit, even if controversial, should be left to individual taste rather than government edict. . . . Let not the government or the courts dictate the reading matter of a free people. Let the parents control the reading matter of their children; let the tastes of the readers determine what they may or may not read'" ("Judge Okays Sale"). Again, Norris's "Guest Columnist" piece quoted additional material from Epstein's decision. "'Average readers,'" the judge argued,

> "are not a captive audience. Reading 'Tropic of Cancer' is their voluntary act. They have the power to be their own censors. Because someone may find the book unpalatable is no justification for depriving others of their free choice to read the book.

"The constitutional right of freedom of speech and press should be jealously guarded by the courts. As a corollary to the freedom of speech and press, there is also the freedom to read. The right to free utterance becomes a useless privilege when the freedom to read is restricted or denied."

Every person his or her own censor—the absolute authority of every separate individual—became problematic even in Epstein's reasoning when the focus turned from individuals to families. As many readers pointed out, not every parent either has or will take the authority to decide what his or her children may or should read. Another point made by Mrs. J. D. Ellis in a letter printed in Mabley's column is that many parents do not have authority over their children. There are "'masses of people, just in Chicago, who will not or cannot guide their children in matters of selection. Many suffer a language difficulty, many are indifferent and many are ignorant. The results are appalling'" ("High School Girl Speaks Out on Smut").

The following exchange of letters in the *Sun-Times,* perhaps more than any other on this issue, reflects the deep differences of opinion on the question of authority and social change. The first letter, headlined "High Schoolers Speak" and signed by Marie Chrupka and three other students identified as "The Class Presidents, Jones Commercial High School," appealed to "the adult citizens of Chicago" and urged them to reconsider their authority where *Tropic of Cancer* is concerned. The letter, quoted here in its entirety, weaves issues of authority, dissociation from censorship, and the last of the issues we will discuss with regard to *Tropic of Cancer,* social value or the causal link between "problem" literature and social ills:

> The City of Chicago should hang its head in shame.
> By permitting the wide-spread sale of a certain obscene book, thereby making it available and accessible to youth, the adult citizens of Chicago have shown their complete disdain and contempt for the healthy minds for which they are directly responsible.
> We regulate the sale of dope, intoxicating liquors and other poisons. We rigidly regulate and guard the physical health of the young. But, alas, we permit the sale of printed corruption which may be purchased by any juvenile old enough to bring money to the vendor.
> Yes, indeed, we must be extremely careful of censorship. But what of the care of impressionable young minds which daily are becoming sicker, as reflected by such symptoms as increased VD rate and rising juvenile delinquency.
> Yes, Chicago should hang its head in shame. It is time when a fellow really needs a friend, a friend mature enough to resist dirty money.

The students' claims that they needed to be protected from the nefarious effects of "a certain obscene book" resonate with impressions discussed above—that Miller and Grove Press had expressly intended *Tropic of Cancer* to harm society by perverting its children.

The students' arguments drew a quick response, however, from readers who would not let the young adults abdicate their own authority so quickly. In a letter headlined "Make Own Decision," Stephanie Lesch argued that individual Americans—unlike those behind the Iron Curtain—have the right, responsibility, and privilege to decide for themselves what they will or will not read: "People have reached a deplorable state of lethargy when they cannot make their own decisions and depend on censorship to do it for them. In contrast, people behind the Iron Curtain would give their lives for this privilege." Characteristically, Lesch dissociated herself from the book, writing, "I can't say anything pro or con for this controversial book in question, as I have not read it, nor do I intend reading it." Nonetheless, she ended the letter by reiterating her demand to exercise her own authority: "Yet I would like to see anyone or any group stop me from doing it, if I had a mind to."

Another letter, by Mrs. M. H. E., headlined "The Antidote," makes the connection between individuals' own authority and the social effects of literature even more forcefully. The writer begins by suggesting that regulation of controversial books and substances is not the answer because such suppression will not work: "I should like to bring aid and comfort to the students from Jones High who feel that the adults of Chicago have thrown them to the wolves via Henry Miller. While it is true that teen drinking is regulated, it is also true that there are teen drunks. And while drug addiction is frowned upon for everyone, teens and adults alike, we still have junkies, teens and adults alike." The writer then uses another part of the students' analogy to her rhetorical advantage, again stressing the social value of literature: "If a dirty book is poison to these young people, I suggest that the antidote must be a clean book. If one so-called obscene book can corrupt our youth, I rejoice at the prospect of what the 74 authors in the Great Books series could do for them. I suggest that the group from Jones High begin their readings with the Areopagitica, which is Milton's famous essay against censorship."

A similar exchange occurred in the *American,* where Jack Mabley ran a letter from Betty Ann Brodzinski, identified as a senior at Holy Family Academy. Like the students from Jones High, this writer appealed to adults for aid and comfort, but not the kind Milton had in mind: "'I am a senior at Holy Family Academy in Chicago. The girls at our school are very disturbed over the court decision in favor of Henry Miller's book "Tropic of

Cancer." Teen-agers are decent and ambitious people. We cannot fight the flood of immorality alone. We need influential and reputable adults to side with us. We can be an effective instrument in banning such trash.'" Mabley's response was quite different from the responses of readers in the *Sun-Times:* "Comment: A lot of words from me, in this column and as a witness in Judge Epstein's court, were decidedly uninfluential. We lost the battle, but we'll keep trying to win the war" ("High School Girl Speaks Out on Smut"). While the battle is long since past—*Tropic of Cancer* has been sold legally and uncontroversially for more than thirty years—the war, a clear consensus one way or the other on the social effects of "problem" literature as opposed to the rights of individuals to publish and read it, is far from over. In the final section of this chapter I analyze how readers argued about the social values and social ills inherent in Miller's novel.

## Social Importance—Social Value or Social Menace?

In *Roth,* Justice Brennan first articulated what has come to be known as the "social value" test, but, as his own words make clear, his criterion was "social importance" rather than "social value": "All ideas having even the slightest redeeming social importance—unorthodox ideas, controversial ideas, even ideas hateful to the prevailing climate of opinion—have the full protection of the guarantees [of the Bill of Rights], unless excludable because they encroach upon the limited area of more important interests." As Felice Flanery Lewis points out in her discussion of *Roth* and the U.S. Supreme Court's summary decision involving *Tropic of Cancer,* the court has waffled on whether the criterion is "social importance" or, as Charles Rembar has articulated, "social value." "This is another example of the significance of semantics in obscenity decisions," according to Lewis. "Rembar's substitution, which was allowed to pass without objection by the Court, undoubtedly had a decided effect on subsequent decisions" (209–10). That *Tropic of Cancer* was important socially is clear from the amount of attention it received as well as the kinds of arguments surrounding it. But what was not at all clear to those in the Chicago-area literary public sphere was whether the book was of social value or a social menace.

Those who argued that *Tropic of Cancer* would have serious social effects—increased rates of sexual deviancy, venereal disease, voyeurism—based their claims on a simple causal model of behavior that also had a history in the courtroom. Judge Curtis Bok of Pennsylvania ruled in the 1949 case *Commonwealth v. Gordon* that several books were not obscene.[15] His reasoning rested on refuting behaviorist claims about the effects of "problem" literature on readers. Bok wondered: "How can any-one say that [the average reader] will infallibly be affected one way or another by one book or another?" Bok articulated the problem of the causal connection between reading and acting when he declared: "The public does not read a book and simultaneously rush by the hundreds into the streets to engage in orgiastic riots" (qtd. in Lewis 172). Yet that same behaviorist model was still legitimate enough in the early sixties to per-suade a great number of Chicagoans that *Tropic of Cancer* would infect their city and suburbs; as the next two chapters suggest, that model is with us still, again implying that public discourses about issues affect social practices as much if not more than court decisions and laws do.

Regardless, both the "social value" test and the assumption upon which many arguments about it rested—that there is a direct connection between what people read and how they act—were frequently recurring *topoi* in public discourses over *Tropic of Cancer*. Invariably, early mentions of the book stressed people's concern about it as a social menace: "Said Police Chief Amasa Kennicott of Des Plaines: 'We're not going to let a thing like that get into the hands of our high school students'" ("Suburb Police Act to Bar Miller Book"). And from *Chicago's American*:

> In the village of Worth, 20 miles west of Chicago, Police Chief Lee Becatti or-dered the paperback off a stand in a drug store after a man angrily complained that his teen-age son had bought one there. Becatti said:
> "The owner of the store and his three employees hadn't read the book. He willingly took the books off the stand when he did read one. Such books should not be printed . . . who knows what damage has been done to the minds of chil-dren." ("Book Shocks Daley, He Orders Probe")

The belief that books could do direct damage to young minds was mani-fest in the way different writers described the book as literal dirt, some-times even contrasting Chicago's moral climate with the litter on its streets. The *Tribune*'s editorial headline "Sent to the Cleaner" stressed the con-nection, as did its copy: "We assume that you don't want filthy books on your shelves any more than you want to bed down with a herd of hogs in your living room. We assume that you would not welcome a visit from a farmhand who hadn't bothered to clean the barnyard off his shoes before entering the house." The book not only tracked dirt; it also smelled: "George Wittenberg, Mount Prospect chief of police since 1931, who evi-dently started the run on banning the book, said he read 'part of it' and alleged it 'smells like last week's fish'" (Wise). In one of the more striking cases of blindness and insight in public discussions about *Tropic of Can-*

*cer,* Mrs. Henry Paul described the book in terms of dirt and disease: "We certainly do not wish to encourage the sewer written literature that has become the cancer of the literary world."

Where the *Tropic of Cancer* as social ill argument got the most attention was, not surprisingly, in *Chicago's American,* where Jack Mabley's crusade against the book used the causal connection more consistently than any other argument did. In the news story on his testimony before Epstein (which ran directly under his weekly column) Mabley was quoted as saying that "a controversial novel is 'damaging to our moral fiber'" ("Book Damaging, Mabley Testifies"). As we have seen, Mabley argued that reading *Tropic of Cancer* was akin to being with a slut or a prostitute; additionally, Mabley argued that this association would have negative consequences: "'Books of this nature degrade the moral fiber and standards of a community in the same sense a person associating with a prostitute degrades himself,' Mabley said" ("Book Damaging, Mabley Testifies").

Mabley's support for Citizens for Decent Literature was not surprising, as the group's main argument against "indecent" literature was that it directly affected the behavior of individuals. As Mabley wrote in "'That Book' to Get Shock Treatment," "These people are deeply concerned about the spread of moral degradation in our community. Perhaps this is difficult to measure. But it may be gauged by the astonishing spread of venereal disease, by the increase of sexual crimes, and by tolerance of filth in other forms—the movies, on TV, and in trash magazines and paperback books." Mabley combined his causal argument with another, that of unlimited development where moral decline is concerned:

> Policemen of the pornography detail said before the decision, "If this book goes, anything goes. We will be helpless."
>
> This has been proven by experience. Test cases are made of books with literary value—"Ulysses," then "Lady Chatterley's Lover" and now "Tropic of Cancer."
>
> Each decision is the signal for the writing of literally millions of paperback obscenities, books which are insults to literature, but which are protected by the court decisions.

Many of Mabley's readers backed him in his causal and unlimited development arguments. Mabley published a letter by W. F. Schultz in his column that questioned Epstein's decision on the question of causality: "'I wrote this to Judge Samuel Epstein: "I cannot agree with you that such books of 'literary merit,' as you put it, are the standards of this community. You claim there is no evidence that the reading of books such as 'Tropic of Cancer' causes juvenile delinquency"'" ("High School Girl

Speaks Out on Smut"). In his letter to Mabley—and in another letter to the *Daily News*—Schultz argued that a 1959 House Postal Operations Subcommittee had found a direct connection between obscenity and juvenile misbehavior. Mabley added a comment to Schultz's letter, again stressing the causal connection and questioning Epstein's authority: "A jury in Los Angeles, which in a simultaneous case found the book obscene, chose to accept the views of police, of J. Edgar Hoover, and of men actually working in the field, who see a direct tie between the flood of obscenity and the increase in sex crimes." Other readers were even more straightforward: "I am worried about the children of Chicago. Sex perverts and maniacs who roam menacingly are influenced by the obscene literature that anyone can buy in our city," wrote E. E. Savickas, who gives examples of recent sex crimes and homicides for which perpetrators have not yet been caught. "Let's clean up Chicago by ridding it of pornographic material that stimulates degenerates."

Mabley also faced readers who disagreed with him, questioning the direct causal connection in different ways. Ray Schubert wrote to Mabley, questioning his faith in institutions to guide and protect children: "'Your main argument against "Tropic of Cancer" seems to be that books of this type will corrupt the morals of impressionable children. This leads me to believe that you have very little faith in the ability of our schools and churches to teach the children the difference between what they believe is right and wrong'" ("It's the Day"). Mabley's response ignored the half-century focus of obscenity legislation on "the average person"; under scrutiny, *loci* of quantity and quality are confused in his response in a way that suggests his main interest was in stoking his readers' fears:

> Comment: The schools and churches do a fine job with the kids they reach. What about the majority who do not attend church? What about the majority of high schoolers who drop out before graduation?
>
> What about the kids with no parents, or parents who can't manage them?
>
> Laws against dope and burglary aren't necessary for 98 percent of the population.
>
> If we accept that good books influence youngsters for good, we must accept that evil books influence them toward evil. And there must be a definition of evil, or pornographic book. I contend the book you mention is evil and pornographic.

Whereas *Chicago's American* focused on the evil nature of the book and the direct causal link between an evil book and evil deeds, the *Sun-Times* focused on its social importance and that no causal link could be proven between reading matter and behavior. Unlike the *American,* the *Sun-Times* gave wide coverage to Epstein's decision, even reprinting much of the decision in one of Norris's columns. "'From all the evidence, the Court concludes that "Tropic of Cancer" is a literary work of substantial merit and, consequently, of social importance. . . . There is no evidence that the reading of books such as "Tropic of Cancer" causes juvenile delinquency because sex criminals usually have such a low educational background they don't read books of this literary caliber,' the judge said" ("Guest Columnist"). While his observation about the nature of sex criminals has since been shown to be untrue, Epstein stressed "contemporary" as much as "community" standards in thinking through the effects of *Tropic of Cancer:* "'By the standards of today the use of dirty words or the description of lewd and vulgar incidents do not seem to have the impact upon our moral sense as they did. Perhaps society is more sophisticated today than it was a generation ago without any loss of its moral values'" ("Guest Columnist"). Perhaps to support its place as the leading newspaper on the question of free press, the *Sun-Times* ran a dissenting opinion from one of its own columnists, the television critic Paul Molloy. In criticizing Epstein's decision, Molloy, like the reader who wrote to Mabley, cites a postal report from several years earlier: "Perhaps the judge is not familiar with this statement from Henry Montague, the nation's chief postal inspector. 'Regardless of the scoffing and ridicule of self-styled intellectuals and sophisticates, to those who live closely with the responsibilities of law enforcement there can be no question that the sale of lewd and suggestive matter is reflected in the mounting and extremely serious problem of juvenile delinquency.'" Like its columnists, readers of the *Sun-Times* were divided on the question of whether *Tropic of Cancer* was of social value or a social menace; as with readers of the *American,* it was clear their worries were being transferred from fear of moral decline and crime in general to specific fears about a specific book.

Epstein's "social value" and "literary merit" criteria were exactly the issues on which the Illinois Supreme Court reversed his decision. As mentioned above, the justices rejected any claims of literary merit because they refused to claim any authority on that question. Since Epstein's social value claim was based on the literary merit of *Tropic of Cancer,* when one went, both went. As reported in the *Sun-Times,* "Justice Harry B. Hershey of Taylorville, who wrote the Illinois court's opinion, said 'the book admittedly has no story, no plot in the usual sense and no character development.'" As a consequence, "'any philosophic theme or portion of the book with literary merit would be lost to the average reader whereas illicit and obscene portions would clearly remain in his mind as the book's dominant

theme'" ("Top State Court Rules 'Cancer,' Bruce Obscene"). With the U.S.
Supreme Court's summary affirmation of *Tropic of Cancer* a few days later,
the "social value" test—no matter its ambiguity—was reaffirmed as a
national standard. The conversations have continued, however, in Chicago
and elsewhere, up to the present.

## Social Value versus Literary Merit

Personal freedoms from flouridation to reflections on Milton's *Areopagi-*
*tica*—those who read and wrote publicly in response to the publication,
sale, and distribution of Henry Miller's *Tropic of Cancer* connected the
novel with many other issues in their lives. Most consistently, they feared
for a world that could produce a book like *Tropic of Cancer,* even though
it is clear that the vast majority of those who wrote about the book had
never read it—and had absolutely no intention of doing so. What readers
tended to focus on—publicity as something to be feared yet exploited,
definitions and implications of "community standards," the authority of
certain groups and individuals in determining what should be read, and
the causal connection between literature and behavior—reflects not only
the concerns of the day but also the issues inherent in reading almost any
written text. Indeed, these *topoi* are with us still, and the next two chapters trace them through two contemporary debates on controversial texts.
While publicity and authority have not changed much as issues, the social
value of literature has come to be seen as a question of whether literary
texts critique or reify certain social practices—or whether it is impossible
for them to do only one or only the other. Even more, however, questions
about the social effects of literary texts are often excluded from public
debate by questions of "literary merit"; to the extent that expert literary
critics become the authorities, the arguments of uncredentialed public critics lose their legitimacy.

As in the case of *Ulysses,* it is clear that public deliberations about *Tropic*
*of Cancer* had some effect on the judicial decisions about the book: both
Epstein's ruling in favor of the novel and the Illinois Supreme Court's ruling against it were informed by passionate arguments put forth by individuals and groups. In addition, an analysis of the public discourses in
response to *Tropic of Cancer* suggests social change does not come through
legal decisions and legislative changes alone; indeed, public discussions can
often so delegitimate institutional power that institutions and their authority need to be reconsidered. Unlike in the case of *Ulysses,* a much wider
circle of citizens got involved in deliberations about *Tropic of Cancer* and

decisions about what should become of the book. While it is ironic that public discussions about the social role of literature in the case of *Tropic of Cancer* took place when social realism was anathema and the new criticism had reached its zenith, this dissonance is not surprising. Just as the authority of legal decisions does not always bear on everyday actions, the authority of professional literary critics does not necessarily affect how people read texts—all the more reason for rhetoricians to study the many different ways people have read and responded to controversial books and the passionate public arguments they have made about the effects of certain books on their shared lives.

NOTES

1. Extended narratives of *Tropic of Cancer*'s battle for U.S. publication can be found in Hutchison; Rembar; Gertz and Lewis; and Wickes. As discussed in chapter 1, such tales tend to participate in master narratives of free speech over censorship, with individual authors, critics, lawyers, and judges acting as heroic agents against the powers of antagonist legal and extralegal censors. Hutchison in particular sees Chicago lawyer Elmer Gertz and Grove Press owner Barney Rosset as fearless leaders in the battle of right (free speech) over wrong (censorship). One example: "A country needs artists and publishers like Henry Miller and Barney Rosset to prick its conscience, to awaken it to internal and external dangers. Whether the fires they set should be smothered by censors or allowed to blaze freely until they die of their own accord—or become larger conflagrations—is the choice that should be left to American citizens. Not to censors" (251).

I do not include excerpts from *Tropic of Cancer* in this chapter because no one in Chicago excerpted it except in private letters sent to "concerned citizens."

2. As Lewis notes, the growing popularity of the paperback novel in the thirties and forties led to the founding of such groups as the National Organization for Decent Literature in 1938 (136; see also Schick); in 1952, concern over the growing post–World War II taste for paperback and erotic fiction led to the formation of the House Select Committee on Current Pornographic Materials, also called the Gathings Committee (Lewis 161). Nonetheless, until the late fifties, censorship forces and judicial decisions focused their attention on such literary problems as "the author's purpose, the relationship of allegedly obscene parts to the whole, the work's effect on an audience, its realism or 'authenticity,' its literary or social merit, and especially the question of whether or not it was 'dirt for dirt's sake'" (Lewis 184). Decades after court decisions had determined certain criteria as valid for making obscenity judgments, those criteria were consistently recognized neither in society at large nor in the courts. Not until *Roth v. United States* (1957) did the U.S. Supreme Court comment on the constitutionality of censoring allegedly obscene materials—literary and otherwise.

3. Rosset, who admired Miller and had written on Miller's work while an undergraduate at Swarthmore (Hutchison 42), used *Lady Chatterley's Lover* as a test case for *Tropic of Cancer.*

4. Massachusetts was the first state to attempt to ban *Tropic of Cancer* (see "Mass. Moves to Ban 'Tropic of Cancer'"; and "Grove Press Will Fight 'Tropic' Ban in Mass"). As Hutchison and others point out, it was the paperback *Tropic of Cancer,* published in October 1961—much earlier than Rosset would have liked because of threats of pirating—that caused the national explosion of legal troubles for Grove Press and Miller (see Hutchison 77–95; and Norris, "'Cancer' in Chicago" 53–54).

5. The suit was "brought in the names of Franklyn S. Haiman, associate professor of speech at Northwestern University and chairman of the North Shore chapter of the ACLU, and Mrs. Isabel Condit, a Morton Grove housewife, whose husband, Carl, is an NU English professor" ("Civil Liberties Unit Sues").

6. In part because the U.S. Supreme Court's June 1964 *per curiam* ruling was in many senses anticlimactic and ambiguous, litigation over the sale of *Tropic of Cancer* at state and local levels continued through the summer of 1966 (Hutchison 242–45; Gertz and Lewis 318).

7. Gertz explained the U.S. Supreme Court's summary decision to Miller in a 24 June 1964 letter:

> There had been a rather poorly handled case in Florida involving *Tropic of Cancer [Grove Press v. Gerstein].* The attorneys, in effect, waived the constitutional issue and this, legally speaking, put us out of court, both as far as the Florida Supreme Court is concerned and the United States Supreme Court. Notwithstanding, Ed de Grazia decided to take what he regarded as a hundred-to-one chance and filed a petition for *certiorari.* This means a petition asking the Supreme Court to consider the case and enter some judgment order with respect to it. (315)

The court ruled on three obscenity cases on 22 June. The first was a movie case—*Jacobellis v. Ohio,* 378 U.S. 184 (1964), involving *The Lovers;* the second was a Kansas case—*A Quantity of Books v. State of Kansas,* 378 U.S. 205 (1964), involving a number of allegedly pornographic paperback books; and the third was the Florida case against *Tropic of Cancer.* Gertz continued:

> At any rate, Monday the United States Supreme Court reversed the obscenity conviction in the movie case, but the justices split all over the lot as to the reasons for the reversal. Justices Brennan and Goldberg wrote an opinion that sounded as if we had dictated it. It confirmed our view of the law, that nothing can be banned unless it is utterly without any redeeming social importance, including in this definition literary and artistic importance. They also decided that the standard to be applied was not of every locality, but a national standard. In other words, if the book or film were generally acceptable throughout the country, it could not be banned in a particular area. . . .
>
> Then, to show the mood in which they were in, the court, by a 5 to 4 vote,

granted *certiorari* (that is, agreed to consider) the Florida *Tropic* case, and summarily (that is, without briefs or argument or loss of time) reversed the Florida decision against the book. This means, as we interpret it, that *Tropic* may be sold anywhere in the United States. But to make absolutely certain of this, Cy [Rembar] and I have been in consultation for days now and are going to take certain steps to see to it that *Tropic* runs into no more trouble anywhere. I will give you the story in detail as soon as I catch my breath. (Gertz and Lewis 315–16)

8. For the most recent and by far most complete secondary bibliography of writings about Miller, see Shifreen, who led me to roughly half of the articles, columns, and letters to the editor in this chapter. A few more citations were culled from references in Gertz and Miller. I found the others by reading issues of the four newspapers on microfilm at Penn State University's Pattee Library (the *Chicago Tribune*) and the Library of Congress (the *Chicago Sun-Times, Chicago's American,* and the *Chicago Daily News*). Chicago had other newspapers, daily and weekly, at the time; an exhaustive study of public discourses about *Tropic of Cancer* in Chicago would include the *Chicago Star,* the *Chicago Defender,* the *Roosevelt Torch,* and many others.

9. The Illinois Supreme Court, in a separate decision the same day, ruled a nightclub performance by Lenny Bruce obscene as well. The front-page story began: "The Illinois Supreme court Thursday declared obscene the book 'Tropic of Cancer,' and a night club performance by Lenny Bruce, who is known as 'Little Boy Blue' because of his offensive material" (M. Jones).

10. In the early sixties, the *Chicago Tribune* and *Chicago's American* were owned by the Chicago Tribune Company. Not until the early seventies did the *Tribune* "shed its image as a parochial midwestern publication, the right wing tool of longtime editor and publisher Col. Robert R. McCormick. . . . For more than a decade after McCormick died [in 1955], his successors remained loyal to his ideas, keeping the pages of the *Tribune* devoted to ethnocentric, conservative views" (Liebovich 174). The *Sun-Times* and the *Daily News* were owned by Marshall Field IV and were considered to be more liberal, though still staunchly Republican. Field's father, Marshall Field III, "began the *Chicago Sun* in 1941 as morning competition for the ultraconservative *Chicago Tribune*" (Ashley xx). *Chicago's American* (sometimes called the *Chicago American* and in its last years called *Chicago Today*) folded in 1974; the *Daily News* folded in 1978. For more on the "Homeric" confrontation between McCormick and the Fields, see Weston (81–87); Schwarzlose; and Norris "'Cancer' in Chicago."

As described in *Tropic of Cancer,* Miller and a few of his friends worked in the Paris offices of the *Tribune.*

11. Norris's "'Cancer' in Chicago" describes the testimony of Norris and Mabley in Epstein's court. For more on the roles of Norris and Mabley see "Debate Set on Controversial Books"; Norris "Flood of Filth"; and "Book Damaging, Mabley Testifies."

12. In his correspondence with Miller, Gertz alludes to several conversations with

people who knew Epstein and told Gertz of the effect the public controversy over *Tropic of Cancer* had on his decisions about the novel (see Gertz and Lewis 24, 29, 39, 61; on the effects of the public controversy on the Illinois Supreme Court, see 169).

13. No letters commenting on Mabley's gendered metaphor were published in any of the four newspapers I researched.

14. The professor of modern literature was Richard Ellmann, then professor of English in the department of literature at Northwestern University. Ellmann testified that *Tropic of Cancer* "describes man's journey through life from despair and emptiness to hope" (Lind; see also Norris "'Cancer' in Chicago").

15. The juryless trial in the Court of Quarter Sessions of Philadelphia County involved James Farrell's *Studs Lonigan* trilogy and *A World I Never Made*, William Faulkner's *Sanctuary* and *The Wild Palms*, Erskine Caldwell's *God's Little Acre*, Calder Willingham's *End as a Man*, and Harold Robbins's *Never Love a Stranger*. Bok's judgment was sustained by the state superior and supreme courts.

# 4

## Publicity, Artistry, and *American Psycho*

During the editing process of "American Psycho," several editors at Random House have privately expressed relief that the war in the Persian Gulf has distracted attention from the book. One said, "'American Psycho' will be published in March or when the land war starts." (Cohen)

One approaches with a fair degree of awe a novel that has inspired the reaction that Bret Easton Ellis's "American Psycho" has done. To have provoked a publisher to reject a finished manuscript without demanding the return of a substantial advance; to have aroused a women's organization to call for a boycott of the book's new publisher—why, it's as if "American Psycho" had returned us to some bygone age when books were still a matter of life and death instead of something to distract us on a flight between JFK and LAX. (Lehmann-Haupt)

Here it is at last, the unspeakable thing. Is there anyone in America who does not yet have an opinion about this book (whether they've read it or not)—the novel Simon & Schuster refused to publish, that inspired the National Organization of [*sic*] Women to boycott not merely this title but everything to be issued in 1991 by Alfred A. Knopf (parent of Vintage, its new publisher), that was excoriated in reviews and "think pieces" before it was even in the bookstores to defend itself? (Bean)

It was much livelier than your ordinary literary blood bath.

The rumors started last spring [1990], four months after Bret Easton Ellis submitted his final version of *American Psycho* to his publisher, Simon and Schuster. A few women refused to work on the book, Ellis's third novel, which describes in excruciating first-person detail the days and nights of a Wall Street–yuppie named Patrick Bateman. The book is so graphic in parts that the marketing division at S&S started questioning whether it should be published at all. Then George Corsillo, the artist who had designed the covers for Ellis's first two books, refused to work on *American Psycho*.

Despite the early warnings, the book inched its way through the editorial corridors at S&S. It met with approval from the editorial board and the company's lawyers, was typeset in galleys and distributed to a few reviewers. By the fall, photocopies of the galleys were making the rounds in New York and Los Angeles. Then the press swung into action.

On October 29th an excerpt from the most violent chapter—describing a woman being skinned alive—appeared in *Time* under the headline "A Revolting Development." In December, *Spy* ran a passage in which the narrator had oral sex with the decapitated head of one of his victims. Suddenly, the book had the attention of Richard E. Snyder, the chief executive officer of Simon & Schuster, and his boss, Martin Davis, the chairman of Paramount Communications, which owns S&S and produces all the *Friday the 13th* movies. Apparently unaware until then of the growing public-relations disaster on his hands, Snyder speed-read the 400 pages over a weekend. Early the next week—and less than a month before the scheduled shipping date—Snyder informed Ellis's agent, Binky Urban, that he was rejecting *American Psycho*, thereby forfeiting the $300,000 advance that S&S had paid Ellis. On November 15th, Snyder made the formal announcement, explaining the decision was "a matter of taste."

The cry went up immediately: Corporate censorship! Within forty-eight hours of Snyder's announcement, however, Sonny Mehta of Alfred A. Knopf (a division of Random House) bought the book for his Vintage Contemporary paperback line. . . . Mehta said he would give the book a light edit and polish and scheduled publication for March.

Enter the feminists, led by Tammy Bruce, the energetic president of the Los Angeles chapter of the National Organization for Women (NOW). Bruce, 28, started the drive for a national boycott of the book and initiated a local hotline on which callers could hear her read gruesome passages aloud. . . . Bumper stickers that read "No Knopf in '91" were printed for the boycott, which would last until December 31st or until the book was no longer being printed.

Now coast-to-coast Bret-bashing began in earnest. The *New York Times Book Review* ran a glib, smirking review by *Life*-magazine columnist Roger Rosenblatt titled "Snuff This Book!" And an opaque *Los Angeles Times* editorial called "Worries About a Book" reached back and slammed Ellis's first novel, *Less Than Zero*, which it said "sketchily—indeed, artlessly—described the lives of a nihilistic circle of college-age hedonists." Gloria Steinem, Kate Millett and other leading feminists jumped on Bruce's bandwagon and wrote to Random House owner S. I. Newhouse Jr. and other executives, supporting the NOW boycott and expressing their outrage at the book.

Even corporate America joined the fray. When American Express learned that Ellis's narrator, a prodigious consumer, used his platinum card to pay for prostitutes and to lift cocaine to his nose, a phone call was placed to Vintage. And if a company was unaware of being mentioned in the book, Tammy Bruce and NOW informed it.

All along, the nagging question of literary merit kept muddying the issue of artistic freedom. The few people who actually read the book called it moronic and sophomoric. The author was called a "dangerously greedy brat." But if such a disturbing book were a masterpiece, what then? Now the literary lions weighed in. In the March issue of *Vanity Fair,* Norman Mailer set out to take measure of the book. Is it art? he asked. Not enough, he said. . . . Let it be published, Mailer concluded, but don't ask me to defend it.

In the middle of all this, the soft-spoken Ellis, 27, has kept his own counsel. Until now. (Love 46)

Robert Love's preface to his April 1991 *Rolling Stone* interview with Bret Easton Ellis offers a taste of the vociferous reaction to *American Psycho,* the names and titles of many of those involved, and, most importantly, some of the *topoi* that were raised by the book and by the scores of news stories and opinion pieces across the country that were written in response to it. Though the many pieces of written discourse disagree on much, they all agree that the controversies surrounding *American Psycho* received—however ephemerally—more and wider public attention than any novel in recent memory.[1] As Richard Bernstein wrote in the *New York Times,* "Even if it does have literary value, Mr. Ellis's book apparently is going to roil the calm more than any other recent cultural product" (C18). Added Roger Kimball of the *Wall Street Journal,* "The chief thing to understand about Bret Easton Ellis's 'American Psycho' is that it counts as an incident in the annals of contemporary American publicity, not American literature."

Initially startled by the immense publicity *American Psycho* received—as well as by its incredibly disturbing content and the variety of public opinions expressed about it—I studied sixty articles about the book that were published between October 1990 and April 1991 in eight major metropolitan daily newspapers and eighteen magazines. While these articles in no way represent the totality of discourses on *American Psycho,* they are representative of deliberation about the novel in the national literary public sphere that formed even before the novel was published and continued until it dropped off the best-seller lists late in the spring of 1991. Whereas publicity played a minimal role in *Ulysses*'s ultimate legal fate and—at least in Chicago—did not work in *Tropic of Cancer*'s favor, arguments about the nature and function of publicity set the contours of much of the public debate over *American Psycho.* While mentioned only in passing in the case of *Tropic of Cancer,* publicity plays the role of an explicit agent in many of the discourses about *American Psycho:* indeed, it could be said that publicity almost kept the novel from being published, then resulted in its being published, and then resulted in its being boycotted; ultimately, publicity resulted in the novel's becoming a best-seller. The strange course of events surrounding Ellis's relationships with two major publishers allowed the novel's publication narrative to garner for it even more public attention. Nearly every public discussion of the book attempted to come to terms with the consequences of publicity—the immense publicity the book had already received and what additional publicity writing about the book might give it. Publicity was always a *topos* in arguments that focused on whether to publish the book, whether to sell it, whether to buy it, and whether to boycott it.

The huge emphasis on publicity as well as the consistent recognition by those who wrote about *American Psycho* that the book was a marketed commodity recall observations Habermas makes about the degeneration of the public sphere in the world of letters in the twentieth century. In the later chapters of *The Structural Transformation of the Public Sphere,* Habermas describes what he calls the transformation from a culture-debating to a culture-consuming public. This transformation—the seeds of which were present in the rise of the bourgeois public sphere—was caused by the laws of the market coming to govern the public sphere. In this structurally transformed public sphere, "rational-critical debate had a tendency to be replaced by consumption," according to Habermas (161). In literary public spheres, this transformation was marked by the commodification of cultural discussion and the sale of outlets for that discussion. "Put bluntly," Habermas writes, before public discussion became a commodity, "you had to pay for books, theater, concert, and museum, but not for the conversation about what you had read, heard, and seen and what you might completely absorb only through this conversation" (167). Habermas's structural analysis helps explain not only how citizen critics have been increasingly excluded from truly public debate about cultural products over the century but also how media that originally had the potential to serve a public function and to foster public debate and democracy (radio in particular) have come to be merely commercial enterprises, bought and sold by private interests for short-term gains (for more on this issue, see McChesney; and Engelman).

Another distinguishing characteristic of the transformation of the literary public sphere is the changed nature of publicity. Here again, Habermas's theory of structural transformation explains how the generation of publicity has changed from bottom-up to top-down; whereas publicity used to be a function of public debates among many, Habermas sees publicity in the social welfare state as controlled or manipulated from positions of power. Since the middle of the twentieth century, Habermas argues, alienation between experts and the great public of the mass media has caused "the public [to] split apart into minorities of specialists who put their reason to use nonpublicly and the great mass of consumers whose receptiveness is public but uncritical" (175). This accounts for the few citizen critics who thought it worth their time to write in public about *American Psycho*. Critical publicity, that is, the process of subjecting interest groups and groups of experts—including literary critics and other intellectuals—to far-reaching publicity, is the only possible solution that may "restore functions of control and critique to the public sphere" (208). With his theory of transformation and concepts of commodification of public debate and critical publicity, Habermas again lends an overall frame of explanation to the changes in literary public spheres in the twentieth century. While the public discourses studied in this chapter reveal *American Psycho* to be a consumer item—ironic in light of Ellis's alleged critique of eighties consumerist culture—they also show that in many ways Habermas's criterion of critical publicity is less rare than he thought in the early sixties, a point I will return to in my conclusion. In any case, publicity is the architectonic *topos* for all other public issues surrounding *American Psycho*.

Given the immense amount of publicity surrounding the book, however, it is important to note that, unlike in the case of *Tropic of Cancer,* only a very few people wrote publicly in defense of banning the book. Nonetheless, definitional and dissociative arguments about the nature and consequences of censorship were common, especially after Simon and Schuster's decision not to publish the novel. *American Psycho* also raised questions about the social role and purpose of literature as well as distinctions between social importance and social value, and those arguments, again, were connected with arguments about publicity.[2] Whereas arguments about the definition and purpose of literature were relatively uncommon in the *Tropic of Cancer* debate in Chicago, such arguments form the substance of many public arguments about *American Psycho*. In fact, the different emphases writers gave to the issues of censorship, obscenity, and literary merit very much affected the shape of public deliberation about the book.

Other than the general issue of publicity, then, the biggest influence on public debate over *American Psycho* was the criterion of literary merit in general and the public discourse of Norman Mailer in particular.[3] Mailer's March 1991 essay on Ellis in *Vanity Fair* shifted the terms of the public debate over *American Psycho* from pragmatic political and social concerns—public concerns—to concerns over the book as art in isolation. Mailer's central questions are Is *American Psycho* art? and Is Bret Easton Ellis an artist? Such questions of aesthetics, if they invite responses at all, invite them only from experts. Whereas the legal system had decided decades before that such novels as *American Psycho* should not be banned, different publics within the literary public sphere that formed in response to its publication persisted in feeling the question should still be open; Mailer's use of the criterion of literary value changed the contour of public debate over the book and transferred ownership of the issue from feminists and social critics to literary experts in the realm of aesthetics.[4]

## *American Psycho* Goes Public

As Robert Love explained in the introduction to his *Rolling Stone* interview with Ellis, *Time* and *Spy* magazines first made public the issue of *American Psycho*—and excerpts of Ellis's text. Many accounts of Simon and Schuster's decision to refuse to publish Ellis's book suggest that these articles, especially the one in *Spy,* caused the cancellation. Hence, the role of "the press" significantly affected *American Psycho*'s publicity from almost the beginning. The first excerpt appeared in *Time* magazine, in an article entitled "A Revolting Development" by R. Z. Sheppard. Sheppard described the excerpt as "one of the tamer examples of Ellis' zombie prose": "I start by skinning Torri alive, making incisions with a steak knife and ripping long strips of flesh from her legs and stomach while she screams in vain, begging for mercy in a thin, high voice. I stop doing this and move over to her head and start biting the top of it, hoping that she realizes her punishment is ending up being comparatively light compared to what I plan to do with the other one." In addition to offering the first glimpse of *American Psycho* to its readers, the *Time* article also raised some of the issues that would circulate around *American Psycho* and those who wrote publicly about it for the next several months.

The article opened by suggesting that *American Psycho* is a mysogynist novel, a *topos* that anyone who wrote publicly about Ellis's novel had to address.[5] Yet Sheppard's suggestion was more subtle than the accusations that would follow. His article began: "Old joke. Two small boys leave a theater after seeing a gushy movie. 'Wasn't it terrible?' says the first boy. 'I didn't think it was too bad,' replies the second. 'During the kissing scenes, I just closed my eyes and made believe he was choking her.'" While Sheppard mentioned that women employees of Simon and Schuster refused to work on the book, he stressed not only that "no one wants to say so on the record," but also that the novel is more nauseating than hateful.

While Sheppard also mentioned that the novel would bring torture onto "the best-seller lists," most of the rest of the article was devoted to stressing that Simon and Schuster planned to, in the words of its trade division publisher, market the novel "aggressively, with muscle and energy." Sheppard said that U.S. publishers' profit margin problems might be behind the planned publication of Ellis's novel: "For S&S, caught in a profit squeeze like many other U.S. publishers, grossing out readers could mean netting a big return on Ellis' advance, estimated at $300,000." According to the article that offered the public its first excerpt of *American Psycho,* then, the novel was disgusting and perhaps hateful. But, above all else, it was a commodity that the publisher hoped would improve its bottom line.

Though the *Time* article was referred to often in summaries of the events surrounding *American Psycho*—in a *New York* article Phoebe Hoban cited "the explosion in *Time* magazine"—the *Spy* magazine article received more attention not only at Simon and Schuster but also in resulting discourses. The article, written by Todd Stiles and entitled "How Bret Ellis Turned Michael Korda into Larry Flynt," ran in the December issue. Stiles's juxtaposition of the mundane in the first sentence—publication announcement and reading tour—with the sadistic in the quotation reflects *Spy*'s characteristic coolness:

> In its current catalog Simon & Schuster announced the January publication of *American Psycho,* by Bret Easton Ellis. Happily, the catalog mentions that Ellis will do a "five-city reading tour." There really is nothing quite like hearing a poet or splendid prose stylist read from his own work. One can just picture Ellis in the wainscoted upstairs room of Atlanta's or Chicago's or Boston's finest independent bookstore, reading from *American Psycho* in effortless cadences:
>
> "I keep spraying Torri with mace and then I try to cut off all her fingers and finally I pour acid into her vagina which doesn't kill her, so I resort to stabbing her in the throat and eventually the blade of the knife breaks off into what's left of her neck, stuck on bone, so I stop. While Tiffany watches, finally I saw the entire head off—torrents of blood splash against the walls, even the ceiling— and holding the head up, like a prize, I take my cock, purple with stiffness and lowering Torri's head to my lap I push it into her bloodied mouth and start fucking it, until I come."

In addition to this sexually violent passage, *Spy,* unlike *Time,* offered another excerpt. The second excerpt gave a sense of what Ellis and his publishers argued was the key to the cultural critique in the novel. "Certainly," Stiles wrote, "gruesome, sadistic murder is not all there is to the book." Stiles then described what he saw as two of Ellis's strategies of social commentary: "the novel pokes fun at materialism by mentioning status brand names a dozen times a page—Cristal, Armani, Blaupunkt[, and] unvary-

ingly, relentlessly, Ellis introduces each character with a fashion report."
Then Stiles gives the second excerpt from the book: "'McDermott is wearing a woven-linen suit with pleated trousers, a buttondown cotton-and-
linen shirt by Basile, a silk tie by Joseph Abboud and Ostrich loafers from
Susan Bennis-Warren Edwards.'" Stiles also suggested in the article how
Ellis might explain having written a book like this, again stressing social
critique: "*I am purposely exaggerating the way yuppie men treat women.
That's the point,* he will say. *I meant to convey the madness of the consumerist eighties.*" And, indeed, that was very like the line Ellis and his
publisher took in defense of the book after its publication. But Stiles was
not convinced, even at this early moment: "Not much could be more sick-
ening than the misogynist barbarism of this novel, but almost as repellent
will be Ellis's callow cynicism as he justifies it." While Stiles defines what
he excerpts as "telling social commentary," he asserts that, nevertheless,
"a number of people have some explaining to do."

The *Time* and *Spy* articles brought public scrutiny to bear on *American
Psycho*. In the scores of articles that would follow, people—journalists,
book reviewers, and other novelists much more than citizen critics—made
arguments endeavoring to change the way other people felt about the book
and the issues it raised. People also wrote to influence what others might
*do* about the book: buy it, boycott it, argue for their right not to buy it,
burn it. Ellis's book and the publicity surrounding it provoked public discussion of issues ranging from publisher responsibility to definitions of
censorship to who gets to tell the story of misogyny—the hated or the
hater?—to how should we read literature—as social critique or as social
reproduction? And those discourses—from the *Spy* article that resulted in
Simon and Schuster's canceling publication to the cries of "corporate censorship" following that decision which resulted in Random House's publishing the novel—also had social functions: to change the way people
viewed an unsettling book with a questionable purpose.

## Publicity

Just as each of the early articles expressed some sort of incredulity about
the violent content of *American Psycho,* each of them referred, in one way
or another, to the fact that publicizing the book was bound to make it sell.
Caryn James, for example, described *American Psycho* as "more an up-
to-the-minute media event than a novel" (1) and Joseph P. Kahn called it
"a cultural lightning rod, wired to attract a supercharged response from

everyone" (72). Thus, as with *Tropic of Cancer,* the *topos* of publicity itself became foregrounded as a subject for deliberation in the literary public sphere that grew up around *American Psycho.*

Publicity has consequences; but what those consequences are was also
a subject for deliberation. Anna Quindlen, for instance, argued in her *New
York Times* op-ed column not only that "the book was derailed by bad
publicity" but also that "this book will sell on controversy alone." Indeed,
the irony of the issue of publicity is that it worked both ways for *American Psycho:* it not only got the book rejected by Simon and Schuster but
also motivated Vintage to accept it a mere forty-eight hours later. In the
words of John Baker, editor-in-chief of *Publishers Weekly,* "the very press
attention that helped kill the book at one publisher will probably ensure
its success at another."

Publicity and its consequences were debated by publishers, by librarians,
by booksellers, by reviewers, by feminists, by other novelists, and by citizens. Joseph Treen's news article on *American Psycho* in the *Boston Globe,*
published before Vintage had accepted the book, showed that publishers
were divided on the question. While Treen quoted Roger Straus of Farrar,
Straus, and Giroux as questioning the effects of publicity—"'This is being built up as a revolting book,' Straus said. 'And so it may not be very
chic to be seen reading it'" (16)—other publishers disagreed. Kent Carroll
of Carroll and Graf said he thought the book would sell well, and he was
hoping to be the publisher. Treen's quote from Carroll contrasts literary
value with social value: "'Historically, we know that what offends people
at any given moment may have much more to do with the social and political climate of the country than it does with the intrinsic value of the
work. . . . If the history of attempting to suppress things tells us anything,
it's that you should bet on the book. More often than not you're going to
be right'" (16). Interested in different *loci* of quality, Carroll still puts
publicity and the promise of big sales at the top of the heap.

Booksellers were faced with a decision about publicity similar to the one
they had had to make just two years earlier, when Salman Rushdie's *The
Satanic Verses* was published. Terry Pristin wrote in the *Los Angeles Times*
that disclaimers were booksellers' latest way to handle the *American Psycho*
conundrum. Pristin described one West Hollywood bookstore that went
so far as to put a disclaimer into each copy of *American Psycho.* The disclaimer read, "'Dear Reader: Book Soup is making this book available to
you because of our commitment to the doctrine of freedom of expression.
This should not be construed to be an endorsement of the contents.'"
Pristin also mentioned that out of concern for sales B. Dalton polled its

eight hundred stores and found that "98% wanted to sell the book, though 90% said it should not be publicized." In a similar piece in the *Atlanta Journal,* Don O'Briant reported that booksellers in the South said they would carry the book but not display it prominently. Booksellers reflected on the publicity surrounding *American Psycho,* some hoping for community protest and others hoping the publicity would die down so that the book would not become a best-seller.

*Publishers Weekly,* too, reported on the deliberations among booksellers, again stressing the conflict between availability and promotion. Madalynne Reuter reported a "profound ambivalence" about the book among booksellers, although the vast majority of them were stocking it. Reuter used one store as a paradigmatic example: "At Cody's in Berkeley, Calif., Nick Setka, the store's manager and chief buyer, said there was quite a bit of instore debate among employees. 'But the ultimate decision was up to store owner Andy Ross, and it was his feeling that we should carry it, but to not go out of our way to promote it to customers.' In the end, Cody's ordered 10 copies of the book despite heated protest from staff, who wrote their complaints into a 'staff log.'" *Publishers Weekly* also interviewed, for its 8 March issue, some booksellers who refused to carry the book but who would special order it "for customers who really want it" ("Vintage 'American Psycho'").

The most active—and most widely publicized—conflict between publicity and suppression focused on the National Organization for Women. As Edwin McDowell reported in the 12 December issue of the *New York Times,* the idea to boycott the book and its publisher came from Tammy Bruce, president of the Los Angeles chapter of NOW. McDowell's article began by quoting Bruce's description of the book, one of the most-often quoted encapsulations: "Outraged by the book its president describes as 'a how-to novel on the torture and dismemberment of women,' the Los Angeles chapter of the National Organization for Women has called for a boycott of 'American Psycho' by Bret Easton Ellis." McDowell reported that Bruce had recorded "a passage from the book about a woman who is raped and tortured with an automatic nail gun" on the Los Angeles NOW chapter's telephone hotline. Yet McDowell stressed that Bruce and other NOW members did not call for the book to be censored and, in fact, were making their appeal on the basis of freedom of expression. Quoting Bruce, McDowell reported, "'We are not telling them not to publish,' Tammy Bruce, the president of the Los Angeles chapter, said. Instead, she said, members are being asked to exercise their right of free expression by refusing to buy the novel so the publisher 'will learn violence against women in any form is no longer socially acceptable.'" McDowell explained that Bruce's purpose in making the tape was to urge those who called in "to write letters of protest to Alberto Vitale, the chief executive of Random House, and to [Sonny] Mehta, who is also the president of Alfred A. Knopf." In an article by Nora Rawlinson in the January issue of *Library Journal*, Bruce further clarified her position, and, once again, the dual nature of publicity was implicated: "In an interview with *LJ*, Bruce said the book offers an 'unprecedented opportunity' to publicize NOW's concerns about violence against women 'and how it is perpetuated by our culture.'" Again, Rawlinson's article stressed that Bruce and NOW were not calling for censorship: "'We are not telling bookstores not to stock the book, we are asking people to show that there is no demand for this kind of literature. We do not see a social commentary in the book, we do not see the reason for the kind of graphicness and misogyny in the book.'"

Bruce's actions—recording an excerpt and risking further publicity by recommending a boycott—were repeatedly addressed in the public discourse that followed. And many, outside and even inside NOW, questioned the ultimate effects of Bruce's methods. Christopher Hitchens, writing in *The Nation*, documented his call to the NOW hotline:

> I have listened often and carefully to the hotline tape that the National Organization for Women has established. The tape performs a number of interlocking and contradictory functions:
>
> 1) It furnishes a graphic reading of a passage from *American Psycho*, in which a woman is so foully raped and dismembered that one replaces the receiver feeling almost distorted with disgust.
> 2) It states that crimes of rape and violence toward women are epidemic and on the rise.
> 3) It quotes numerous distinguished feminist writers as saying that no such description of the torture and slaying of a Jewish or black person would be permitted by Sonny Mehta.
> 4) It says that the publication by a "reputable" house promotes the action described to the level of "Americana."
> 5) It calls for a boycott and other forms of punishment of the publisher.

After this description Hitchens questions Bruce's analysis of the social problem of violence against women as well as her analysis of the solution to the problem of Ellis's book: "Given that crimes of violence against women are on the rise, for example, why does it follow that the fictional portrayal of such crime should be furiously deplored?" On the other hand, if *American Psycho* is, as Bruce has argued, a "how-to manual," why publicize that through the hotline? Again, in Hitchens's words, "If the offending passage is held to be an incitement to imitative or similar crimes, why put a tape of it on the wire for all to hear?" Finally, Hitchens questions Bruce's assertion that depicting crimes leads to more of those crimes being committed: "Why imply that depictions of lynching or gassing would not or, much more suggestive, *should not,* be put in print? And why, if as NOW claims one in three American women will be raped in her lifetime, should one decry the elevation of a fictional recognition of the subject to the presumably privileged height of 'Americana'?"

Booksellers, too, questioned the consequences that publicity about the hotline and the boycott would have on sales. Terry Pristin, for example, reported in the 1 March issue of the *Los Angeles Times* that many booksellers blamed Tammy Bruce and NOW for the brisk sales of *American Psycho:* "Glenn Goldman, owner of Book Soup, which ordered an undisclosed number of books and stuffed them with disclaimers, blamed NOW for the interest in the book. Within a day of its arrival, the store sold 18 copies, he said." According to Pristin, Goldman claimed that such issues as women's rights suffer from publicity: "'If you're talking about women's civil rights, it's probably better to have as little publicity as possible,' he said."

Even within NOW—from the top, in fact—Bruce's use of publicity was publicly questioned. In a sidebar entitled "NOW Members Split over Call for Boycott of 'American Psycho,'" Maureen Downey reported on 8 March in the *Atlanta Journal* that across the United States, NOW members were deeply divided over whether to support Bruce's call for a boycott. Downey reported that NOW president Molly Yard opposed the boycott and contended that it "elevates a book panned by critics into a controversial cause celebre. 'My own personal feeling is that the more they talk, the more they publicize the book,' [Yard] says, adding that NOW mail is divided." Downey also put Yard and Bruce in direct conflict, quoting Bruce's attempt to shift the *locus* of the arguments from publicity to women's welfare: "'Molly Yard needs to realize that the issue here is not the book,' Ms. Bruce says. 'The bigger issue here is that women are dying. . . . For Molly to take the opinion that we should remain silent is what has gotten women in this position in the first place.'"

Within NOW as well as among booksellers and publishers, opinion was sharply divided over whether publicizing *American Psycho* would cause more harm or more good. This profound questioning of the phenomenon of publicity suggests Habermas's account of top-down publicity should be expanded to include questions of the potentially contradictory effects of publicity. Nonetheless, it is clear that the mechanisms of publicity about

*American Psycho* were set off by two publishers concerned more about their profit margins than about any social consequences Ellis's book might have.

## Censorship

Publicity and censorship—censorship variously defined—have an odd kind of reciprocal relationship, one that controversial and obscene or blasphemous books especially bring to the fore. As David Streitfeld noted in the *Washington Post:* "Any boycott against *American Psycho* will have to take into consideration the fact that such protests often simply increase a book's audience. Not for nothing did publishers once advertise books as 'Banned in Boston.'" Again, as Love noted in his introduction to the *Rolling Stone* interview, early reactions to Simon and Schuster's cancellation of *American Psycho*'s publication centered on charges of corporate censorship. That issue, and different definitions of the concept, became subjects for deliberation in the literary public sphere that formed in response to the novel.

After making his announcement that Simon and Schuster would not publish *American Psycho,* Chairman Richard Snyder was asked by Madalynne Reuter of *Publishers Weekly* whether his decision constituted censorship. Reuter reported Snyder's reply in a 30 November article: "'It's not a First Amendment issue,' [Snyder] told *PW.* 'It's not a right of free expression issue. I was advised that the book could be placed elsewhere.'"

Anna Quindlen of the *New York Times* was among the first to assail Snyder's reasoning. In her column of 18 November, she questioned the grounds of Snyder's decision as well as, implicitly, his view of art: "The eternal question about violence in art is whether it simply reflects our worst behavior or inspires it. We are so terrified of inspiration that sometimes we are moved to suppression. But reflection is essential because it often leads to thought, and occasionally to understanding. That is why we publish troubling books. A publisher who makes safe decisions has abdicated. He is, according to a quip repeated often last week, not a publisher, but a printer." While Quindlen did not accuse Snyder of being a censor, she did argue that, by his decision, he revealed that he was not a true publisher. Yet Quindlen's further argument—that Paramount Communications's ownership of Simon and Schuster suggested Snyder might have been forced into his decision—did raise the specter of corporate censorship, albeit indirectly: "Writers feared the conglomeration of publishing. They believed the day would come when men who know little about books—'but I know what I like!'—would make publishing decisions guided by profits and press coverage." Quindlen also quoted an authority figure who seconded her opinion: "Robert K. Massie, president of the Authors Guild, called the cancellation 'a black day,' adding, 'It's a day the guild has been predicting would come since giant corporations started buying distinguished American publishing houses.'" Quindlen ended her article by calling the decision "cowardice"; she never called it censorship.

Many others dissociated what Simon and Schuster did from censorship. In the 30 November issue of *Publishers Weekly,* Calvin Reid interviewed several writers, publishers, and booksellers to get their reactions. Again, Massie of the Authors Guild was quoted as stressing that the incident was one of breach of contract and showed the evils of corporate publishing. Wendy Strothman of Beacon Press maintained that the Ellis case is "not a First Amendment issue." Roger Straus of Farrar, Straus, and Giroux commented, "I do not consider this a First Amendment matter—it is a matter of taste." Martin Garbus of Frankfurt, Garbus, Klein, and Selz replied that "there is no First Amendment to stop publishing houses from censoring books—the First Amendment only applies to state censorship." And Joyce Maskis of the Tattered Cover Bookstore stressed censorship versus selection: "Publishers and booksellers have the First Amendment right to choose what to publish and what to sell," she said.

The only newspaper editorial I found in my reading about the reaction to Ellis's novel—a 16 January editorial in the *Los Angeles Times* entitled "Worries about a Book"—also rejected as censorship Simon and Schuster's decision not to publish *American Psycho.* The editorial addressed the definition of censorship directly by using two analogies, one well known and the other relatively obscure. First, however, the editors argued that books can do harm; sorting through the issue of judgment versus censorship "begins with the candid admission that words and other forms of expression do matter. If they did not, the constitutional protection extended to them in the First Amendment of our Bill of Rights would be folly—and the Founding Fathers were not fools. But that which has the power to edify, enlighten and ennoble also has the power to do harm." Then the editors argued by analogy using Harriet Beecher Stowe's *Uncle Tom's Cabin* and the contemporaneous *Awful Disclosures* by Maria Monk, described as "the memoirs of a young woman who, after converting to Roman Catholicism, entered a convent where she was forced into clerical concubinage, orgies and the ritual murder of children." While many people argued upon its publication that *Awful Disclosures* should be banned because, according to the editorial, "as the bible of the Nativist Movement, [it] helped foment deadly anti-Catholic violence in Boston and Philadelphia," nineteenth-century America "survived" the book just as it benefited from *Uncle Tom's*

*Cabin.* "If the former had been suppressed as a provocative calumny," the editors asked in the concluding sentence, "what of the latter?"

Regardless of the legal definition of censorship, the word continued to be used in many different ways in the literary public sphere. Terry Pristin quoted a bookseller who had come to her own definition of the term: "Before ordering five copies, Terry Baker, co-owner of the mystery annex of Small World Books in Venice, said she had read everything that she could find on the controversy surrounding the book. Though she does not approve of it, 'If I do not carry this book, I believe I'm participating in censorship,' she explained." And a 17 November *Chicago Tribune* article written by Marianne Taylor and Kenneth R. Clark included another implicit definition of censorship. William Rickman, president of the twenty-store Kroch's and Brentano's chain, remarked that the stores would carry the books and "'let our customers make the censorship choice themselves'" (8).

Christopher Hitchens raised the question of corporate censorship in his *Nation* article, using as his point of comparison a book that Simon and Schuster did not reject, Ronald Reagan's "memoir" entitled *An American Life.* Hitchens opened his article by reacting to Reagan's most recent explanation for his visit to the Bitburg cemetery, which he had been repeating in interviews during his publicity tour for the book: "Backed by the resources of a distinguished publisher, a former American President sweetens the memory of the Waffen SS. By any standards, this is a fine day's work. But by prevailing standards, a work of nonfiction that prettifies real-world atrocities is nothing when compared with a work of fiction that depicts imaginary ones." Hitchens argued in the article that Reagan's new explanation, financed by Simon and Schuster, and the publisher's decision to publish *An American Life* in the first place are in much poorer taste than is Ellis's book. And to buttress this argument he, as mentioned above, critiqued NOW's boycott as misguided. At the end of the article, Hitchens brought these different subjects together: "'There's no more a market,' says Tammy Bruce of Los Angeles NOW, 'for fiction about the torturing and skinning of women than there is for, say, fiction about the torturing and the gassing of Jews.' Think about that statement, think about Ronald Reagan and Simon and Schuster and their real-world falsifications, and say if you think fiction is the problem. Which deserves the title of 'Americana': *An American Life* or *American Psycho?* Try reversing the authors and titles for a start."

The issue of quality was raised as well by John Leo, writing in *U.S. News and World Report.* While not explicitly rejecting claims that the ghostwritten Reagan memoir is in questionable taste, Leo deflected any comparison of Reagan's memoir to Ellis's novel. Leo dissociated his support for Simon and Schuster's decision not to publish *American Psycho* from censorship and put the question more generally:

> How can we get this dangerous junk out of the culture? Short of censorship, everything possible ought to be done, beginning with a serious national debate. Maybe it will come down to boycotts. In the meantime, maybe we should recycle Nancy Reagan's slogan, "Just say no." The career of Andrew Dice Clay began to unravel the day that Nora Dunn and Sinead O'Connor stood up and refused to perform with him on "Saturday Night Live." That touched off a chain reaction of noes that included Jay Leno, David Letterman, MTV and more and more of the public.

Instead of calling for legal or even corporate censorship, Leo called for extralegal efforts to suppress cultural texts that are believed to be offensive. Further, although relatively few public citizens were active participants in this literary public sphere, Leo's argument invokes an active public—in addition to celebrities, of course—as antidote to cultural "junk."

Without calling it censorship, the syndicated columnist Joan Beck called for editors, publishers, and readers to "just say no" to cultural texts that offend them. Beck assailed "those who keep pushing the limits of social tolerance for their own purposes and profits" and compared *American Psycho* to the Madonna video "Justify My Love," which MTV refused to air, citing the video's questionable taste. "What is welcome, though," writes Beck, "are the rare voices that quietly say, 'This one is not for us' and 'We don't want our name on a book of questionable taste.' May they increase and prevail."

Finally, an unsigned editorial in the 10 December issue of *The Nation* equated Simon and Schuster's decision to cancel publication of *American Psycho* with U.S. government actions to stop broadcasts of taped phone conversations of deposed Panamanian official Manuel Noriega. Entitled "Backdoor Censors," the article began: "Two recent setbacks for freedom of the press possess a fortuitous symmetry. One involves prior restraint and the other what might be called posterior restraint." While the Noriega case involves the rights of a broadcast organization to be free from prior restraint, the article argued, Simon and Schuster's decision—and the late date at which it was made—raises the question of the independence of corporate publishers: "And so the issue of free speech, corporate censorship division, does arise. If *American Psycho* is as exploitative as it sounds, we find ourselves once again defending sleaze. At any rate, Ellis's book will not be suppressed. Another publisher, Vintage Contemporaries, snapped it up and is expected to make a bundle. We plan to rush out to our neighborhood bookstore and not buy it." By aligning the two situations, *The Nation* article attempted to maintain a balance among citizens' rights to information, questions of taste, and increasing corporate control of media and publishing in this country. *The Nation* article agreed with other voices in the literary public sphere by concluding that there are definitions of censorship other than the strictly legal one that pertain in the case of *American Psycho.*

## "Is It Art?" and Is Ellis an Artist?

Demonstrating that its editors were undaunted by the challenge to free speech absolutism inherent in Ellis's graphic prose, *Vanity Fair* published not only a long feature by Norman Mailer on *American Psycho* but also a long excerpt from the novel. Mailer's article, which received more response than any other piece written about Ellis's book, set out to answer the question "What is art?" through making the person, Ellis, coextensive with the act of his novel. In other words, Mailer's primary criterion for judging the novel was his sense of the artistry of its author. More writers responded directly or in passing to Mailer's article than to anything else published on *American Psycho.*

Mailer opened his article by commenting that he "cannot recall a piece of fiction by an American writer which depicts so odious a ruling class— worse, a young ruling class of Wall Street princelings ready, presumably, by the next century to manage the mighty if surrealistic lever of our economy" (154). Mailer followed this commentary by quoting in its entirety—"uncut from the original manuscript" (156)—one of the most graphic scenes in the novel, in which the protagonist, Patrick Bateman, has a conversation with, taunts, tortures, and finally murders a homeless man. This is the longest excerpt of *American Psycho* to appear in print:

> Bags of frozen garbage line the curbs. The moon, pale and low, hangs just above the tip of the Chrysler Building. Somewhere from over in the West Village the siren from an ambulance screams, the wind picks it up and it echoes and then fades.
>
> The bum, a black man, lays in the doorway of an abandoned antique store on Twelfth Street on top of an open grate, surrounded by bags of garbage and a shopping cart from Gristede's loaded with what I suppose are personal belongings: newspapers, bottles, aluminum cans. A handpainted cardboard sign attached to the front of the cart reads: I AM HUNGRY AND HOMELESS PLEASE HELP ME. A dog, a small mutt, short-haired and rail thin, lies next to the bum,

its makeshift leash tied to the handle of the grocery cart. I don't notice the dog the first time I pass the bum. It's only after I circle the block, walking up to him that I see it laying in a pile of newspapers, guarding him, a collar around its neck with an oversized nameplate that reads: Gizmo. The dog looks up to me wagging its skinny, pathetic excuse for a tail and when I hold out a gloved hand it licks at it hungrily. The stench of some kind of cheap alcohol mixed with excrement hangs over the bum like a thick, invisible cloud and I have to hold my breath, before adjusting to the stink. The bum wakes up and opens his eyes, yawning, exposing remarkably browned, stained teeth between purple lips.

The bum is fortyish, heavy-set, and when he attempts to sit up I can make out his features more clearly in the glare of the streetlamp; a few days growth of beard, triple-chin, a ruddy nose lined with thin brown veins. He's dressed in some kind of tacky looking lime-green polyester pantsuit with washed-out dated Sergio Valente jeans worn *over* it (this season's homeless person's fashion statement) along with an orange and brown V-neck sweater ripped and stained with what looks like burgundy wine. It seems he's very drunk—either that or he's crazy or stupid. His eyes can't even focus in on me when I stand over him, blocking out the light from a streetlamp, covering him in shadow. I kneel down.

"Hello," I say, offering my hand, the one the dog licked. "Pat Bateman."

The bum stares at me, panting with the exertion it takes to sit up. He doesn't shake my hand.

"You want some money?" I ask gently. "Some food?"

The bum nods and starts to cry, thankfully.

I reach into my pocket and pull out first a ten dollar bill then change my mind and hold out a five to him instead. "Is this what you need?"

The bum nods and then looks away, shamefully, his nose running and after clearing his throat, sobs quietly, "I'm so hungry."

"It's cold out too," I say. "Isn't it?"

"I'm so hungry," the bum moans again and he convulses once, twice, and a third time, then embarrassed, looks away.

"Why don't you get a job?" I ask, the bill still held in my hand but not within the bum's reach. "If you're so hungry, why don't you get a job?"

He breathes in, shivering, and between sobs, admits, "I lost my job . . . oh lord . . ."

"Why?" I ask, genuinely interested. "Were you drinking? Is that why you lost it? Insider trading? Just joking. No, really—were you drinking on the job?"

He hugs himself, in between sobs, chokes, "I was fired. I was laid-off."

I take this in, nodding. "Gee, uh, that's too bad."

"I'm so hungry," he says, then starts crying hard, still holding himself. His dog, the thing called Gizmo, starts whimpering.

"Why don't you get another one?" I ask. "Why don't you get another job?"

"I'm not . . ." He coughs, holding himself, shaking miserably, violently, unable to finish the sentence.

"You're not what?" I ask softly. "Qualified for anything else?"

"I'm hungry," he whispers, imploringly.

"I know that, I know that," I say. "Jeez, you sound like a broken record. I'm trying to help you . . ." My impatience rises.

"I'm hungry," he repeats.

"Listen. Do you think it's fair to take money from people who *do* have a job?" I ask him. "Who *do* work?"

His face, still contorted with sobs, crumples and he gasps, almost crying out, his voice raspy, "What am I gonna do?"

"Listen, what's your name?" I ask.

"Al," he says.

"*Speak* up," I tell him. "Come on."

"Al," he says, louder.

"Get a goddam job, *Al*," I say, earnestly. "You've got a negative attitude. That's what's stopping you. You've got to get your act together. *I'll* help you."

"You're so kind mister. You're kind. You're a kind man," he blubbers. "I can tell."

"Ssshhh," I whisper. "It's okay." I start petting the dog.

"Please," he says, grabbing my wrist, but lightly, with kindness. "I don't know what to do. I'm so cold."

I ask him, "Do you know how bad you smell?" I whisper this soothingly, stroking his face. "The *stench,* my God . . ."

"I can't . . ." he chokes, then swallows, shaking. "I can't find a shelter."

"You *reek,*" I tell him again. "You reek of . . . shit . . ." I'm still petting the dog, its eyes wide and wet and grateful. "Do you know that? Goddamnit Al, look at me and stop crying like some kind of *faggot,*" I shout. My rage builds then subsides and I close my eyes, bringing my hand up to the bridge of my nose which I squeeze tightly, then sigh, "Al . . . I'm sorry. It's just that . . . I don't know, I don't have anything in common with you."

The bum's not listening. He's crying so hard he's incapable of a coherent answer. I put the bill slowly back into the other pocket of my Luciano Soprani jacket and with the other hand stop petting the dog and reach into the other pocket. The bum stops sobbing abruptly and sits up, looking for the fiver or, I presume, his bottle of Thunderbird. I reach out and touch his face gently, once more with compassion and whisper, "Do you know what a fucking loser you are?" He starts nodding helplessly and I pull out a long thin knife with a serrated edge and being very careful not to kill the bum push maybe half an inch of the blade into his right eye, flicking the handle up, instantly popping the retina and blinding him.

The bum is too surprised to say anything. He only opens his mouth in shock and moves a grubby, mittened hand slowly up to his face. I yank his pants down and in the passing headlights of a taxi can make out his flabby black thighs, rashed because of constant urinating in his pant-suit, the stench of shit rises quickly into my face and breathing through my mouth, on my haunches, I start stabbing him below the stomach, lightly, in the dense matted patch of pubic hair. This sobers him up somewhat and instinctively he tries to cover himself with his hands and the dog starts barking, yipping really, furiously, but it doesn't attack, and I keep stabbing at the bum now in between his fingers, stabbing the backs of his hands. His eye, burst open, hangs out of its socket and runs down his face and he keeps blinking which causes what's left of it inside the wound to pour out, like red, veiny egg yolk. I grab his head with one hand and push it back and then with my thumb and forefinger hold the other eye open and bring the knife up and push the tip of it into the socket, first breaking the protective film so the socket fills with blood, then slitting the eyeball open sideways and he finally starts screaming once I slit his nose in two, spraying me, the dog with blood, Gizmo blinking trying to get the blood out of his eyes. I quickly wipe the blade clean across his face, breaking open the muscle above his cheek. Still kneeling I throw a quarter in his face, which is slick and shiny with blood, both sockets hollowed out, what's left of his eyes literally oozing over his lips, creating thick, webby strands when stretched across his screaming open mouth. I whisper calmly, "There's a quarter. Go buy some gum, you crazy fucking nigger." Then I turn my attention to the barking dog and when I get up, stomp on its front paws while it's crouched down ready to jump at me, its fangs bared, and immediately crunch the bones in both its legs and it falls on its side squealing in pain, its front paws sticking up in the air at an obscene, satisfying angle. I can't help but start laughing and I linger at the scene, amused by this tableaux. When I spot an approaching taxi, I slowly walk away.

Afterwards, two blocks west, I feel heady, ravenous, pumped-up, as if I've just worked out heavily, endorphins flooding my nervous system, my ears buzzing, my body tuning in, embracing that first line of cocaine, inhaling the first puff of a fine cigar, sipping that first glass of Cristal. (156–57)

Of the many things Mailer could have said about the excerpt, the first judgment he made was that the novel is "a radioactive pile" (157). At once, Mailer made clear his criteria for evaluating the book—judgments about its author: "The writer may have enough talent to be taken seriously. How one wishes he were without talent!" (157).

After summarizing the publishing history and public response to the novel, Mailer described the process of reading *American Psycho* and explained that he devoted so much time and publication space to write about "a book like this" (159) because he had to determine whether it was true art. *American Psycho* rests squarely on the line between art and its opposite, whatever that is—"The novel is not written so well that the art becomes palpable, declares itself against all odds, but then, it is not written so badly that one can reject it with clear conscience" (158); as a result, without Mailer's critical efforts, the novel "is bound to rest in unhallowed ground if it is executed without serious trial" (159).

The serious trial that Mailer had in mind centered on the question of true art. In his words, "What is art? What can be so important about art that we may have to put up with a book like this?" (159). Mailer articulated his criteria before he offered his ultimate judgment: the book is "boring" and "intolerable"; it involves "the worst and dullest characters a talented author has put before us in a long time" (158). In the balance of the article, Mailer argued that the book should be defended because talented authors have the right to create whatever they want. *American Psycho,* however, is not artful enough to warrant enduring its extreme violence. Art should tell us more about its subject, Mailer argued, and *American Psycho* does not tell us anymore about "the criminal mind" than we knew when we began the book. Mailer concluded that Ellis is not artful enough in distancing himself from his main character to be able to inform us about what makes a serial murderer tick. Verdict: Ellis is a talented writer but not an artist; thus, his book is not art. Mailer ended the article by again asserting that it is his act of judgment that is important: "So I cannot forgive Bret Easton Ellis. If I, in effect, defend the author by treating him at this length, it is because he has forced us to look at intolerable material, and so few novels try for that much anymore" (221). Mailer thus first moves the *locus* of debate from social consequences to aesthetics and then rejects Ellis and further discussion of his book on the basis of aesthetic criteria.

Mailer also responded to some of the earlier worries about the consequences of *American Psycho.* But he argued that *American Psycho* was so revoltingly shocking that it would serve to critique society's values rather than to reinforce them by getting men to confront their misogyny:

> While it is certainly true that the fears women have of male violence are not going to find any alleviation in this work, nonetheless I dare to suspect that the book will have a counter-effect to these dread-filled expectations. The female victims in *American Psycho* are tortured so hideously that men with the liveliest hostility toward women will, if still sane, draw back in horror. "Is that the logical extension of my impulse to inflict cruelty?" such men will have to ask themselves, even as after World War II millions of habitual anti-Semites drew back in similar horror from the mirror of unrestrained anti-Semitism that the Nazis had offered the world. (221)

Mailer capped his ruminations on the social effects of Ellis's novel by imagining himself in the role of publisher and reiterating his sense of the purpose of literature: "If I had been one of the authors consulted by a publisher, I would have had to say, yes, publish the book, it not only is repellent but will repel more crimes than it will excite. This is not necessarily the function of literature, but it is an obvious factor here" (221).

Responses to Mailer's piece were many. Caryn James wrote in the *New York Times* that Ellis's novel ups the ante for violence in popular culture: "'American Psycho' can raise the ante only if readers and other writers accept it on its own pretentious terms, if they fall for the claim that it says something about the criminal mind" (21). "Audiences may not have got into Norman Bates's mind, but at least they knew that he, and Hitchcock, had one. It is impossible to say the same about 'American Psycho'" (21). James thus asserts that *American Psycho* will not have any effect because it will not be taken seriously, unlike the cultural text she contrasts with *American Psycho,* Jonathan Demme's film adaptation of Thomas Harris's novel *The Silence of the Lambs.* James prefers *The Silence of the Lambs* to *American Psycho* solely on the basis of artistic merit:

> Mr. Demme and Ms. [Jodie] Foster have made some legitimate claims for the feminism implicit in the strong heroine's role. Gay activists have made less convincing charges that Mr. Demme exploits homophobic stereotypes: the uncaptured serial killer, though not a homosexual, is a man who wants to be a woman. Both attitudes reflect the society that shaped the film, but both are ultimately beside the point. Like [Hitchcock's] "Psycho," "The Silence of the Lambs" succeeds artistically because it entangles viewers with demented individuals, not social symbols or case studies. (20)

Finally, James wrote that *American Psycho* is "mindless" (21) and "peabrained" (1); "violence itself does not damn the work" (21), but it is "inept and pretentious, an exploitation book dressed up with an epigraph from Dostoyevsky and a title allusion to Hitchcock" (21). James suggested that works that would cross the boundaries of taste must be "artistically successful" and that *American Psycho* cannot be taken seriously because it is not.

Jonathan Yardley, in an article entitled "Norman Mailer's Shock Schlock," wrote in the *Washington Post* that Mailer's defense of Ellis on the grounds that *American Psycho* takes on difficult subjects misses the point: Ellis has taken on the wrong difficult subjects and in the wrong form. In an argument that made implicit claims about the scope and purpose of fiction, Yardley argued:

> Our novelists are indeed afraid of big and troubling subjects, and richly deserve disdain for their cowardice. But the "intolerable material" that should command their attention is not the stuff of pulp function, what Mailer himself calls the "horror shop plastic" of Ellis's novel. It is rather the stuff of real American life: not the fantasy of a cruel and imperialist America that thrives in the hyperventilated imaginations of the literati, but America as it actually is, a blend

of hope and despair, achievement and disappointment that can be seen in revealing miniature in the daily affairs of any American community.

It is possible to find that America in books now being written, but this will give Mailer no comfort because they are not books by novelists. Nothing in current American fiction even approximates the painfully gritty slices from our national life to be found in two new works of nonfiction by writers who have the effrontery to be journalists: "The Promised Land," by Nicholas Lehmann, and "There Are No Children Here," by Alex Kotlowitz. Both books deal with life in the projects of Chicago, "intolerable material" if ever there was such; both tell us more about America, its occasional victories and hard failures, than can be found in a single sentence of Ellis's exploitative, sophomoric pornography.

Yardley's distinction between "the fantasy of a cruel and imperialist America that thrives in the hyperventilated imaginations of the literati" and "the painfully gritty slices from our national life" suggests that, for him, American fiction has not met its potential in the way that American journalism has.

Yardley's comments make implicit statements about whether literature should and does describe society's values, subvert them, or reproduce them. This issue came up directly in many of the articles about *American Psycho;* it is one of the most deliberated questions about Ellis's book. Many writers in the literary public sphere feared the potential of *American Psycho* to reproduce society's values, that is, to cause more violence toward women and more conspicuous consumption—of things and of people. For example, Marilyn Gardner, who wrote on *American Psycho* for the *Christian Science Monitor,* asked, "How much violence is too much? And when is a certain measure of violence socially redeeming, serving a particular theme within a specific context?" Gardner discussed the gray areas she maintained individual readers must negotiate for themselves. But, she stressed, Ellis's tone of coolness complicates the matter for many readers:

> Ellis—and though he goes to excess he is not alone—deliberately takes an aloof, unfeeling stance as if the object is to be "cool." The only thing worth registering shock over, it seems, is the fact that anyone in the '90s could still be shocked.
>
> But to witness the shocking without being shocked is a working definition of being dehumanized. If readers and spectators, the final tastemakers, become brothers and sisters of numbness with the amoral antiheroes themselves, we can no longer blame Ellis or anyone else. We, too, will have joined the monsters, and like him, the price we pay will be moral obliviousness.

Some writers assumed or asserted that *American Psycho* might merely describe rather than reproduce society's values; again, Anna Quindlen was among the first to bring that issue into the literary public sphere: "Is it heartening to read novels in which men and women treat one another with affection and respect, and kindness is the overweening emotion? Yes. Does that reflect the world? Hardly. The eternal question about violence in art is whether it simply reflects our worst behavior or inspires it." Quindlen argued that that problem was in society, not in the fictional portrayal of it, a sentiment shared by several other writers.

In his review of *American Psycho,* however, Henry Bean takes the idea that the novel describes society further. Bateman, wrote Bean, "has, does and is everything the children of Reagan were promised they could have, do and be. True, he's sort of alienated and also commits serial murders, some of which he describes in disturbing detail, but, hey, in deregulation you live with the bumps. Let the marketplace take care of it." Despite his tone, Bean argued that Ellis's intention was to critique eighties consumerist values. And in a claim disputed by many—from the first *Spy* article on— Bean wrote that the book committed no more violence against women than against other groups: "The loudest attacks have accused the novel of misogyny, exploitation of and unremitting violence toward women. Yet of the 18 people (not to mention assorted animals) tortured and murdered by the narrator, eight are women, nine are men, and one is a small boy; of the book's 400 pages, fewer than 40 are devoted to these events. In the other 360, Ellis is unusually attentive to daily instances of racism, anti-Semitism, homophobia. And he repeatedly mocks the perfunctory sexism of his upper-class mates." Bean conceded "that some of the torture and dismemberment, especially of the women, is performed with particular zeal." Yet, again, he argued that, given the prevalence of violence against women in contemporary society, "it must surely be an appropriate subject for fiction. (One can imagine NOW demanding such books instead of boycotting them.) And it is difficult to conceive of anybody reading these passages without being moved to disgust, grief and finally pity." Bean sees the rape and dismemberment and murder of women as just one of the ills of the eighties. Because those acts receive no moral judgment in the novel, Bean sees Ellis as having written effective social commentary. Bateman, according to Bean, "sins and no one cares. It almost seems that no one knows. What Ellis fully understands is the politics of social irresponsibility, that electoral strategy initiated by Richard Nixon but which has reached full flower in the Reagan-Bush years. 'American Psycho' tells of the greed and soullessness to which we have all yielded in our way and that leads inexorably to gratuitous murder, to murder as our final expression of disgust and plea for judgment."

Bean concluded that Ellis was trying to describe eighties America to get Americans to see their own emptiness and to attempt to subvert it, a view with which Joseph Coates, writing in the *Chicago Tribune,* agreed strongly. After describing Bateman and his associates Coates wrote: "There is no doubt that such people exist in significant numbers among the elite crowd who run things and make the most money in this country, and that they are incredibly shallow, ignorant and sometimes dangerous despite the expensive colleges from which they come and whose names they use as status credit cards" (5). Coates spent quite a bit of his review entertaining the idea that Ellis might have written the book as a social critique of aesthetics. Coates pointed out that the first person Bateman kills is a homeless man and commented that

> Bateman and his friends apparently see the whole social problem of poverty and homelessness as a matter of urban decor aggravated by a subconscious sense of guilt they don't have the resources to confront.
>
> In the scene in which the derelict is killed, Ellis effectively shows us how all Bateman's values—despite a Harvard education—have effectively hardened into a sense of taste: ethics are all aesthetics for him, and he is enraged when they are violated.
>
> Bateman has to kill him—and does, slowly and painfully—merely to reaffirm his own sense of who he is. This dehumanizing attitude can be found in people with much less money than Bateman and his friends—people who have merely been drenched with a generation's worth of consumerist brainwashing on television. (5)

What is especially striking about Coates's review is that at the end of his commentary, which suggested a deep understanding and appreciation for the social function of the book, Coates concluded: "I only wish that Ellis had written a better book to illustrate it" (5).

Some writers flatly rejected the idea that *American Psycho* could serve as social criticism. Roger Kimball responded to such arguments by reminding readers that Ellis is being manipulated by the publishing industry: "Like his other books, 'American Psycho' is utterly unredeemed by moral sensibility or critical distance. It is a symptom, not criticism, and is no more a 'commentary' than is 'Deep Throat.'" Similarly, Joseph P. Kahn commented in the *Boston Globe:* "What thinking reader can wade through 400 pages narrated by a smug serial killer—a Wall Street yuppie, no less—who dispatches his victims with knife, nailgun and (above all else) studied indifference and not say, whoa, Bret, this can *not* be part of the solution; ergo, it must be part of the problem" (67).

But the most thorough treatment of the question of whether *American Psycho* describes, subverts, or reproduces social values came from Mim Udovitch's review in the *Village Voice*. Udovitch wondered how so many people could misunderstand that Ellis meant the book to critique American values: "Every line, chapter, and train of thought proceeds ineluctably on parallel tracks, past the same scenery, to a single destination of social indictment," she wrote (65). Udovitch continued this line of reasoning by calling the Los Angeles NOW boycott "misguided" (65). Bruce's encapsulation of the work as a "how-to novel on the torture and dismemberment of women" is, according Udovitch,

> a pure lucid syllogism. Its major premise (that sexual violence requires a manual), its minor premise (that *American Psycho* is such a manual) and its conclusion (that publication would thus promote as well as reflect real acts of violence against women) are all demonstrably false. . . .
>
> To justify the second [premise] would be to imply that Ellis's amorality play condones the acts it describes, when they are clearly, indeed crudely, condemned on both literal and allegorical levels, not to mention being so flatly written that they are hardly memorable, let alone shocking. Some of the scenes of rape and dismemberment are positively childish: Look Ma, no hands. And the conclusion is thus dubious—and to the extent that it siphons off energy that could be better employed against real rather than imagined misogyny, destructive—as any of the numerous parallel assaults on pornography and the arts that so often proceed from the same faulty reasoning on the Jesse Helms–Andrea Dworkin continuum. (65)

Fears that *American Psycho* will reinforce the misogyny already present in society went so far as to prompt a news story on violence toward women. In the *Atlanta Constitution*, Maureen Downey wrote a story headlined "Every Woman's Nightmare" that not only discussed *American Psycho* and *The Silence of the Lambs* but also featured interviews with women who confront violence every day. "Although 'The Silence of the Lambs' is far less salacious than 'American Psycho,'" Downey wrote, "both give substance to a woman's worst nightmare of ending up a victim of male violence" (G1). The article continued with statistics on violence against women and is the one article on or about *American Psycho* that did not employ aesthetic criteria to evaluate the book. Downey interviewed women about their reactions to the book and the film and stressed that cultural texts do have consequences:

> Peg Ziegler needs no reminder of the vulnerability of women. She sees it every day as director of the Rape Crisis Center at Grady Memorial Hospital.

So she avoids movies and books with any manner of violence. But that doesn't mean she escapes the consequences.

"I have to live in the world with potential assailants who do see those films and read those books," she says.

"And I don't mean the handful of sociopaths who grin when they murder somebody. It's more likely the man in the three-piece suit, the apparently normal man who sees in these films and books the message that it is permissible at times to abuse someone else." (G4)

By focusing on the real-life effects of cultural texts, Downey offers a series of *topoi* in counterpoint to arguments about Ellis's artistry.

## Worries about a Shared World

Reading and studying *American Psycho* and the public discourses that were written in response to it was a painful process, and it is clear that many of those who wrote publicly about the book found it painful too. But I have suggested in this chapter that, regardless of how painful Ellis's book is and no matter how despicable the motives of those who published it might have been, the book at least temporarily resulted in communication in public by journalists, booksellers, librarians, and a few citizen critics about issues of common concern. That publicity was one of the major issues raised by and about *American Psycho* both confirms and refutes some of Habermas's conjectures about the nature and function of publicity in late capitalism while supporting his narrative of structural transformation. Those who argued about the *topos* of publicity regarded it as a social problem or issue; thus, publication of Ellis's book encouraged at least some discussion of publicity as manipulation in late capitalism in a media culture that is ultimately controlled by only a very few elites (see also McChesney; and Engelman).

Despite the way Mailer's argument changed the contours of the nationwide literary public sphere that formed in response to the publication of *American Psycho*, these discourses demonstrate that literature can serve a social function, even today, by engendering rational-critical debate in a discursively formed public sphere among real individuals who share substantial common interests. The most substantial common interest in the case of deliberations about *American Psycho*, I believe, is a concern for the state of our society and for the safety and security of our selves and those we love. Whatever the writers of these discourses disagreed on, they were genuinely and deeply concerned for the future of a world that could produce a book like *American Psycho*.

NOTES

1. Salman Rushdie's *The Satanic Verses* would be a contender for this title since it received a great deal of global publicity in 1989. For a discussion of publics theory and the controversy over Rushdie's novel, see Domenig.

2. As discussed in chapter 3, the 1957 *Roth* decision left unclear whether "social value" and "social importance" were equivalent. The 1966 U.S. Supreme Court decision on *Fanny Hill* included "utterly without redeeming social value" as one criterion for obscenity. That criterion was woven with publicity in the 1966 obscenity trial of William S. Burroughs's *Naked Lunch*. In her analysis of the case, Felice Flanery Lewis explains, "Noting that the record contained 'many reviews and articles in literary and other publications discussing seriously this controversial book,' the Massachusetts court decided it could not say that *Naked Lunch* had no redeeming social importance" (213).

3. Mailer had served as a witness in the Boston obscenity trial of *Naked Lunch* (Lewis 214–15); his third novel, *The Deer Park*, had a publication history similar to that of *American Psycho*, Ellis's third novel: Rinehart, who had published Mailer's first two novels, refused to publish the third on the grounds that it was obscene but paid Mailer for the privilege of not publishing it. After six other publishers turned down the novel, Putnam finally agreed to publish it (Rembar 15).

The *Chicago Tribune* book critic Joseph Coates alluded to Mailer's novel when writing about *American Psycho*: "Ellis gives us a deer park full of people so absorbed in status that they are what they own, and this 'minimal self' as the social critic Christopher Lasch called it, is continually threatened by not having exactly the right things at the right time—as well as by people who have nothing" (5).

4. In his study of discourse and social will-formation in public debates on drinking and driving, Joseph R. Gusfield uses the metaphor of "ownership" to argue that in debates about public problems, different groups struggle to determine what the stakes of an issue are and whose views will be legitimated: "The concept of 'ownership of public problems' is derived from the recognition that in the arenas of public opinion and debate all groups do not have equal power, influence, and authority to define the reality of the problem. . . . Even if opposed by other groups, [owners] are among those who can gain the public ear" (10). Specific to his case study, Gusfield argues that, because such institutions as the medical profession, universities, and the sciences were unprepared to deal with the public debate on drinking and driving, institutionalized religion came to own the problem and thus it became a moral rather than a social issue.

5. In his study of the social construction of serial homicide, Philip Jenkins points out that the controversy over *American Psycho* took place in the context of several other public discussions of serial murder. The August 1990 murders of five University of Florida students revived public concern over a number of other unsolved serial murders; the film *Silence of the Lambs* was released in February 1991;

and in July 1991 the Jeffrey Dahmer serial murder case became "one of the best known serial murder incidents worldwide" (93). Further, Jenkins argues that feminist theory has since the late seventies interpreted the serial murder of women as "gynocide" or "femicide" and represented it as "the ultimate manifestation of sexual abuse" (172).

# 5

## Andrea Dworkin's *Mercy:*
## Pain and Silence in the "War Zone"

The following excerpt of *Mercy* was published as a sidebar in the *New York Times Book Review* on 15 Sept 1991:

> You try to make them understand that yes something did happen honest you aren't lying and you say it again, strained, thicklipped from biting your lips, your chest swollen from heartbreak, your eyes swollen from tears all salt and bitter, holding your legs funny but you don't want them to see and you keep pretending to be normal and you want to act adult and you can barely breathe from crying and you say yes something did happen and you try to say things right because adults are so stupid and you don't know the right words but you try so hard and you say exactly how the man sat down and put his arms around you and started talking to you and you told him to go away but he kept holding you and kissing you and talking to you in a funny whisper and he put his hands in your legs and he kept rubbing you and he had a really deep voice and he whispered in your ear in this funny, deep voice and he kept saying just to let him . . . but you couldn't understand what he said because maybe he was mumbling or maybe he couldn't talk English so you can't tell them what he said and you say maybe he was a foreigner because . . . he talked funny and you tried to get away but he followed you and then you ran and you didn't scream or cry until you found your momma because he might hear you and find you so you were quiet even though you were shaking and you ran and then they say thank God nothing happened.

Two reviewers took two different approaches to the novel:

> Ms. Dworkin's argument, proceeding from pain, may be moving, but it is also intolerant, simplistic, and often just as brutal as what it protests. Ms. Dworkin advocates nothing short of killing men. The last chapter ends: "I went out; at night; to smash a man's face in; I declared war. My *nom de guerre* is Andrea One;

I am reliably told there are many more; girls named courage who are ready to kill." One cannot argue here, any more than Mr. Rushdie could, that statements in literature are not equivalent to statements in the real world. (Steiner)

The question becomes how to speak about rape—or other self-destroying experiences—in a way that makes its gravity inescapable without further erasing the individual selves of those who endure it, or don't. (Kaplan)

This excerpt appeared in the *Michigan Quarterly Review:*

I barely know any words for what happened to me yesterday, which doesn't make tomorrow something I can conceive of in my mind; I mean words I say to myself in my own head; not social words you use to explain something to someone else. I barely know anything and if I deviate I am lost; I have to be literal, if I can remember, which mostly I cannot.

## The "War Zone"

Unlike *Ulysses* and *Tropic of Cancer,* which have become canonical enough to amass storied accounts of their battles for publication against state censorship, and even unlike *American Psycho,* whose journey to publication received immense publicity precisely because its sexually violent and graphic subject matter caused it to be rejected by one publisher and readily accepted by another two days later, Andrea Dworkin's *Mercy* has not received a public account of its struggle toward U.S. publication. This is curious since Dworkin's narrator explicitly calls for abused women to kill men at random, while Ellis's novel was interpreted as an implicit argument for men to rape, kill, and dismember women. The absence of a public quest narrative for publication as well as the dearth of public reaction to the novel—*Mercy* received fewer than ten reviews while *American Psycho* received more than seventy reviews and several other feature stories—point to the main *topoi* concerning *Mercy:* the lack of public attention it received before and after its publication and the relationship among that lack of attention, the subject matter of the novel—rape specifically and sexual abuse of women in general—and the argumentative strategies of Dworkin and her critics.

Dworkin's ninth book and second novel, *Mercy* was first published in England in September 1990 by Secker and Warburg. Though a few reviewers refer to Dworkin's difficulty in finding a U.S. publisher, the only full account of this struggle was written by Dworkin herself, in an author's note published with a short excerpt from *Mercy* in the Winter 1990 issue of *American Voice:* "The following is an excerpt from *Mercy,* a novel that was published in England this fall but has no Amerikan publisher. I have been working on it for over two years; it has had a publisher in England for most of that time. I think it is fair to say that in the U.S.A., it is suppressed writing" (24). Dworkin has written repeatedly about her difficulties in getting most of her books published, which she views as a constant battle to get her books into the hands of women who desperately need them. This battle for publication and publicity is one of the recurring themes of Dworkin's nonfictional *Letters from a War Zone*. Ultimately, the relative silence about a novel that so unabashedly addresses a controversial social and political issue raises questions about the relationship among fiction, politics, and social change as well as about the nature and function of literary public spheres in late twentieth-century U.S. culture. After providing background on Dworkin's other work and on *Mercy*, I will analyze the public discourses and silences about *Mercy* and Dworkin's other writings during the period after *Mercy* was published. Ultimately, I suggest that Dworkin's argumentative strategies prior to *Mercy*, her rhetorical choices in the novel, and her critics' insistence on responding to her as a *topos* of radical feminism severely limited the possibility that reviewers and other readers could construct a common discursive space in which to discuss her book and ideas. In this literary public sphere the issue is Andrea Dworkin, and the architectonic argumentative structure is *ad personam*. I conclude by suggesting that Dworkin's rhetorical choices in *Mercy* and her critics' representations of her as writing solely out of personal pain and victimization—and these rhetorical strategies as paradigmatic of public discussions about issues that concern what have long been considered "private" issues—raise troubling questions about the possibilities of public discourse and argumentation when it is seen to require a dispassionate, impartial, or disinterested point of view for productive argumentation to ensue (Habermas, *Structural Transformation* 25–26, 161–62; Perelman and Olbrechts-Tyteca 14, 61). Ultimately, this chapter raises the question of the status and the discursive consequences of personal experience in a literary public sphere, especially when that sphere is figured as a "war zone."

Dworkin is an appropriate subject for the study of the possibility of literary public spheres in part because she states explicitly in her writing and implies through certain aspects of her writing practice that she believes fictional discourse can play an important role in public debate; in addition, as she tells it, her publication history suggests that her work has been structurally if not intentionally suppressed by the very institutions that have the power to get people talking with one another about literature and the political issues it might raise. In *Letters from a War Zone*, a collection of essays, speeches, interviews, and book reviews she wrote between 1976 and 1989, Dworkin introduces each selection with information about its rhetorical situation and reception and argues that the press refused to publish or review the great majority of her work precisely because the issues her writing raises threaten the power of the press as an institution and expose connections among the publishing industry, pornographers, and organized crime:

> These essays and speeches present a political point of view, an analysis, information, arguments, that are censored out of the Amerikan press by the Amerikan press to protect the pornographers and to punish me for getting way out of line. I am, of course, a politically dissident writer but by virtue of gender I am a second-class politically dissident writer. That means that I can be erased, maligned, ridiculed in violent and abusive language, and kept from speaking in my own voice by people pretending to stand for freedom of speech. It also means that every misogynist stereotype can be invoked to justify the exclusion, the financial punishment, the contempt, the forced exile from published debate.[1] (6)

While Dworkin's definition of "censorship" is clearly not the legal definition—indeed, she has published nine books in two decades without any government interference—the reception her books have received as well as her inability to publish articles in periodicals most likely to foster public debate about political issues prompt her to evoke censorship. Even when her work is discussed in the press, asserts Dworkin, making a claim similar to Gayatri Chakravorty Spivak's in "Can the Subaltern Speak?" she is not given the chance to speak in her own voice; instead, others misrepresent her by speaking for her.

The work that Dworkin has published concerns, primarily, pornography and sexual abuse. She is the author of the nonfiction works *Woman Hating* (1974), *Our Blood* (1976), *Pornography* (1981), *Right-Wing Women* (1983), and *Intercourse* (1987), as well as the coauthor with Catherine A. MacKinnon of *Pornography and Civil Rights* (1988) and ordinances that define pornography as a civil rights violation against women.[2] In addition, she has published a collection of short stories, *The New Woman's Broken Heart* (1986), and a novel, *Ice and Fire* (1985).[3] She published a second collection of essays, *Life and Death,* in 1997. Despite this record of publication, Dworkin devotes much of *Letters from a War Zone* to her failure to get most of what she has written published and much of what she has published discussed or reviewed publicly. Early in *Letters from a War Zone,* for instance, Dworkin chronicles the publication history of each piece in the collection: four were "published in mainstream magazines with decent, not wonderful, circulations," three in *Ms.,* one in *Mother Jones.* "Most of these essays and speeches were published in tiny, ephemeral newspapers, most of which are no longer publishing," Dworkin writes. "Seven of these pieces have never been published at all; four have been published in English but have never been published in the United States; one, 'Letter from a War Zone,' has been published in German and Norwegian but never in English" (5). Dworkin is especially bitter that larger-circulation, relatively liberal U.S. magazines will not publish her work and will not give her space to respond to the criticisms of her work that they have published repeatedly:

> None of these pieces, despite repeated efforts over years, were published in *The Nation, The New Republic, The Progressive, The Village Voice, Inquiry,* left-liberal periodicals that pretend to be freewheeling forums for radical debate and all of which have published vicious articles with nasty, purposeful misrepresentations of what I believe or advocate. . . . I have never been given any right of response. And none of these pieces, despite repeated efforts over years, have been published in the magazines that presume to intellectual independence: for instance, *The Atlantic* or *Harper's.* And I have never been able to publish anything on the op-ed page of *The New York Times,* even though I have been attacked by name and my politics and my work have been denounced editorially so many times over the last decade that I am dizzy from it. And I have never been able to publish in, say, *Esquire* or *Vogue,* two magazines that publish essays on political issues, including pornography, and also pay writers real money. (5–6)

Indeed, after *Letters from a War Zone* was published, the work of anti-pornography feminists was criticized in a lead essay by the novelist John Irving in the *New York Times Book Review.* The *Times* printed a nearly full-page response by Dworkin, but because it was run as the first and longest letter among others responding to Irving, the *Times* did not have to pay Dworkin for her work. Hence, intimately connected to the questions of publication and publicity is, for Dworkin, the material issue of being able to make a living from writing.[4]

In addition to her concerns about publicity and finances, Dworkin is concerned that her difficulty in getting published and reviewed keeps her work from reaching the women who need it: she is unapologetic that she is writing for a particular audience and with a specific purpose. Indeed, while she is skeptical about society's ability to accept writers, she is unequivocal in her belief that writers are primary agents of social change; Dworkin believes not only in the importance of the individual vision of the individual writer but also in the power of public debate about that vision. "Writers get underneath the agreed-on amenities, the lies a society depends on to maintain the status quo, by becoming ruthless, pursuing the truth in the face of intimidation, not by being compliant or solicitous," Dworkin writes (4). Clearly, her purpose in writing is to change society:

> I wrote [the selections in *Letters from a War Zone*] because people are being hurt and the injury has to stop. I wrote them because I believe in writing, in its power to right wrongs, to change how people see and think, to change how and what people know, to change how and why people act. . . . I wrote these pieces because I believe that women must wage a war against silence: against socially coerced silence; against politically preordained silence; against economically choreographed silence; against the silence created by the pain and despair of sexual abuse and second-class status. And I wrote these essays, gave these speeches, because I believe in people: that we can disavow cruelty and embrace the simple compassion of social equality. I don't know why I believe these things; only that I do believe them and act on them. (5)

Yet at the same time that Dworkin articulates a belief in "people," she seems distrustful of "society" and its reaction to the writer. No society is grateful for the writer: "We think that contemporary western democracies are different but we are wrong. The society will mobilize to destroy the writer who opposes or threatens its favorite cruelties: in this case, the dominance of men over women" (4). A particular section of "society," reviewers, comes under fire in some of Dworkin's writings. Dworkin's assertion that "every misogynist stereotype can be invoked" (6) to keep her work from being published and reviewed suggests that misogyny is most likely the reason that her work is sometimes not published or reviewed; in addition, such assertions cause critics to become defensive when they do review her work. This assertion of misogyny and consequent defensiveness seems to have occurred after Dworkin published *Intercourse*. Because of the nature of her argument—"that getting fucked and being owned are inseparably the same; together, being one and the same, they are sex for women under male dominance as a social system" (66)—critics who did not review the book positively could be seen as in collaboration with male dominance, as, in Dworkin's words, "participat[ing] in the fuck, giving it its power as possession" (79). Critics who did not review Dworkin's work positively were, in Dworkin's view, simply not interrogating their own sexual practices adequately. Thus, Dworkin's beliefs—articulated in as well as performed through her writing—suggest two distinct views of those who might read her books: first, that society in general (and reviewers in particular) cannot be trusted to appreciate the writer's ability to tell the truth and, second, that women can nonetheless wage a war against misogyny and silence.

These different visions suggest again that Dworkin writes for a particular audience, and her statements about why she writes bear this out. As she writes in *Letters from a War Zone,* "these essays and speeches speak for and to vast numbers of women condemned to silence by . . . misogyny, . . . sadistic self-righteousness, . . . [and] callous disregard for human rights and human dignity" (6). In her discussion of doing research for *Pornography,* she further clarifies her purpose and audience:

> In writing my new book, I experienced the most intense isolation I have known as a writer. I lived in a world of pictures—women's bodies displayed, women hunched and spread and hanged and pulled and tied and cut—and in a world of books—gang rape, pair rape, man on woman rape, lesbian rape, animal on woman rape, evisceration, torture, penetration, excrement, urine, and bad prose. . . . I became frightened and anxious and easily irritable. But the worst was that I retreated into silence. I felt that I could not make myself understood, that no one would know or care, and that I could not risk being considered ridiculous. The endless struggle of the woman writer to be taken seriously, to be respected, begins long before any work is in print. It begins in the silence and solitude of her own mind when that mind must diagram and dissect sexual horror.
>
> I had to study the photographs to write about them. I stared at them to analyze them. It took me a long time to see what was in them because I never expected to see what was there, and expectation is essential to accurate perception. I had to learn. A doorway is a doorway. One walks through it. A doorway takes on a different significance when one sees woman after woman hanging from doorways. A lighting fixture is for light until one sees woman after woman hung from lighting fixtures. The commonplace world does not just become sinister; it becomes disgusting, repellent. Pliers are for loosening bolts until one sees them cutting into women's breasts. Saran Wrap is for preserving food until one sees a person mummified in it. . . . Writing is not a happy profession. It is viciously individual: I, the author, insist that I stand in for us, women. In so doing, I insist on the ultimate social meaning of writing: in facing the nightmare, I want another generation of women to be able to reclaim the dreams of freedom that pornography has taken from me. (33–36)

While Dworkin resists a facile view of a reading public able to immediately understand her vision and act on it, she seems to have faith that, if writers continue to write—continue to "face the nightmare"—the injuries of the past may begin to heal. The quantity and quality of the public reception of her books, however, casts a long shadow on whatever optimism Dworkin maintains about the power of her fiction to promote social change and raises questions about whether her rhetorical strategies can ever foster the kind of readership, public discussion, and change she says she believes in and wants to effect in women's lives.

## *Mercy* in Public

*Mercy* was published in the United States in August 1991 by Four Walls Eight Windows. Though short excerpts of the novel were published as sidebars to a few reviews, the only substantive ones were the publication of half of chapter 9 in the Fall 1990 issue of *Michigan Quarterly Review*[5] and a short excerpt from chapter 11 in the Winter 1990 issue of *American Voice*.[6] As with *American Psycho,* I searched for reviews and other discussions of *Mercy* in *Lexis/Nexis, Newspaper Abstracts on Disc, Periodical Abstracts on Disc, Book Review Digest,* and *Book Review Index.* Compared to Ellis's book, *Mercy* received few reviews; more significantly, *Mercy* was not the subject of feature stories in the newsweeklies. Even *Ms.* played down the book; the very short, unsigned review was tucked into the magazine's "Bookwatch" section, perhaps because of Dworkin's unpopularity among many liberal feminists.

Indeed, *Mercy* received substantive discussion in only the *Women's Review of Books,* a publication geared to what Nancy Fraser would call a subaltern counterpublic. Even there, however, no letters to the editor followed the review. Also, unlike what followed publication of Ellis's book, media coverage of *Mercy*—or in this case, the lack of media attention—did not become a public issue; the U.S. media's failure to come to terms with or, with very few exceptions, even to mention a book that not only described rape graphically but also called for women to kill men did not itself get any attention in the major media. In addition, even in publications that reviewed the book and in which editors explicitly and regularly solicit reader correspondence, I could find no letters to the editor either about *Mercy* or about the reviews it received. The dearth of public response to *Mercy*—especially compared to the intense publicity garnered by Ellis's *American Psycho*—suggests that access to publicity and perhaps public debate of any kind is a consequence of power. Even before *Mercy* was published in its entirety in the United States, Laurence Goldstein, editor of the *Michigan Quarterly Review,* stressed the intense publicity surrounding the issue of women's bodies in his introduction to the special issue of the journal in which an excerpt of *Mercy* appeared:

> The female body is, as Margaret Atwood writes, "a hot topic" being scrutinized in a multitude of recent books, in college courses and conferences, and with increasing sophistication in feminist publications in every professional field. Social issues like abortion, pornography, rape, and new technologies of reproduction have guaranteed a continuing, perhaps eternal, controversy about the rights and violations of the female body, not to mention the no less political

matter of medical treatments related to anorexia, hysterectomy, PMS, mortal illnesses, and other conditions surveyed in this issue. (485)

Given the "hot topic" that *Mercy* addresses, why did its publication attract little attention and virtually no public discussion? *Ms.* did not give the book much attention, but the unsigned review dubbed it controversial and praised it highly: "So controversial that it appeared abroad before finding a courageous publisher in the U.S., Dworkin's new novel is her best yet: brilliant, provocative, relentless, hypnotic, and powerful. A must for those who read Dworkin—and a must for those who haven't yet" (76). On the whole, treatment of *Mercy* can be characterized by this review in *Library Journal:*

> In this work, the well-known author of numerous books on women, feminism, and pornography has created an unusual, highly charged, and formally provocative account of one woman's life of increasingly horrific violence and sexual abuse by men. The book begins when the protagonist, Andrea, is nine years old and has just been the victim of a sexual assault by a stranger in a movie theater. From that point on, the reader is carried at a dizzying pace through chapters in Andrea's progressively darker and more disturbing life until Andrea, at 27, comes to the decision that the only response to the kind of violence she's suffered all her life at the hands of men is simply to start killing them. Unfortunately, the compelling, stream-of-consciousness pacing of the narrative begins to break down early in the book, becoming a harsh diatribe that, ultimately, Dworkin's skill as a writer is not sufficient to carry. (106–7)

Instead of addressing the social issues raised by the book, reviewers are on the whole more likely either to make "the person" coexistent with "the act" (Perelman and Olbrechts-Tyteca 293–321)—and thus write about Dworkin rather than the novel—or to change *stasis* by attributing the novel's failure to Dworkin's lack of writing skill or by redefining the novel as a "diatribe," "manifesto," or "polemic" (Perelman and Olbrechts-Tyteca 415–44), all of which are ultimately *ad personam* attacks. Perelman and Olbrechts-Tyteca distinguish between *ad hominem* arguments, "which the speaker knows would be without weight for the universal audience, as he conceives it" (111), and *ad personam* arguments, which are personal attacks that aim at disqualifying the opponent from debate (111, 318; see also Johnstone). In studying the reviews of *Mercy* and five other articles about Dworkin in U.S. print media after *Mercy*'s publication, I found these were the major *topoi* critics used: the genre of *Mercy;* associations and dissociations of Andrea Dworkin and Andrea the main character/narrator; redefinitions of the novel and its purpose; representations of Dworkin;

and language and style in the book. Especially given the outcry over *American Psycho* and the striking similarities between the political and social issues the two novels raised, the public reactions *Mercy* did and did not receive deserve study.

In early autumn 1990, *Mercy* made its first public appearance in the United States when approximately half of what would be chapter 9 appeared in the *Michigan Quarterly Review* in a special issue entitled "The Female Body." The issue included poetry and fiction as well as essays, and Dworkin's chapter, "In October 1973 (age 27)," was marked as fiction even though the narrator's name is Andrea and (though this is not mentioned in the journal) many scenes in the novel closely parallel events in Dworkin's life. Unlike with *American Psycho,* no extended excerpts from *Mercy* appeared in general-circulation magazines before or after the novel was published; hence, I have chosen to offer part of the excerpt that appeared in the *Michigan Quarterly Review* for three reasons: first, this part of the novel appeared first in public (though admittedly to very few readers); second, an excerpt provides a sense of the novel for those who have not read it; and third, this excerpt introduces an issue that became one of the major themes in public discourses about the novel: distinctions between autobiography and fiction and the consequences for public discourse of intentionally blurring the two.

> I am writing a certain very serious book about life itself. . . . My book is a very big book about existence but I can't find any plot for it. It's going to be a very big book once I get past the initial slow beginning. I want to get it published but you get afraid you will die before it's finished, not after when it can be found and it's testimony and then they say you were a great one; you don't want to die before you wrote it so you have to learn to sustain your writing, you take it serious, you do it every day and you don't fail to write words down and to think sentences. It's hard to find words. It's about some woman but I can't think of what happens. I can say where she is. It's pretty barren. I always see a woman on a rock, calling out. But that's not a story per se. You could have someone dying of tuberculosis like Mann or someone who is suffering—for instance, someone who is lovesick like Mann. Or there's best-sellers, all these stories where women do all these things and say all these things but I don't think I can write about that because I only seen it in the movies. There's marriage stories but it's so boring, a couple in the suburbs and the man on the train becoming unfaithful and how bored she is because she's too intelligent or something about how angry she is but I can't remember why. A love story's so stupid in these modern times. I can't have it be about my life because number one I don't remember very much and number two it's against the rules, you're supposed to make things up. The best thing that ever happened to me is these walls and I don't think you could

turn that into a story per se or even a novel of ideas that people would grasp as philosophical: for instance, that you can just sit and they provide a framework of dignity because no one's watching and I have had too many see too much, they see you when they do things to you that you don't want, they look, and the problem is there's no walls keeping you sacred. . . . There's nothing imaginary about walls, or eating, nothing fictive as it were, but more especially there's nothing imaginary about them when they're missing. . . . You're supposed to make things up, not just write down true things, or sincere things, or some things that happened. My mother who you can't make up either because there's nothing so real as one named me Andrea as if I was someone: distinct, in particular. She made a fiction. I'm her book, a made-up story written down on a birth certificate. You could also say she's a liar on such a deep level she should be shot by all that's fair; deep justice. If I was famous and my name was published all over the world, in Italy and in Israel and in Africa and in India, on continents and subcontinents, in deserts, in ancient cities, it would still be cunt to every fucking asshole drunk on every street in the world; and to them that's not drunk too, the sober ones who say it to you like they're calling a dog; fetch, cunt. If I won the Nobel Prize and walked to the corner for milk it would still be cunt. And when you got someone inside you who is loving you it's still cunt and the ones who'd die if they wasn't in you, you, you in particular, at least that night, at least then, that time, that place, to them it's still cunt and they whisper it up close and chill the blood that's burning in you; and if you love them it's still cunt and you can love them so strong you'd die for them and it's still cunt; and your heartbeat and his heartbeat can be the same heartbeat and it's still cunt. It's behind your back and it's to your face; the ones you know, the ones you don't. It's like as if nigger was a term of intimate endearment, not just used in lynching and insult but whispered in lovemaking, the truth under the truth, the name under the name, love's name for you and it's the same as what hate calls you; he's in you whispering nigger. It's thugs, it's citizens, it's cops, it's strangers, it's the ones you want and the ones you deplore, you ain't allowed indifference, you have to decide on a relationship then and there on the spot because each one that passes pisses on you to let you know he's there. There's some few you made love with and you're still breathing tight with them, you can still feel their muscles swelling through their skin and bearing down on you and you can still feel their weight on you, an urgent concentration of blood and bone, hot muscle, spread over you, the burden of it sinking into you, a stone cliff into a wet shore, and you're still tangled up in them, good judgment aside, and it's physical, it's a physical memory, in the body, not just in the brain, barely in the brain at all, you got their sweat on you as part of your sweat and their smell's part of your smell and you have an ache for them that's deep and gnawing and hurtful in more than your heart and you still feel as if it's real and current, now: how his body moves against you in convulsions that are awesome like mountains moving, slow, burdensome, big, and how you move against him as if you could move through him, he's the ocean, you're the tide, and it's still cunt, he says cunt. He's indelibly in you and you don't want redemption so much as you want him and still it's cunt. It's what's true; Andrea's the lie. It's a lie we got to tell. Jane and Judith and Ellen and whomever. It's our most desperate lie. My mother named me Andrea. It means manhood or courage. It means not-cunt. She specifically said: not-cunt. This one ain't cunt, she declared, after blood spilled and there was the pain of labor so intense that God couldn't live through it and wouldn't which is why all the pain's with us and still she brought herself to a point of concentration and she said: not-cunt. This one's someone, she probably had in mind; a wish; a hope; let her, let her, something. Something. Let her something. Don't, not with this one. Just let this one through. Just don't do it to this one. She wrote: not-cunt, a fiction, and it failed, and the failure defeated her and turned her cold to me, because before I was even ten some man had wrote "this one's cunt," he took his fingers and he wrote it down on me and inside me, his fingers carved it in me with a pain that stayed half buried and there wasn't words I had for what he did, he wrote I was cunt, this sweet little one who was what's called a child but a female one which changes it all. My mama showed that fiction was delusion, hallucination, it was a long, de-ranged lie designed to last past your own lifetime. The man, on the other hand, was a pragmatist, a maker of reality, a shaper of history, an orchestrator of events. He used life, not paper, bodies, not ink. (629–32)

A novel written by a person named Andrea in which the main character and narrator is named Andrea (Dworkin nowhere gives the narrator a last name) and in which the prologue and epilogue are authored by "Not Andrea" problematizes the concepts of fiction, genre, and ethos. Because Dworkin uses her own first name for the main character of the book and because the main character's biography has much in common with Dworkin's, many reviewers made the question of genre and, consequently, the author herself part of their analysis of the novel. One of the earliest commentaries on whether *Mercy* is autobiography or fiction came in a short review in *Publishers Weekly*'s "Forecasts" section in July 1991. Without attributing its claim that Dworkin "admitted" the novel was autobiographical, *PW* wrote that Dworkin "gives her own name to the protagonist/narrator of this powerful, almost frenzied, admittedly autobiographical novel that chronicles her life and sexual victimization" (Steinberg).[7]

Of much more consequence to public discussion than the theoretical question of genre, however, is that reviewers took Dworkin's conflation of fact and fiction as an opportunity to write about the person—Andrea Dworkin—rather than the act—her novel. By its status as a novel, *Mercy* makes operative claims that it is fiction. Yet critics consistently refused to treat it as fiction, using strategies of association and dissociation of concepts (Perelman and Olbrechts-Tyteca 415)—in this case fact and fiction—

to attempt to come to terms with Dworkin's arguably incommensurable claims: this book both is and is not "true." In a *Los Angeles Times* review of *Mercy,* Constance Casey opened with an excerpt from the first page of the book—"'I wasn't raped until I was almost 10, which is pretty good it seems when I ask around because many have been touched but are afraid to say'"—and then goes on to make connections between the main character and Dworkin: "This is the beginning of the story from age 10 to 27 of a woman named Andrea, born in 1946 in Camden, N.J. Andrea is a character in a work of fiction by a prominent American feminist also named Andrea, also born in 1946 in Camden." Casey at times synthesizes Andrea and Dworkin: she refers to them at one point as "the two of them." Cindy Jenefsky makes a similar move in the *Women's Review of Books,* using "Andrea and Dworkin" as the subject of many sentences and finally calling *Mercy* "Andrea/Dworkin's story" (7). The *Chicago Tribune* reviewer, Madison Smartt Bell, picking up on Dworkin's references to Malcolm X in *Mercy,* wrote that "If Andrea Dworkin is the Malcolm X of feminism, then this novel is her version of his 'Autobiography.'"

Yet other reviewers were less likely to accept the novel as autobiography without pausing to question the implications of that definitional argument and the incommensurable nature of "fact" and "fiction." The critic who most adamantly questioned Dworkin's blurring of Andrea and Dworkin was the *New York Times Book Review*'s Wendy Steiner, who wrote that *Mercy* "denies the difference between the metaphorical and the literal. In 'Mercy,' women's experience *is* the ovens; women *are* the mass suicides of Massada. Andrea is not a persona or a character but Ms. Dworkin herself; art *is* life." What Steiner reacts to most strongly in Dworkin's erasure of the distinction between fact and fiction, literal and figurative, centers on the suggestion by Dworkin that women kill men:

> One cannot argue here, any more than Mr. Rushdie could, that statements in literature are not equivalent to statements in the real world. Ms. Dworkin's pain erases the boundary between the two spheres, declaring the distinction a male trick to justify pornography and rape. Either her book must be absolved of murderous intent through special pleading—the invocation of that very magic circle around art that she has worked so hard to deny—or else we must accept that we are reading a political manifesto justifying and inciting illegal acts. Either way, we are caught in a bind. We must either deplore Ms. Dworkin's duplicity, which would be unfeeling, or have her arrested, which would mean we were assenting to the literalism that is our own undoing.

In taking Dworkin at her word, Steiner articulates the dilemma of interpreting Dworkin's rhetorical choice of naming her character Andrea and having her confess to killing men: the critic must either be relentlessly literal-minded—as were some readers of *American Psycho*[8]—or "deplore" Dworkin's rhetorical maneuverings in the text, a move that would be "unfeeling." Steiner thus suggests the high degree of difficulty of reviewing Dworkin; by using the word *unfeeling,* she also points to the difficulty of responding to narratives of personal pain in literary public spheres. Besides declaring the book a "manifesto," Steiner also dubs the book a monologue, again suggesting the difficulty critics have of responding to—entering into dialogue with—discourse that comes from personal experience: "'Mercy' is a monologue that almost makes [Andrea's] deviance seem normal; its voice speaks in extremis out of a pain so compelling that patience and reason appear to be obscenely insensitive responses."

Steiner's charge of "manifesto" was echoed by other critics, most notably Madison Smartt Bell in the *Chicago Tribune.* Bell focused on how *Mercy* deviated from accepted novelistic convention and concluded that it was, therefore, more polemic than novel: "There's hardly any plot in the conventional sense and not really any characters, except Andrea; the others are just more heads on the hydra that's out to crush and devour her," Bell writes. "All the men are rapists and all the women let her down somehow. . . . Her only real friend is her dog." Bell concludes, "The book carries too heavy a polemical burden to work very well as a novel. . . . But very likely Dworkin is more interested in producing a politically effective text than an esthetic object" (5). Another reviewer claimed that Dworkin's purpose in writing *Mercy* was to raise controversy and thus publicity, not to write serious and "honest" literature. Writing in the *Los Angeles Times,* Constance Casey argued, "If 'Mercy' has value, it is not as fiction, but as an event. Dworkin's book doesn't want to teach or touch or entertain. It wants to kick out a window. Someone will come along later, someone mercifully skilled and subtle, and the existence of 'Mercy' may free her— or him—to write honestly about rape." That Casey would support her claim that *Mercy* is not honest about rape on the quality of Dworkin's writing—she is neither "skilled" nor "subtle"—moves the political to the aesthetic as Mailer's arguments about Ellis did.

Yet another definitional strategy emerged in public responses to *Mercy:* arguing that the novel itself is pornography and thus accusing Dworkin of reproducing the very social artifact that her life's work is intended to critique. Given that definitions of pornography are still legally and socially undecided, this definitional *topos* in the literary public sphere takes on potential importance (see Hauser "Defining Publics"; Dworkin and MacKinnon 24–32, 36–41, 67–70; and Russell). Because of *Mercy*'s stylistic strategies, Steiner argues, the book is a kind of supraprurient anti-pornography-pornography:

> "Mercy" itself is meant to provide a new representational strategy. Andrea's language is lyrical and passionate—a cross between the repetition of the early Gertrude Stein and, ironically, the unfettered flights of Henry Miller. She describes sexual violence in graphic terms, risking the prurience of the pornography she deplores. But unlike any antipornography text that I know, "Mercy" defeats prurience. It is to pornography what aversion therapy is to rape. The titillating language of violation—"one hand's holding my neck from behind and the other's pulling off my T-shirt, pulling it half off, ripping it"—becomes noxious with Andrea's terror and pain and the inhuman viciousness and betrayal of the men she has trusted. Her stylistic breathlessness—repetition, rhythm, loss of control—conveys not rising passion but the desperate need to have the violence end.

Other critics struggled in similar ways to define and represent *Mercy,* in particular regarding its connection with pornography. Writing in the *Los Angeles Times,* Constance Casey asserts but does not argue that *Mercy* is pornography: "The novel, which repeats some of the same violent sexual incidents Dworkin included in her first novel, 'Ice and Fire,' is essentially pornography. This is noteworthy because Dworkin is best known as a crusader for the abolition of pornography." Whether Casey's criterion for pornography is "violent sexual incidents" is unclear.

A more developed discussion of *Mercy* as a kind of pornography came from Esther Kaplan, writing in the *Village Voice.* "Andrea Dworkin's new novel, *Mercy,* is the sexual coming of age story of a young woman, meaning it's a book about rape," Kaplan writes. Kaplan sees Dworkin using the novel to make a definitional argument about rape: "The novel is a serious attempt to describe rape, in all its emotional brutality and destruction of the self, not as an exceptional circumstance, but as part of a culture-wide continuum of threat and violence." However, because of the way Dworkin represents Andrea in the novel, Kaplan sees *Mercy* as voyeurism rather than as politically effective fiction: "The question becomes how to speak about rape—or other self-destroying experiences—in a way that makes its gravity inescapable without further erasing the individual selves of those who endure it, or don't. While battling the onslaught that constitutes this culture of misogyny, we need to be able to see ourselves not as caged animals, but as people capable of resistance, solidarity, and selfhood. I want to be a sister to Andrea, not a voyeur, but Dworkin won't let me." Kaplan concludes that because Dworkin leaves Andrea isolated from other women, a point I will return to below, the novel's effect on its readers is tantamount to pornography: "The world of this novel is that of an isolated, mutilated woman surrounded by her rapists, familiar as the terror of horror movies in which a woman has no recourse, either to rationality or to friends, and in which her hysteria is more likely to give pornographic pleasure than to provoke rage."

Taking a very different view of how to represent Dworkin's novel, Cindy Jenefsky defined *Mercy* as an attempt to confront and come to terms with the pain of sexual abuse. Writing in the *Women's Review of Books,* Jenefsky situated her discussion within bell hooks's call to "remember the pain": "In contrast to the notion, popularly advocated by academic feminists, that focusing on women's pain accentuates our victimization and powerlessness and thereby denies our agency, hooks claims that speaking from that place of pain is transformative—that it is the necessary location from which one learns about oppression and learns what is necessary to overthrow it." Jenefsky argues that *Mercy* is written from inside "that place of pain" and that the novel's purpose is to illustrate "how male domination is maintained through 'ordinary' sexual practices." The book, Jenefsky writes, is meant to be transformative for the reader as much as for the writer. In light of that, Jenefsky writes, it is important not to define *Mercy* as entertaining reading: "*Mercy* is not a book to pick up if you're looking for light, weekend leisure reading; in the manner of Toni Morrison's *Beloved,* this book compels the reader to experience the pain the protagonist suffers. Even if you don't like Andrea—either her behavior or her ways of thinking—you still cannot escape feeling her pain; the agony, confusion, terror, humiliation and anguish are built into the form of Dworkin's writing and, therefore, built into the experience of reading the work" (6). Yet, as both Steiner and Kaplan point out, the question of how to represent pain in fiction depends largely on one's audience and purpose. Steiner ends her review by musing on the difficulties of a novel that defines itself as a conduit for the expression of pain:

> The question is how we can deal with pain, conviction, compulsions that we do not share. Or alternately, the question is whom Ms. Dworkin thinks she is speaking to. By reading "Mercy" we are meant to experience her pain, to know it as our own. Will we take the next step—as women, becoming Andrea Two or Three or Ten, or as men, bending to the task of describing the blood that has stained us? Or is the matter put in terms too crude, too intellectually violent, to offer us the possibility of action? If all women are either victims or collaborators and all men are rapists, can the cry for mercy fall on any but deaf ears?

Given Dworkin's incommensurate views of the power of writing, the question of whom she is writing to in *Mercy* takes on special resonance. If *Mercy* was written just for women who have been sexually abused, it is unlikely that the book could be productively discussed among the diversity of reviewers. Further, Dworkin's rhetorical choices represent the issue in such extreme terms that the possibility of action or change appears unlikely. Yet the lack of responses to Jenefsky is difficult to interpret: did the review, in a subaltern literary public sphere, lead to further reading and discussion of the book? Again, it is impossible to support a claim based on silence. What is clear, however, is that the subaltern space of the *Women's Review of Books* was a safer space than was *Ms.* or any other publication for a lengthy article on Dworkin's novel, which—as does her other work—offers critiques of academic and liberal feminisms.

Just as defining and representing Dworkin's novel was an issue in reviews of *Mercy*, representing Dworkin was also a site of struggle. Closely connected to the issue of representing *Mercy* is the issue of representation in general. In most public discourses about *Mercy*, Dworkin's work as an antipornography activist as well as her reputation among feminists and the larger public received as much if not more attention than did the novel in question. What each publication or reviewer chose to emphasize about Dworkin reflects how each wanted to represent her to their readers. Hence, how different writers and reviewers defined the writer of *Mercy* reveals the grounds of much of the public discourses about the book.

Perhaps most obvious to issues of representation is physical appearance, and Dworkin's body was mentioned in a few of the public discourses written after the publication of *Mercy*. While not making Dworkin's body either equivalent (Perelman and Olbrechts-Tyteca 210) or coexistent (293) with *Mercy*, Joan Frank, in her *San Francisco Review of Books* interview, offered a narrative and physical description to contrast Dworkin's physical appearance with her writing style: "Meeting Andrea Dworkin is a shock," Frank writes, adding that Dworkin is "quite demure in person" and noting "her large earth-mother body" (9). Frank continues: "Frizzy salt-and-pepper hair frames her face, which wears an expression of sad forbearance. Her voice is gentle, her words simple and deliberate" (9). Frank's opening manifests not only a connection between the essence of a writer and the writing but also that it is acceptable to make such connections explicit.

Frank's characterization of Dworkin differs markedly from Camille Paglia's in a *Playboy* article on Dworkin and Catherine A. MacKinnon. In her article, "The Return of Carry Nation," Paglia makes Dworkin's and MacKinnon's bodies absolutely equivalent and coextensive with their political and social beliefs and projects. Paglia surmises that Dworkin's

"boiling emotionalism and self-analytic, self-lacerating Jewishness" provide an antidote to "MacKinnon's pinched, cramped, body-denying Prot-
estant culture" (36). Dworkin, Paglia writes, "pretends to be a daring truth
teller but never mentions her most obvious problem: food" (36). Paglia
continues, describing MacKinnon as well as Dworkin in a tone appropriate to the magazine's subtitle, "Entertainment for Men":

> Dworkin, wallowing in misery, is a "type" that I recognize after 22 years of teach-
> ing. I call her The Girl with the Eternal Cold. This was the pudgy, clumsy, whiny
> child at summer camp who was always spilling her milk, dropping her lollipop
> in the dirt, getting a cramp on the hike, a stone in her shoe, a bee in her hair. In
> college, this type—pasty, bilious and frumpy—is constantly sick from fall to
> spring. She coughs and sneezes on everyone, is never prepared with a tissue and
> sits sniffling in class with a roll of toilet paper on her lap. (36)

Paglia's comments are textbook cases of *ad personam* attacks: endeavoring to disqualify Dworkin and MacKinnon from the public debate over
pornography by making fun of their bodies, personalities, and motivations.
   More pertinent than using physical appearance to dismiss Dworkin's
work is the question of how to define the kind of work she does. In its notes
on contributors, the *Michigan Quarterly Review* stressed that Dworkin is
a writer of fiction as well as nonfiction; in addition, her work with
MacKinnon was mentioned—"[Dworkin] and Catherine A. MacKinnon
wrote a law for the City of Minneapolis that recognizes pornography as a
violation of the civil rights of women" (481)—but that the ordinance had
been ruled unconstitutional was not. While it did not review *Mercy,* the
*San Francisco Review of Books* ran a news story on Dworkin (she read
excerpts from *Mercy* to and addressed the American Psychological Association) and a brief interview with her in its Fall 1991 issue. Again, that
Dworkin is both novelist and activist was reflected in the blurb on the
magazine's contents page: "Novelist and anti-pornography campaigner
Andrea Dworkin talks to Joan Frank."
   Much more complex than attempting to give a balanced or unbiased view
of Dworkin as one of several contributors to a journal or one of several
subjects in a magazine is the issue of connecting or not connecting
Dworkin's fiction with her nonfiction and her activism. In her review of
*Mercy,* Casey finds it difficult to write about the novel without immediately putting it in the context of Dworkin's nonfiction work: "'Mercy' is
less a story than a catalog of sexual attacks. (In her nonfiction book 'Intercourse,' Dworkin argued that the penis is a weapon and that every act
of heterosexual intercourse is an attack.) The people are scarcely more than

bodies—Andrea, the victim, and almost every male, the rapist. All that dawns on Andrea is that she and other women should kill the men who caused them pain." Madison Smartt Bell used a similar parenthetical reference to situate and ultimately interpret *Mercy* in light of Dworkin's nonfiction: "(readers of 'Intercourse' will know that in Dworkin's larger scheme of things any woman's desire for penetration by a man is merely the product and mechanism of her enslaved degradation)." Reviewers' connections of Dworkin's fiction with her nonfiction and activism is a recurring *topos* in public discourses about *Mercy*.

Previous negative reactions at once put the novel in the context of her other work and provided another context for the public reception of *Mercy*. In what was by far the widest-circulation review of *Mercy*, Wendy Steiner opened her *New York Times Book Review* article with a narrative:

> This past spring in London, with an hour to kill in a bookstore, I decided to read the first few pages of as many new novels as I could. Among the recent releases was "Mercy," a second novel by the controversial feminist Andrea Dworkin, better known to me for her nonfiction tirades against pornography, against intercourse, against men. She was not a writer I would normally be drawn to, but in the spirit of experimentation I read through the first chapter. It was a representation of sexual trauma through a 9–year-old child's bewilderment, and I found myself utterly transfixed; I had to keep on reading.

Steiner's narrative betrays discomfort at reading Dworkin; as such it appears to be an attempt to explain why Steiner would write about a book that many people would find—by the very fact of its author—embarrassing or distasteful.

In her *Village Voice* review, "Rapes of Wrath," Esther Kaplan makes a similar move to inform readers about Dworkin's reputation: "Now, I've always known of Dworkin as a pariah among feminists, her radical critiques of intercourse, virginity, and the valorization of sex foundering in the face of her censorious reputation and her antiporn alliance with the Right." Kaplan sees *Mercy* not as a novel but as "a long autobiographical prequel to her theoretical writings," "a defense of her whole project, as if her lifetime of angry essays will at last make sense in the face of this testimonial about rape and abuse." Just as it figured into genre discussions, Dworkin's reputation as a political activist colored how she was described in public discussions; in particular, Kaplan's representation is colored by criticisms of Dworkin's "antiporn alliance with the Right," a topic I will return to below.

In addition to deciding how to represent Dworkin and her reputation,

reviewers of *Mercy* found themselves in the middle of battles between liberal and radical feminists over pornography and free speech and thus had
to decide how to depict her radicalism. Again, such negotiation is one of
Wendy Steiner's main points. After initially saying that she picked up *Mercy*
only as an experiment, Steiner admits that, in hindsight, the novel is quite
different from what she first thought it was: "I now see Ms. Dworkin's
book in a larger context—as another salvo in the war between liberals and
radicals. Once again the noddy head of tolerance is pummeled by the
unbrookable demands of outraged pain." Steiner, along with other critics, is especially concerned about Dworkin's use of another voice to begin
and end *Mercy,* a voice she calls "Not Andrea" and who narrates the prologue and epilogue. "The repulsiveness of the Not Andrea voice is the great
scandal of our times—reason's inability to offer an acceptable answer to
the pain that everywhere surrounds us. This weakness is the undoing of
liberalism . . . the failure of communication between feminists inside the
system and those outside it" (11). Steiner concludes that the epilogue is
"cheap. The issues are important enough to be raised by a character whose
liberalism is not so obviously corrupt." Again, reviewers' vehemence about
the "Not Andrea" voice suggests that Dworkin's consistent critique of liberal and academic feminisms is at the heart of responses to her work.

Again reading Dworkin more generously than most critics, Cindy
Jenefsky describes Dworkin's use of the Not Andrea voice as the "literal
framing of the novel within its own critique" and argues that it "represent[s] both Andrea's and Dworkin's struggles to overcome others' denial
of the destructive nature of sexual abuse in women's lives. Dworkin, then,
accuses critics in advance of colluding in women's oppression; for, in the
context of the narrative, those who minimize Andrea's words help to perpetuate abuse" (7). Jenefsky here articulates what has perhaps most angered those who read and reviewed *Mercy* and, given the terrain of feminist politics, felt they were unable to create an uncharged or unlabeled space
from which to write about it: that to write or to speak is automatically to
be situated and to be judged. Complicating this, Jenefsky writes, is that
any woman who writes about *Mercy* has to do so from a site of particular
experience with issues of gender and sexual abuse:

> What is probably going to anger Dworkin's critics the most, however, is her
> implicit claim that the root of feminists' denial of Andrea/Dworkin's story is
> women's resistance to recognizing sexual victimization in their own lives. "Not
> Andrea" concludes the epilogue: "I have been hurt but it was a long time ago.
> I'm not the same girl." Dworkin implies that academic feminists in particular
> have adopted an intellectual analysis of sex at the expense of their (or other

women's) concrete experiences with sex. Accordingly, both the prologue and epilogue are written in an analytic style, borrowing vocabulary from feminist theoretical debates on sexuality. (7)

Dworkin's politics come in for other criticisms as well. Madison Smartt Bell dislikes Dworkin's "uncompromising demonization of all members of the enemy group"—men—and argues that the analogy Dworkin makes between race and gender does not fit. "For irony, compare the fictional Andrea's murders of winos with Eldridge Cleaver's rape of white girls," Bell writes. "The real catch is that while black separation is at least theoretically possible, female separatism is not."

The most scathing critique of Dworkin's location among debates about race, class, and gender—and the only one to suggest that Dworkin's radicalism is not nearly radical enough—came from Esther Kaplan. Kaplan writes that while what happens to Andrea in the book is "nauseating and terrifying," the events are "unfortunately . . . submerged in doltish musings about God, Poetry, Freedom, and the War that become progressively more bitter, but never develop politically." In short, Kaplan writes, Dworkin's politics are inconsistent at best and, at worst, have no practical results, a point that the lack of citizen-critic responses to her novel and its reviews at least potentially supports: "Andrea's geopolitics: she's against the bomb and for peace. Her class analysis: 'He's been low; he knows.' She goes from idealizing the famed men of Western literature ('I would have enjoyed a cup of coffee with Camus in my younger days') to seeing all writings by men as based on rape ('I've got enough semen dripping in me for a literary renaissance'), but she never seems to read any women writers." What concerns Kaplan most is that Dworkin never allows Andrea to join forces with other people; Andrea, Kaplan writes, is never allowed any human connection as a source of regeneration:

> The book—for all its attempts to be down with the black man (a figure Dworkin tosses in to signify the sorrows of the downtrodden) and the broke, and to inspire empathy with women who are raped—views those who experience oppression as being utterly without pride, absolutely debased. Dworkin's character ends up serving as a testimonial to the total efficacy of misogynist practice in the destruction of human beings, playing out as she does the kind of animalistic vision of women found mostly in certain men's fantasies. The only rebellions in the novel are solitary and violent. Andrea has visions of mass resistance—"I think one day they will gather, the women, outside where he lives. I think there will be thousands of them. I think it will be a crowd, a mob, a riot, a revolution"— but she never organizes other women or even maintains connections with any (female characters, in fact, are few and minor). She strikes out alone.

It is Dworkin's "antiporn alliance with the Right" and her refusal to write about the potential of women acting collectively rather than individually that color Kaplan's critique of Dworkin's radicalism.

Finally, Camille Paglia locates Dworkin and MacKinnon among versions of feminism in her *Playboy* article. Calling to mind a scene from *Mercy* in which Andrea is throat-raped soon after the movie *Deep Throat* was released (the novel refers to Linda Marchiano in several places), Paglia disagrees with Dworkin's and MacKinnon's claims that pornography can cause incidents of sexual abuse: "MacKinnon and Dworkin, like most feminists today, lack a general knowledge of criminology or psychopathology and hence have no perspective on or insight into the bloody, lurid human record, with its disasters and triumphs" (38). She argues that, led by sympathizers of Dworkin and MacKinnon, feminism has degenerated into "a catch-all vegetable drawer where bunches of clingy sob sisters can store their moldy neuroses. . . . Let's get rid of Infirmary Feminism, with its bedlam of bellyachers, anorexics, bulimics, depressives, rape victims and incest survivors" (38). The consequences of such feminism, Paglia writes, keep women alienated from their own bodies. "The demons are within us," Paglia concludes: "MacKinnon and Dworkin, peddling their diseased rhetoric, are in denial, and what they are blocking is life itself, in all its grandeur and messiness. Let's send a message to the Mad Hatter and her dumpy dormouse to stop trying to run other people's tea parties" (38). Paglia's "the demons are within us" argument is less obviously *ad personam* when it is directed, for example, against the Report of the Special Committee on Human Sexuality of the Presbyterian Church U.S.A. ("The Joy of Presbyterian Sex") or even when it is part of a larger argument at the *stasis* of consequence against academic feminism ("It's a Jungle out There, so Get Used to It!"). But because the level of discussion in her *Playboy* article has dropped to the low point of "entertainment for men," no productive discussion can ensue about the grounds social science uses to ascertain harm from pornography. Indeed, if and when a space opens up for such a discussion, one response to Paglia might be, "I don't need studies and statistics to tell me that there is a relationship between pornography and real violence against women. My body remembers" (Russell 120).

Closely related to representations of *Mercy* as a kind of novel or autobiography are attempts by critics to come to terms with Dworkin's language. Critics consistently commented on the rough language yet less consistently endeavored to explain why she might use it; Dworkin was criticized for being repetitive and numbing readers to the horrors of sexual assault. Constance Casey remarked that while other feminist writers, notably Marge

Piercy, use language that is "raw and rough" they also write novels in which "you turn the page because you care what happens next." Casey continues: "Turn the pages of 'Mercy' and you get the equivalent of a slap in the face. Dworkin believes only violent language can communicate violent events; the ironic effect of violent language numbingly repeated, however, is to make the reader say: 'What happens to this character doesn't matter.'" Casey responds to comments Andrea makes in *Mercy* about Holocaust literature, that it is "almost funny" in the way it attempts to represent atrocities clearly and precisely: "Andrea may be right that no amount of clarity and precision can describe pain," Casey writes. "But more people would read 'Mercy' past the first three pages if it had more clarity and precision. And if you believe Holocaust and other horrors can't be described in words, perhaps you have no business writing and publishing a book."

Other critics saw Dworkin's stylistic choices differently. For instance, Madison Smartt Bell characterized the novel as an attempt to "sustain a scream for over 300 pages." Bell thus argues that Dworkin's "long tumbling run-on sentences . . . achieve a powerful effect." Esther Kaplan saw Dworkin's "swampy prose" as communicating yet another message: "The narrator is consistently overwhelmed: her language is obsessive and repetitive; she has no steady alliances or sources of comfort; her destruction as an adult is well under way in childhood."

Most interesting about reviewers' discussions of Dworkin's style, however, is that they led to antithetical interpretations of the book. On the one hand, the writer of the unsigned review in *Publishers Weekly* decided that the style mirrored Andrea's disintegration over the course of the book: "The novel's unparagraphed prose—like Andrea, intense, jumpy, impassioned—brilliantly captures the narrator's mental and physical degradation. As her life disintegrates, she repeats three facts—her name, her place of birth and the poet Walt Whitman's address in Camden, N.J., on a street where she was born—as a mantra anchoring her to reality." On the other hand, Cindy Jenefsky, writing in the *Women's Review of Books,* argued that Dworkin's style has two objectives. First, it reflects "Andrea's gradual empowerment," her "shift from self-annihilation to self-defense," given that "self-determination" has shown itself to be illusory (7). Second, it communicates Andrea's constant battle for language and for the power to tell her story. After an excerpt from early in the book (similar to the one that opened this chapter) Jenefsky explains Dworkin's use of language:

> As Andrea's parents continue to ask questions and make comments that minimize and trivialize her feelings, the young girl's story becomes progressively more convoluted. Each time her parents minimize the abuse, her confusion and panic

intensify, culminating at the end of the chapter in a breathless sentence that spans three pages. The form of the text thus compels the reader to *feel* some of the panic the child experiences. Unlike everyone else in Andrea's life who hears her story, the reader is not encouraged to collaborate in denying the pain. (6)

Jenefsky argues that Dworkin's style in the main body of the book contrasts with the highly intellectualized style of the prologue and epilogue, and that the intellectualized style used by academic feminists allows people to ignore the experiences of suffering women: "The artistic form of *Mercy* fulfills its own political directives. It does what it says needs to be done to stop the cycle of violence against women: it confronts the pain of sexual abuse" (7).

Indeed, the battle for language, for the power to tell, is another of Dworkin's major themes. "The formal writing problem, frankly, is that the bait can't write the story," Andrea says at one point in the excerpt. "The bait ain't even barely alive" (634). In another part excerpted in the *Michigan Quarterly Review,* Dworkin described this search for language and struggle for the power to tell:

You're supposed to make things up for books but I am afraid to make things up because in life everything evaporates, it's gone in mist, just disappears, there's no sign left, except on you, and you are a fucking invisible ghost, they look right through you, you can have bruises so bad the skin's pulled off you and they don't see nothing; you bet women had the vapors, still fucking do, it means it all goes away in the air, whatever happened, whatever he did and however he did it, and you're left feeling sick and weak and no one's going to say why. . . . No one else ever did anything, certainly no one now in this fine world we have here; certainly not the things I think happened, although I don't know what to call them in any serious way. You just crawl into a cave of silence and die; why are there no great women artists? Some people got nerve. Blood on cement, which is all we got in my experience, ain't esthetic, although I think boys some day will do very well with it; they'll put it in museums and get a fine price. Won't be their blood. It would be some cunt's they whispered to the night before; a girl; and then it'd be art, you see; or you could put it on walls, make murals, be political, a democratic art outside the museums for the people, Diego Rivera without any conscience whatsoever instead of the very tenuous one he had with respect to women, and then it'd be extremely major for all the radicals who would discover the expressive value of someone else's blood and I want to tell you they'd stop making paint but such things do not happen and such things cannot occur, any more than the rape so-called can happen or occur or the being beaten so bad can happen or occur and there are no words for what cannot happen or occur and if you think something happened or occurred and there are no words for it you are at a dead end. . . . So it doesn't feel right to make things up, as you must do to write fiction, to lie, to elaborate, to elongate, to exaggerate, to distort, to get tangled up in moderations or modifications or deviations or compromises of mixing this with that or combining this one with that one because the problem is finding words for the truth, especially if no one will believe it, and they will not. I can't make things up because I wouldn't know after a while what's blood, what's ink. I barely know any words for what happened to me yesterday, which doesn't make tomorrow something I can conceive of in my mind; I mean words I say to myself in my own head; not social words you use to explain something to someone else. I barely know anything and if I deviate I am lost; I have to be literal, if I can remember, which mostly I cannot. No one will acknowledge that some things happen and probably at this point in time there is no way to say they do in a broad sweep; you describe the man forcing you but you can't say he forced you. If I was a man I could probably say it; I could say I did it and everyone would think I made it up even though I'd just be remembering what I did last night or twenty minutes ago or once, long ago, but it probably wouldn't matter. The rapist has words, even though there's no rapist, he just keeps inventing rape; in his mind; sure. He remembers, even though it never happened; it's fine fiction when he writes it down. Whereas my mind is getting worn away, carried out to sea, layer by layer, fine grains washed away, a thin surface washed away, then some more, washed away. I am fairly worn away in my mind, washed out to sea. It probably doesn't matter anyway. People lead their little lives. There's not much dignity to go around. There's lies in abundance, and silence for girls who don't tell them. I don't want to tell them. A lie's for when he's on top of you and you got to survive him being there until he goes; Malcolm X tried to stop saying a certain lie, and maybe I should change from Andrea because it's a lie. It's just that it's a precious thing from my mother that she tried to give me; she didn't want it to be such an awful lie, I don't think. So I have to be the writer she tried to be—Andrea; not-cunt—only I have to do it so it ain't a lie. I ain't fabricating stories, I'm making a different kind of story. I'm writing as truthful as the man with his fingers, if only I can remember and say; but I ain't on his side. I'm on some different side. I'm telling the truth but from a different angle. I'm the one he done it to. (634–36)

Again, nowhere but in the *Women's Review of Books* does public discourse about *Mercy* attempt to explain within the context of the novel why Dworkin would write the way she does: "Much of this novel concerns Andrea's struggle with the inadequacy of words" (6), Jenefsky writes, focusing not only on Andrea's assault in a movie theater when she was nine but also on her rape by prison doctors with a steel speculum while she was jailed for civil disobedience during the Vietnam War. Andrea, Jenefsky writes, "is unable to comprehend the experience *as rape* because 'no one said rape'; 'it wasn't rape,' explains Andrea, 'because it wasn't a penis and it was doctors'; and since she 'had never heard of any such thing happen-

ing before . . . it didn't seem possible to [her] that it had happened at all'"
(6). Even when Andrea begins to understand what is happening to her—
when she is being repeatedly beaten and raped by her husband, for example—"she wants to stand up in a public theater and scream out his
abuses, but she refrains because she knows she will not be taken seriously,"
Jenefsky writes (6). She concludes: "While the inadequacy of Andrea's
language keeps her isolated and hinders her from obtaining help from
others, her poverty and progressive self-annihilation increasingly erode her
capacity for meaningful speech: the success of one's words in *Mercy* corresponds to the degree of social, economic and political power one already
possesses" (6).

## Private Experience in Public

Jenefsky's words point to one conclusion about the different receptions of
*American Psycho* and *Mercy:* Simon and Schuster's last-minute refusal to
publish *American Psycho* garnered Ellis and his novel a lot of publicity and
"social power," power that Andrea Dworkin does not have, in part because she is seen as a "pariah" (Kaplan) and in part because of her rhetorical strategies. Defining the literary public spheres that form around her
work as "war zones" has consequences for the quality and quantity of
public discussion of Dworkin's work: guerrilla rhetorical tactics—judging
critics in advance and seeing all men and anyone else who does not agree
with her as partly responsible for individual and systemic sexual abuses
of women—do not foster open debate or a common space for productive
discussion, for "creating meaning together" (Hauser and Blair 142).

Another factor complicating the reactions to both *American Psycho* and
to *Mercy* is their first-person narrators and close connections to actual
events—whether, in the case of *American Psycho,* actual serial killings and
femicide, or, in the case of *Mercy,* Dworkin's autobiography and increasing publicity about violence against women. In his account of the structural changes in the public sphere in the world of letters, Habermas argues
that one of the distinguishing characteristics of a moribund public sphere
and a politicized social sphere is a move to narrative in news coverage and
an erasure of "the line between fiction and report" (*Structural Transformation* 170). As a result of this conflation, "the public sphere itself becomes
privatized in the consciousness of the consuming public: indeed, the public sphere becomes the sphere for the publicizing of private biographies,
so that the accidental fate of the so-called man in the street or that of systematically managed stars attain publicity, while publicly relevant devel-

opments and decisions are garbed in private dress and through personalization distorted to the point of unrecognizability" (171–72). Habermas's account of structural transformation delegitimizes personal accounts as expressed in public in a way that raises questions about how individuals might ever gain a voice in public as well as about narrativity as a means to political legitimation.

Yet critiques of enlightenment ideologies that linger within notions of publics and public spheres suggest that Dworkin's guerrilla tactics are themselves the result of a starting point of unequal power. Like Habermas's account, Dworkin's work in general and *Mercy* in particular raise the question of how to speak one's personal experience in public. In many ways *Mercy* is anecdotal evidence about the effects of pornography on the life of an individual woman. As such, it has much in common with testimony before the Meese commission on pornography and during hearings on The Ordinance to Add Pornography as Discrimination against Women—the law Dworkin co-wrote—in Minneapolis. Given critiques of the credibility of such reports in public that ask for more objective analysis (Hauser "Defining Publics") and models of public discourse and argumentation that call for disinterestedness (Habermas *Structural Transformation;* Perelman and Olbrechts-Tyteca), we may not be able to credibly and productively discuss issues usually considered "private" in literary public spheres. As suggested above, Nancy Fraser's concept of subaltern counterpublics might help explain why only in the *Women's Review of Books* was *Mercy* understood as sending a coherent message to an audience who needs it. Yet the lack of written response to Jenefsky's review offers nothing but silence. As I have suggested, whether labeled as fiction or not, such accounts of the effects of pornography and sexual abuse as *Mercy* exemplifies tend not to be discussed on their own terms in public debate but are instead addressed in terms of their literary merit—a criterion that may not apply.

NOTES

1. Dworkin is more explicit about organized crime–publishing industry connections in Dworkin and MacKinnon (26, 83–84).

2. The Ordinance to Add Pornography as Discrimination Against Women was passed twice in Minneapolis by two different city councils and was vetoed both times by the mayor. In Indianapolis, the ordinance passed and became law. Within one hour, the city was sued for passing the law, which was later ruled unconstitutional by the Seventh U.S. Circuit Court of Appeals. That decision was summarily affirmed by the U.S. Supreme Court (see Dworkin and MacKinnon 63–65, 95; and Stoltenberg 72–75).

3. Dworkin includes the following among the front matter of *Ice and Fire:* "This book is fiction and no resemblance to actual events, persons or locations is intended or should be inferred." *Mercy* includes no such disclaimer.

4. Neither Dworkin (through the Markson Agency) nor Dworkin's individual publishers would release Dworkin's sales figures or earnings (personal correspondence with Stephanie Hawkins, Elaine Markson's assistant).

5. Pages 214–32 of the Four Walls Eight Windows edition of *Mercy* were published as part of a special issue, "The Female Body," of the *Michigan Quarterly Review,* a literary review with a circulation of eighteen hundred.

6. Pages 316–24 of the Four Walls Eight Windows edition of *Mercy* were published as part of a special issue, "Silencing," of *American Voice.* The literary review, founded in 1985 and published by the Kentucky Foundation for Women, has a circulation of two thousand.

7. The only published comments by Dworkin about *Mercy* that I could find were, again, from the author's note before the *American Voice* excerpt: "It is a book about multiple rape, its effects on women's freedom and consciousness. The book is set up such that each chapter represents a rape experience of some sort. I have written two endings for it, my plan from the beginning, which will be published sequentially, the first a suicide, the second where the woman responds with physical aggression against men. This is an excerpt from the second ending. It is certainly taboo material" (24).

8. Steiner seems to have in mind here those who read speech qua action, an approach similar to the one Dworkin and MacKinnon take on pornography (58–65).

# 6

# Beyond the Aesthetic: Citizen Critics and Protopublic Classrooms

In the four preceding chapters I have studied the processes through which actual readers attempted to come to terms with controversial texts by writing publicly about them. While in the final two cases the critics were largely journalists, book reviewers, and other professional writers, in the first two cases citizens also felt a sufficient sense of agency to write publicly about *topoi* raised by literary texts and other discourses written in response to those texts in literary public spheres. As I suggested in chapter 1, this study and others like it can offer rhetoricians, literary critics, political scientists, and social theorists an empirical basis for building probabilistic theories about how arguments in literary public spheres might have actually affected certain social practices in this country during the twentieth century. If, in Dewey's terms, artists are the "real purveyors of news," *Citizen Critics* has attempted to show how actual readers struggled to understand and come to terms publicly with *topoi* invented from the news delivered by Joyce, Miller, Ellis, and Dworkin. In addition, I have suggested that the "news" these writers offered was to some degree excluded from public debate by discussions of the aesthetic merit of their work or by a media culture that increasingly does not invite citizens to understand their views of cultural products as anything other than demographic preferences. Fewer and fewer people have a say in naming and using *topoi* raised by cultural texts and other products. In that sense, the history of literary public spheres in this country in the twentieth century mirrors the history of participatory democracy more generally. As Michael X. Delli Carpini and Scott Keeter have argued, democracy as practiced in late capitalism is marked by "political institutions and processes designed to allow citizens to have a voice in their own governance, while at the same time limiting the impact of that voice" (2; see also McChesney; Engelman; and Schudson).

*Citizen Critics* posits an alternative history of criticism in the twentieth century, focused on a relatively large number of citizen critics, journalists, reporters, and other writers rather than a very few institutional or expert literary critics rationalizing how "the reader" reads. *Citizen Critics* also suggests a pedagogy, and I end this chapter and the book with a discussion of classrooms as protopublic spaces in which students can form and enter literary public spheres and choose whether to join wider public spheres. It has become, of course, a commonplace in discourses public and private that we live in an age "when people across the political spectrum decry the decline of 'civic life' . . . [and when] government, politicians, and even politics itself have become objects of indifference and contempt" (Brinkley 5; see also Gitlin; McChesney; Fishkin; Delli Carpini and Keeter; and Batstone and Mendieta). Yet, as Delli Carpini and Keeter argue in *What Americans Know about Politics and Why It Matters,* the condition of our public life "is neither inevitable nor benign. Rather, it results from systematic distortions in the development and practice of democracy in America. And it results in substantial inequalities in who participates, in how effective their participation is, and in who benefits from the actions of their government" (3). The pedagogy of classrooms as protopublic spaces, one I use in my undergraduate courses, is offered here as a potential means of improving not only the quality of public discourse but also the practice of democracy, locally and nationally.

In his book *The Good Citizen* Michael Schudson argues that citizenship in this country has proceeded through four distinct eras. During the era of the founders, politics operated by the personal authority of "gentlemen" and through a politics of assent. In the nineteenth century, the development of political parties heralded a politics of affiliation. Mass democracy in the first three-fourths of the twentieth century "celebrated the private, rational 'informed citizen' that remains the most cherished ideal in the American voting experience today" (6). Schudson concludes that "we require a citizenship fit for our own day" (9), and *Citizen Critics* attempts—through its focus on inventional reading and on pedagogy—to enter the conversation about how new forms of citizenship might come into being.

Again, I both confirm and critique Habermas's account of structural transformation and the structural role of literary public spheres as we have transformed from culture-debating to culture-consuming publics. As discussed in chapter 4, Habermas underestimated the extent to which publicity would become a *topos* for critical publicity. At least where highly publicized novels are concerned, participants in literary public spheres seem more able to question the sources of publicity than Habermas imagined. Yet—and this is a central point—few citizens feel willing or able to join the fray anymore, and thus most novels do not become public issues, at least not in the sense that their publicity leads to democratic participation and public judgment. Since novels and other cultural products—radio talk shows, films, television programs, advertising campaigns, political advertisements—are read by experts who focus on *topoi* from their particular areas of expertise, these texts often fail to become public issues. Just as importantly, then, *Citizen Critics* provides a point of departure for definitional claims about the different forms literary public spheres have taken in the twentieth century and might take in the future, thus further complicating Habermas's master narrative of structural transformation. In chapter 2 I examined a literary public sphere institutionalized through a particular publication, the *Little Review,* and composed of relative cultural elites. In chapter 3 I suggested that a literary public sphere can be limited geographically, and that geography can help describe the shared interests of the varied participants. Of the four case studies in this book, nonexpert citizen critics were most active in the literary public sphere that grew around *Tropic of Cancer,* perhaps because the novel was a local concern to the vast majority of those who wrote about it in public. In chapter 4 I argued that a literary public sphere can be a national phenomenon, though it is less clear in the case of *American Psycho* what caused the silence among citizen critics: has literature become so much a discourse of aesthetic experts and the media so controlled by monied elites that citizens simply assume their views will not be heard? The silence in the wake of *American Psycho* suggests this happens when the First Amendment comes to structurally distort all debate about a cultural product. Finally, in chapter 5 I suggested that certain metaphors, when used to describe literary public spheres, systematically exclude so many voices that it is unclear whether a literary public sphere can be said to exist at all; at the same time, I suggested that the many *topoi* raised by Dworkin found few places—and no published place—to grow. Overall, it is clear from this project that the processes through which literary texts affect social practices can be studied empirically by analyzing the contours of public debate as reflected in the rhetorical strategies of participants' discourses.

More specifically, in chapter 2 I argued that the discourses of Margaret Anderson and Jane Heap, reflecting the view of the artist as genius, set the discursive stage for the Woolsey decision by moving all questions about *Ulysses* as addressed to them by the "Reader Critics" of the *Little Review* to the *topoi* of "true art" and "the true artist." For Anderson and Heap, Joyce's novel—and Joyce himself—were more a matter of belief than of reason; to question Joyce's intentions or the intelligibility of his novel was to betray oneself as not of the elect. As Felice Flanery Lewis points out, popular efforts to censor literature in this country began about 1890 in connection with the efforts of Anthony Comstock (8–9); John Sumner, the agent behind the first trial of *Ulysses,* succeeded Comstock as head of the New York Society for the Prevention of Vice. As early as thirty years after Comstock's first efforts, the *topos* of "literary merit" was fast becoming the authoritative legal standard for deciding whether contemporary books—historically distant "classics" such as Boccacio's *Decameron* had for the most part already been cleared—should gain legal publication and distribution. Through their arguments, Anderson and Heap helped transform what was perceived as an "improper" novel into a "contemporary classic," thus asserting what would come to be known as canonicity as a refuge against charges of obscenity. The legitimacy of that refuge would be an issue for Henry Miller's *Tropic of Cancer.*

Arguably the most censored and litigated book in the history of this country, *Tropic of Cancer* resulted in more than sixty court cases at local, state, and national levels between 1961 and 1964. In the three decades since the Woolsey decision, change had come slowly to censorship law. While the U.S. Supreme Court had ruled in the 1957 *Roth* decision that obscenity was not constitutionally protected speech or press, Justice Brennan's five criteria for obscenity in *Roth* were ambiguous and led to interpretations that have never resulted in legal or social consensus. Given that ambiguity, public discourses in Chicago's four major daily newspapers in the wake of publication of *Tropic of Cancer* reflect a literary public sphere's attempt to come to terms with the issues of community standards, the social value of literature, the criterion of literary merit, and the arbiters of obscenity. In chapter 3 I argued that the *topoi* in public discourses about *Tropic of Cancer* in Chicago helped shape legal decisions and further debates on issues of censorship and social change during a time when courts around the country—from municipal and county courts to the highest court in the land—were deeply divided at even the definitional *stasis* on nearly every obscenity case. Most specifically, I suggested that the *topos* of literary merit—as legitimated in Judge Epstein's decision as well as in the U.S. Supreme Court's summary affirmation of the Florida decision—excluded to a large degree further debate about the social consequences of such controversial books as *Tropic of Cancer.*

Though changes in obscenity law over three decades allowed a book as sexually violent as Bret Easton Ellis's *American Psycho* to avoid any legal censorship challenges, some readers and many reviewers were deeply troubled about the consequences of a book that Tammy Bruce, president of the Los Angeles chapter of NOW, called a "how-to novel on the torture and dismemberment of women" (McDowell). In chapter 4 I argued that the public questioning of the nature and role of publicity surrounding Ellis's book suggests that Habermas underestimates the potential of critical publicity in late capitalism. In any case, the shifting of questions of the social and political effects of *American Psycho* to questions of aesthetics—a shift begun by Norman Mailer in his *Vanity Fair* article on the novel—most changed the contours of the national debate over Ellis's book, excluded or delegitimated the arguments of those who questioned the social effects of the novel, and took *American Psycho* out of the realm of public comment and into the expert realm of aesthetics. Mailer's argument shifts ownership of the problem of *American Psycho* from feminists and other social critics to an aesthetic elite. Only time will tell—as the novel does or does not become canonical according to one set or another of aesthetic criteria—whether citizen critics or literary and other expert critics will ultimately determine judgments about *American Psycho*.[1]

The first three case studies in this project suggest a continual shift in public discussions of controversial novels from questions of social and political impact to questions of literary merit—either in courtrooms or in literary public spheres themselves—and a concomitant exclusion of public debate about the social effects of literature. One founding assumption of this study was that fictional texts, or texts usually considered literary, have the potential to do work in the world and that studying public discourses might provide a more empirical sense of how that process works. In other words, I never assumed that a *literary* public sphere would in any way be by definition an *aesthetic* public sphere: Habermas's claim about the central role played by fiction in the eighteenth century in no way posits people in coffeehouses or bourgeois families in their homes discussing the artistic unities of a popular novel. Instead, the *topoi* invented and used in discussions in the public sphere in the world of letters allowed these people to reflect on their own political conditions: "In the *Tatler*, the *Spectator*, and the *Guardian* the public held up a mirror to itself. . . . The public that read and debated about this sort of thing read and debated about itself" (*Structural Transformation* 43). Yet the shape of arguments across the twentieth century about books that raised certain social and political issues suggests that, ultimately, the *topos* of literary merit has often had the effect of calming the waters, removing books from the literary public sphere and inserting them into a sphere of experts, where judgments about the quality of writing were often made but rarely supported in a way that nonexperts could, in turn, judge those arguments. In chapter 5, I suggest that Dworkin so personalized the "war zone" of the literary public sphere that most reviewers moved the *locus* of debate from Dworkin's subject matter—violence against women—to the craft of her writing or to Dworkin herself. More so in Dworkin's case than in any of the other three, discussion of the political *topoi* of an explicitly political novel was systematically excluded from the literary public sphere that grew up around it.

Given the distinctions I am drawing here, the question most assuredly will be asked: If Dworkin (and perhaps Ellis and perhaps even Miller) wanted to write a book about social ills, why did she choose to write a novel? And given that she chose to write a novel, why shouldn't her novel be judged by aesthetic criteria? This study provides additional support for claims that aesthetic criteria are not and should not be seen as universal or ahistorical; what is "good writing" in one case may very well not be "good writing" in another. Joyce provides the least suspect warrant for this assertion: that his stylistic innovations had such influence on writing of all kinds over the twentieth century merely suggests that the aesthetic criteria of high modernism have been legitimated by expert literary critics and professional reviewers. Many actual readers would still feel about Joyce the way one of the *Little Review*'s "Reader Critics" did: "I consider myself fairly intelligent. I have read more than most. There are some few things I expect of a writer. One of them is coherence. Joyce will have to change his style if he wants to get on" ("What Joyce Is Up Against"). Turning Anderson and Heap's headline on itself, each of the novels in this study were "up against" leftover aesthetic criteria that ultimately kept readers from addressing the arguments these books made about the world around them. The movement of political and social questions to aesthetic questions has especially complicated results for writers who, like Dworkin, seem to feel that novels are one way to enable the private experiences of groups of people—subalterns, in Fraser's and Spivak's terms—to enter wider public spheres and gain legitimation. But until narratives are judged by criteria other than the solely aesthetic in literary public spheres—and until teachers of reading and writing change the criteria by which responses to texts are judged and encourage students to become active participants in public discussions of controversial cultural texts—subaltern narratives have little chance of bringing the concerns of underrepresented groups into mainstream publics.

The exclusion of deliberations about the political and social consequences of literary texts is manifested in another phenomenon of the twentieth century: the rise of the professional literary critic and the decline of the citizen critic. As Lewis documents, judges were deeply divided through the early sixties on whether to allow the testimony of literary critics into the courtroom when the social effects of novels were in question (see also Rembar); yet soon after the authority of literary critics emerged as legitimate and then ultimate on those questions, censorship of literary texts became rare. Though the question of censoring literary obscenity was settled in courts of law, as I suggest in chapters 4 and 5, the question is still not settled for many in other, wider publics. *Citizen Critics* has suggested that whereas institutionalized literary critics, lawyers, and judges have accepted the criterion of "literary merit" as warrant for no longer censoring or suppressing most works of fiction, citizen critics—individuals writing publicly in literary public spheres about works of fiction that concern them—are less settled about whether "literary merit" (or the possibly less elite "good writing") is in itself a legitimate or ultimate criterion.

A parallel development, and one that deserves further study, is the emergence of social science research as legitimate and then ultimate in deciding what causal relationship might exist between cultural texts and behavior. Again, as professional literary critics and social scientists have come to own the issue of the social effects of controversial cultural texts, individual and in some cases group narratives of harm have been excluded from public debate. Indeed, literary public spheres do not form around only "literary" texts. Though not within the scope of this book, literary public spheres have formed around radio shows, films, television shows, and other cultural products—even texts as complicated as the Starr report. In fact, news coverage and public debate over the impeachment of President Clinton suggest that *topoi* do have lives of their own. When the Starr report was released over the Internet, it was repeatedly referred to as a "tawdry dime-store novel," and when Rep. Henry Hyde of Illinois was asked by CNN reporters, as he prepared to read the Starr report, for his definition of an impeachable offense, he said—echoing U.S. Supreme Court Justice Potter Stewart's operational definition of obscenity—"We'll know it when we see it."

Only time—and our efforts as teachers and citizen critics—will tell whether controversial novels will continue to be perceived and described in metaphors of unpleasantness—the *Tribune* called *Tropic of Cancer* a "stinker," and Mailer saw the publicity over *American Psycho* as a "tidal wave of bad cess" (157; see also Mailloux, *Reception Histories* chap. 6). It is my hope that we might return, in the words of Christopher Lehmann-

Haupt, "to some bygone age when books were still a matter of life and death instead of something to distract us on a flight between JFK and LAX."

## Classrooms as Protopublic Spaces

In the balance of this chapter, I will sketch a pedagogy that helps literary and other cultural texts matter by giving students the choice to become citizen critics. It is a pedagogy that focuses on publics and public spheres rather than on audiences, readers, or communities and that attempts to move toward counteracting the narrative of structural transformation articulated by Habermas and revised by his many commentators. At the heart of this pedagogy is a passion for the habit of public writing as a means of reinvigorating public life and citizenship.

In an essay reflecting on their 1984 article "Audience Addressed/Audience Invoked," Andrea A. Lunsford and Lisa Ede suggest that many teachers and scholars simplify the concept of audience in their writing classrooms. While they argued in 1984 that "previous commentators had generally taken a partial view of an unusually rich and complex concept," Lunsford and Ede maintained in 1996 that even their own work on audience has largely continued to limit the heuristic power of asking students to think about, for example, "the ways in which audiences can not only enable but also silence writers and readers" (170). Indeed, Lunsford and Ede argue, the concept of audience has long enabled teachers and students to obscure that "the classroom is not a magic circle free of ideological and institutional influence" (171). Lunsford and Ede suggest that the concept of audience has simply not yet been put into practice in ways complex enough to withstand the complications of praxis in writing classrooms. Invoking bell hooks, Lunsford and Ede call for writing classrooms to be rhetorical spaces that teachers and students open up to the play and struggle of difference. "We must work hard," they write, "to understand the complex choices, multiple responsibilities, and competing representations that communication always entails" (175).

Before Gregory Clark argued for a rescue of "the discourse of community," Joseph Harris made a point similar to Lunsford and Ede's regarding the notion of "community" in writing instruction. Following Raymond Williams, Harris argues that, because "community" has no "positive opposing" term, it "can soon become an empty and sentimental word" (13). "Community," Harris argues, "tends to mean little more than a nicer, friendlier, fuzzier version of what came before" (13). "As teachers and theorists of writing," Harris concludes, "we need a vocabulary that will allow us to talk about certain forces as social rather than communal, as involving power but not always consent. Such talk could give us a fuller picture of the lived experience of teaching, learning, and writing in a university today" (20–21). A pedagogy of publics and public spheres, in which the classroom plays a processual role as a protopublic space, would extend the picture many of us wish for even further, including but going beyond the university and into the different kinds of public realms that our students and we read and write in after we have left high school and perhaps college, after we have gone home for the evening or the morning— all the kinds of writing we might engage in for the duration of our lives, the writing we do as citizen critics.

Another of Harris's concerns about the concept of *community* in the writing classroom is that it leads away from the empirical world:

> Most of the "communities" to which other current theorists refer exist at a vague remove from actual experience: The University, The Profession, The Discipline, The Academic Discourse Community. They are all quite literally utopias— nowheres, meta-communities—tied to no particular time or place, and thus oddly free of many of the tensions, discontinuities, and conflicts in the sorts of talk and writing that go on everyday in the classrooms and departments of an actual university. For all the scrutiny it has drawn, the idea of community thus still remains little more than a notion—hypothetical and suggestive, powerful yet ill-defined. (14)

Unlike concepts of audience, reader, and community, which can lead students to think in general terms, realizing the classroom as a protopublic space and encouraging students to see themselves as agents in different and overlapping publics can help them realize the particular and situated nature of rhetoric and the need for rhetoric to respond to particular needs of particular publics at particular times.

While I have written elsewhere about two specific writing courses that functioned as protopublic spaces ("'Everywhere You Go, It's There'"), here I want to argue more generally about how publics theory and rhetoric combined can help students imagine themselves as—and then act as—citizen critics. First of all, classrooms can never be truly public spaces because of the presence of the teacher and because of the institutional constraints and supports that necessarily follow from that structure. So, at best, the classroom can be a protopublic space, or a space where students can engage in the praxis of rhetoric, an art whose *telos* is *krisis,* or judgment. The prefix *proto-* is meant to suggest that from the classroom, with its institutional structures that keep it from being a public space, students can study and practice the discourses of literary public spheres as well as write arguments that they may choose to send out for publication, thus engaging with and possibly even forming publics.

Realizing classrooms as protopublic spaces requires a few fundamental pedagogical shifts of value. Instead of focusing on just the formal qualities of texts—novels, poems, films, editorials—students and teachers focus on the *topoi* generated by those texts. In other words, texts are neither meant to be "taught" nor meant to be means to discrete and specific pedagogical goals. Instead, texts are inventional prompts for discussion about various publics and their possible reaction to the texts in question. How does this pedagogy proceed? After studying and internalizing theories of the *stasis* questions and *topoi,* students work together to generate as many *topoi* as possible from the texts under discussion. Mapping these *topoi* is a helpful means of seeing possible ways that the *topoi* may be in relation (see Yates). In addition, texts are discussed in relation to other texts written in response to them, including student writing meant for eventual publication.[2] The most difficult part of realizing the classroom as a protopublic space is helping students learn to practice discoursing with one another, in speech as well as in writing, in the shared space of the classroom. Similarly, it takes much of the term for most students to realize not only that their thoughts are valued in the classroom as much as the published writers we read but also that entering public deliberations on all kinds of public issues is as straightforward as sending a letter or op-ed to the local newspaper. Assigning students to listen to local talk radio—and then to call a show, make an argument, support it, and record it on audiotape—is a possible means of getting students to begin to imagine themselves as participants in local public discourse.[3]

Participating in and studying the discourses of literary public spheres have advantages over traditional literary criticism and English studies pedagogies, both in the protopublic space of the classroom and beyond, in wider nonacademic and extraliterary publics. First, studying and producing discourses that form or sustain literary public spheres can help create a public-oriented agency or subjectivity in students that transcends the limits of liberal democratic citizenship as well as formalist criteria for ethos— "good sense, good will, and good moral character."[4] The Aristotelian trinity is not adequate either for studying and teaching transitions from private to public subjectivities or for studying and teaching subjectivity-formation on the World Wide Web and in other computer-mediated settings. Habermas emphasizes in his narrative of structural transformation that the emergence of the bourgeois public sphere required a split in subjectivity between *bourgeois* and *homme,* a split that does not have to occur in literary public spheres. Whereas political questions often bifurcate the subject's interests over questions of property, discussions of literary and other cultural texts do not necessarily have to cause a split in subjectivity. Further, Sennett's account of presentation versus representation, which I understand as an account of public subjectivity, offers rhetors a means of thinking about how they might construct various *ethe* to invent and present themselves in different publics or at different points in a public's process of forming, acting, possibly disintegrating. Studying literary public spheres and making arguments in them allows a place for the process through which the private self may emerge in public discourse: a place for individual experience, memory, and identity to find—through arguments about literary or cultural texts in the classroom realized as a protopublic space— collective voice. The process—the *praxis*—through which these things can happen is rhetoric.

Second, publics theory and rhetoric together allow for the study of how publics form and, perhaps, disintegrate. Dewey's emphasis on private people recognizing common interests through reading and writing together suggests a sense of how publics move through processes of being inchoate: thinking, reading, writing, and speaking about the consequences they might share; recognizing themselves as publics; deliberating about the qualities of possible conjoint actions; and, quite possibly, disintegrating as mutually recognized publics. In classrooms, this sense of process can fit very well not only with students' writing processes in general but also with invention specifically. For instructors who teach the *stasis* questions as an inventional tool, this sense of publics-in-process can help students practice making judgments about which arguments to make and how to make them for which publics in which situations.

Rhetoric matters in literary public spheres—in protopublic classrooms and beyond—because of the collective nature of reading and writing together that defines the activities and goals of literary public spheres. Rhetoric matters because, in literary public spheres, rhetoric—which demands engagement with the living—enables literary and other cultural texts to matter. Rhetoric offers readers the opportunity to move from the *vita contemplativa* of private reading to the *vita activa* of literary public spheres. Studying the rhetorics of literary public spheres and encouraging students to practice rhetoric in local ones offers promise as a post–English studies pedagogy because it allows literary and other cultural texts to matter—to become inventional prompts not to mere contemplation but to real-world and shared, that is, *public* rhetorical exchanges. The classroom, as Lunsford and Ede write, is not a magic circle; neither are public spheres three-ring circuses in which spectacle and silence are the only means and entertainment and oppression the only ends.

Again, whereas theories of audiences or readers tend to focus on their fictional nature, psychological constituents, or demographics, such theories do not account for the empirical rhetorical processes through which publics come to recognize themselves, form, act, and, perhaps, disintegrate. For teachers and students in writing classrooms, studying the formations of publics, the different subjectivities students might try out for different publics at different points in their formation or disintegration, the gradations of publicness and expertise in academic and professional writing, and the processes through which subalterns choose or do not choose to join larger or wider publics provides a rich and complex alternative to studying individual arguments tailored to ideal, prefabricated, homological audiences. Publics theories enable teachers and students and critics to bring reading and writing together and to stress the social and processual natures of both. *Publics* as a term to replace *readers* or *audiences* or *communities* allows students to experience writing as wholly processual and as practiced within and for real groups of people who need their discourses. Notions of publics and counterpublics encourage a productive combination of expressivist and public discourse in classrooms; and classrooms as protopublic spaces rather than as communities allow teachers and students—and citizen critics—to engage in education as practice for democratic public life.

## NOTES

1. A film version of the novel started production in March 1999.

2. Graff's "teach the conflicts" pedagogy focuses on expert critics and theorists rather than on citizen or student responses to texts. While classrooms as protopublic spheres may include the discourses of cultural elites, they emphasize letters to the editor, newsgroups, and other venues where citizen critics might be published.

3. This assignment is, of course, not without its risks. I have included my assignment sheet (see the appendix) to suggest how to work with those risks and how to give students as much support as possible as they move from a protopublic space to the open airways. A more vexing problem is that as huge national and international media corporations buy and sell radio stations, chances for public discourse fade as fewer and fewer stations allow discourses that are not "entertainment"—if they air any local talk at all.

4. This view of subjectivity includes both "modernist" and "postmodernist" inclinations toward the individual, as discussed by Faigley (17, 111–31).

# Appendix:
# Short Assignment 1:
# Call to Local Radio Talk Show

This assignment is as straightforward as the others in this class. But it might make you a different kind of nervous. I have asked students in previous classes to call local radio talk shows and make arguments, and, while they have hated the idea *before* they made the call, they unanimously were glad they had gone through with it after it was over. So: here goes.

This assignment asks you first to listen to and study and then to participate in the discussion on a local talk radio show. Whichever show you choose to call, you will want to listen a few times before you enter the conversation. Why? Ethos. Knowing the rules of the game more or less is one way to sound credible.

In class, we will review what local radio talk shows you might want to listen to and participate in. But you are welcome to choose one we have not discussed in class. The only kinds of radio talk shows that are not acceptable in this assignment are those that are geared toward information rather than discussion: car care shows or gardening shows or health care shows or psychology shows. The idea of this assignment is to get you in public in yet another way and in yet another medium, radio. Also, this assignment does not ask you to call state or national shows; it and we are focusing on local discourse as mediated by radio.

A word about local radio in an age of commercialization: radio stations are, for the people who own them, first and foremost investments. And radio stations are being bought and sold more and more quickly, as ways to make a lot of money in a short period of time. So one thing we will have to remember is that radio shows are seen by the industry as investments first and entertainment second rather than as *topoi* for public debate and comment. This reality will form part of the context for our discussions of public discourse as the semester progresses.

Still, local radio talk shows, regardless of the industry's purposes, can be used for public purposes. That's where you come in. What I'm asking you to do in this assignment is to enter the entertainment-oriented sphere of local talk radio and use it to make an argument about something you feel requires comment. So you will want to pick an issue about which you hold some opinions. And here's the radical part of this assignment (at least as far as talk radio is concerned!): you have to support your opinions with one or more of the *topoi* we're learning in this class.

So, in summary: this assignment asks you to call a local radio talk show that you have listened to enough to get a sense of how it works and to make an argument and support it. It might be in your best interest not to identify yourself as "doing this for a class"—a strategy which has in the past pretty much destroyed the on-air credibility of the students who have used it. Remember, as with the other assignments in this class, we want to make it as real as we can get it. So pick something that you truly have opinions about. Listen to the radio, find something that you can't let pass without comment, and make an argument and support it. Oh: you also have to record yourself, so if you don't have a boombox or stereo that records the radio, you'll have to borrow one. Let me know if this is a hardship, and you can borrow mine.

# Works Consulted

Allor, Martin. "Relocating the Site of the Audience." *Critical Studies in Mass Communication* 5.3 (Sept. 1988): 217–33.

"Among the Best Selling Books in the Midwest as Reported by Leading Booksellers and Wholesalers." *Chicago Tribune* 20 Aug. 1961, sec. 4: 4.

Anderson, Margaret. *My Thirty Years' War.* New York: Horison, 1969.

———. "An Obvious Statement (for the Millionth Time)." *Little Review* 7.3 (Sept.–Dec. 1920): 8–16.

———. "To the Book Publishers of America." *Little Review* 6.8 (Dec. 1919): 65–67.

Apeland, Casper. Letter. *Chicago Tribune* 24 Aug. 1961: 16.

Aristotle. *Rhetoric.* Trans. John Henry Freese. Loeb Classical Library. Vol. 193. 1926. Cambridge, Mass.: Harvard University Press, 1991.

———. *Topics.* Trans. E. S. Forster. Loeb Classical Library. Vol. 391. Cambridge, Mass.: Harvard University Press, 1960.

Arnold, Bruce. *The Scandal of* Ulysses. London: Sinclair-Stevenson, 1991.

Aronowitz, Stanley, and Henry A. Giroux. *Postmodern Education: Politics, Culture, and Social Criticism.* Minneapolis: University of Minnesota Press, 1991.

Ashley, Peter J. Introduction. *Twentieth-Century American Newspaper Publishers.* Ed. Peter J. Ashley. Vol. 127 of *Dictionary of Literary Biography.* Detroit: Gale Research, 1993. xi–xxii.

"Author and Publisher of THAT Book File Suit." *Chicago's American* 24 Oct. 1961, 2d ed.: 4.

B., S. S. "What Joyce Is Up Against." Letter. *Little Review* 4.2 (June 1918): 54.

"Backdoor Censors." Editorial. *Nation* 10 Dec. 1990: 720.

Baker, John. "Publisher Responsibility and Bret Easton Ellis." *Publishers Weekly* 30 Nov. 1990: 7.

"Ban on Miller's 'Tropic' Overruled in Wisconsin." *Chicago Tribune* 21 May 1963: 5.

Barnes, Djuna. "James Joyce." *Vanity Fair* Apr. 1922: 65, 104.

Bartlett, Anne. "Prohibition Era." Letter. *Chicago Daily News* 25 Oct. 1961: 12.

Batstone, David, and Eduardo Mendieta, eds. *The Good Citizen.* New York: Rout-ledge, 1999.

Bean, Henry. "Slayground." *Los Angeles Times Book Review* 17 Mar. 1991: BR1.

"Beatnik Poets Find Backer." Associated Press story. *Chicago Sun-Times* 23 Oct. 1961, 1st ed.: 16.

Beck, Joan. "Sex, Hype, and Videotape Drown Out Voices of Reason." *Chicago Tribune* 6 Dec. 1990, sec. 1: 21.

Bell, Madison Smartt. "Sustaining a Scream: Andrea Dworkin's Novel Depicts a Life of Politics, Poverty, and Rape." Rev. of *Mercy,* by Andrea Dworkin. *Chicago Tribune* 15 Sept. 1991, sec. 14: 5.

Berlant, Lauren, and Michael Warner. "Sex in Public." *Critical Inquiry* 24 (Winter 1998): 547–66.

Bernstein, Richard. "'American Psycho,' Going So Far That Many Say It's Too Far." *New York Times* 10 Dec. 1990: C13+.

Berry, John N., III. "Bean Counting Replaced Editorial Judgment Years Ago: American Psycho Is Not the Problem." Editorial. *Library Journal* Jan. 1991: 6.

Berthold, Hildegarde. Letter. *Chicago Tribune* 18 Aug. 1961: 10.

"Best Selling Books in the Midwest as Reported by Leading Booksellers and Whole-salers." *Chicago Tribune* 13 Aug. 1961, sec. 4: 3.

Billimack, C. R. Letter. *Chicago Tribune* 18 Aug. 1961: 10.

Bitzer, Lloyd. "The Rhetorical Situation." *Philosophy and Rhetoric* 1.1 (1968): 1–14.

———. "Rhetoric and Public Knowledge." *Rhetoric, Philosophy, and Literature: An Exploration.* Ed. Don M. Burks. West Lafayette: Purdue University Press, 1978. 67–94.

Bleich, David. *Subjective Criticism.* Baltimore: Johns Hopkins University Press, 1978.

Bloem, Dan F. "Michigan Reader." Letter. *Chicago Sun-Times* 13 Mar. 1962: 29.

"Book Damaging, Mabley Testifies." *Chicago's American* 24 Jan. 1962, 2d ed.: 3.

"Book Is Dirty, but Not Obscene, Judge Decides." *Chicago's American* 22 Feb. 1962, 1st ed.: 5.

"Book Shocks Daley, He Orders Probe." *Chicago's American* 13 Oct. 1961: 3.

"Bookwatch." Rev. of *Mercy,* by Andrea Dworkin. *Ms.* 2 (1991): 76.

Booth, Wayne C. "The Rhetorical Stance." *College Composition and Communication* 14 (Oct. 1963): 139–45.

———. *The Rhetoric of Fiction.* 2d ed. Chicago: University of Chicago Press, 1983.

Boyle, Thomas E. "On Censorship." Letter. *Chicago Sun-Times* 26 Oct. 1961: 43.

B[radley], V[an] A[llen]. "'Tropic' Reaches Stores." Rev. of *Tropic of Cancer,* by Henry Miller. *Chicago Daily News* 17 July 1961: 17.

Brinkley, Alan. "Unceremony: The Conventions Will Come to Order. Too Much Order." *New Yorker* 12 Aug. 1996: 4–5.

Brown, Elsa Barkley. "Negotiating and Transforming the Public Sphere: African American Political Life in the Transition from Slavery to Freedom." *The Black Public Sphere.* Ed. Black Public Sphere Collective. Chicago: University of Chicago Press, 1995. 111–50.

Burke, Kenneth. *Attitudes towards History.* 2d rev. ed. Los Altos, Calif.: Hermes, 1959.

———. *Counter-Statement.* Berkeley: University of California Press, 1931.

———. *Permanence and Change.* 2d rev. ed. Los Altos, Calif.: Hermes, 1954.

Casey, Constance. "A Catalogue of Violence against Women." Rev. of *Mercy,* by Andrea Dworkin. *Los Angeles Times* 27 Aug. 1991: E10.

"A Change Is Made." *Chicago Tribune* 20 Aug. 1961, sec. 4: 4.

Chrupka, Marie, et al. "High Schoolers Speak." Letter. *Chicago Sun-Times* 19 Mar. 1962: 21.

"Civil Liberties Unit Sues to Halt Ban on 'Tropic.'" *Chicago Sun-Times* 17 Oct. 1961, 1st ed.: 21.

Clark, Gregory. "Rescuing the Discourse of Community." *College Composition and Communication* 45 (Feb. 1994): 61–74.

Coates, Joseph. "'Psycho': A Shocking Bore." *Chicago Tribune* 6 Mar. 1991, sec. 5: 1+.

Cohen, Roger. "Editorial Adjustments in 'American Psycho.'" *New York Times* 18 Feb. 1991: A13.

Collins, Joseph. "James Joyce's Amazing Chronicle." Rev. of *Ulysses,* by James Joyce. *New York Times Book Review and Magazine* 28 May 1922: 6, 17.

"Court Puzzled by Experts on Book's Morals." *New York Tribune* 15 Feb. 1921: 5.

"Court Rules on 'Tropic.'" Editorial. *Chicago's American* 22 June 1964: 6.

Cromie, Robert. "The Bystander." *Chicago Tribune* 4 Mar. 1962, sec. 4: 7.

Crowe, Charles M. Letter. *Chicago Tribune* 18 Aug. 1961: 10.

"Current Books and Their Rights." *Publishers Weekly* 23 Aug. 1991: S15.

Cushman, Ellen. "Opinion: The Public Intellectual, Service Learning, and Activist Research." *College English* 61 (Jan. 1999): 328–36.

Dawson, N. P. "The Cuttlefish School of Writers." *Forum* 69 (Jan. 1923): 1174–84.

Day, K. C. Letter. *Chicago Tribune* 17 Aug. 1961: 16.

"Dealer Charged in Smut Case." *Chicago's American* 11 Oct. 1961, 2d ed.: 3.

"Debate Set on Controversial Books." *Chicago Sun-Times* 3 Mar. 1962, 1st ed.: 16.

Delli Carpini, Michael X., and Scott Keeter. *What Americans Know about Politics and Why It Matters.* New Haven: Yale University Press, 1996.

Dewey, John. *The Public and Its Problems.* New York: Holt, 1927. Athens, Ohio: Swallow, 1980.

Domenig, Kathleen. "The Rushdie Crisis in the United States: A Rhetorical Analysis of Contemporary Publics and the Mass Media." Diss. Penn State University, 1995.

Dove, Joyce M. "Agrees with Judge." Letter. *Chicago Sun-Times* 26 Mar. 1962: 29.

Downey, Maureen. "Every Woman's Nightmare." *Atlanta Constitution* 8 Mar. 1991: G1+.

———. "NOW Members Split over Call for Boycott of 'American Psycho.'" *Atlanta Journal* 8 Mar. 1991: G4.

Dreyfus, Hubert L., and Paul Rabinow. *Michel Foucault: Beyond Structuralism and Hermeneutics.* 2d ed. Chicago: University of Chicago Press, 1983.

Duff, Charles. *James Joyce and the Plain Reader.* London: D. Harmsworth, 1932.

Dworkin, Andrea. "April 30, 1974." Excerpt from *Mercy. American Voice* 6 (Winter 1990): 24–32.

———. *Ice and Fire.* New York: Weidenfeld and Nicolson, 1987.

———. "In October 1973 (Age 27)." Excerpt from *Mercy. Michigan Quarterly Review* 29.4 (Fall 1990): 623–36.

———. *Letters from a War Zone: Writings, 1976–1989.* New York: Dutton, 1989.

———. *Mercy.* New York: Four Walls Eight Windows, 1991.

———. "Pornography and the New Puritans: Letters from Andrea Dworkin and Others." *New York Times Book Review* 3 May 1992: 15.

Dworkin, Andrea, and Catherine MacKinnon. *Pornography and Civil Rights: A New Day for Women's Equality.* Minneapolis: Organizing against Pornography, 1988.

E., Mrs. M. H. "The Antidote." Letter. *Chicago Sun-Times* 26 Mar. 1962: 29.

Eagleton, Terry. *The Function of Criticism: From the* Spectator *to Post-Structuralism.* London: Verso, 1984.

———. *The Ideology of the Aesthetic.* London: Blackwell, 1990.

Eastman, Max. "The Cult of Unintelligibility." *Harper's Monthly Magazine* Apr. 1929: 632–29.

Eberly, Rosa A. "'Everywhere You Go, It's There': The UT Tower Shootings and Public Memory." *Rhetoric and Public Memory.* Ed. David Henry and Stephen Browne. New York: Sage, forthcoming.

Ede, Lisa, and Andrea A. Lunsford. "Audience Addressed/Audience Invoked: The Role of Audience in Composition Theory and Pedagogy." *College Composition and Communication* 35 (May 1984): 155–71.

Edwards, Mike. "Other Filth in City." *Chicago Sun-Times* 17 Mar. 1962: 15.

"Eight Suburbs Dismissed in Book Ban Suit." *Chicago Tribune* 19 Dec. 1961, sec. 2: 9.

Elbow, Peter. "Closing My Eyes as I Write: An Argument for Ignoring Audience." *College English* 49 (Jan. 1987): 50–69.

Ellis, Bret Easton. *American Psycho.* New York: Vintage, 1991.

Ellmann, Richard. *James Joyce.* New York: Oxford University Press, 1959.

Elshtain, Jean Bethke. *Public Man, Private Woman: Women in Social and Political Thought.* Princeton: Princeton University Press, 1981.

Engelman, Ralph. *Public Radio and Television in America: A Political History.* Thousand Oaks, Calif.: Sage, 1996.

Ernst, Morris L. *The Censor Marches On.* New York: Doubleday, 1940.

Ernst, Morris L., and Alan U. Schwartz. *Censorship: The Search for the Obscene.* New York: Macmillan, 1964.

Fahnestock, Jeanne, and Marie Secor. "The Rhetoric of Literary Criticism." *Textual Dynamics of the Professions: Historical and Contemporary Studies of Writing in Professional Communities.* Ed. Charles Bazerman and James Paradis. Madison: University of Wisconsin Press, 1991. 76–96.

———. "Stases in Scientific and Literary Arguments." *Written Communication* 5.4 (Oct. 1988): 427–43.

Faigley, Lester. *Fragments of Rationality: Postmodernity and the Subject of Composition.* Pittsburgh: University of Pittsburgh Press, 1992.

Faulkner, Joseph M. Letter. *Chicago Tribune* 18 Aug. 1961: 10.

Fish, Stanley. *Is There a Text in This Class? The Authority of Interpretive Communities.* Cambridge, Mass.: Harvard University Press, 1980.

———. *There's No Such Thing as Free Speech . . . and It's a Good Thing, Too.* New York: Oxford University Press, 1994.

Fishkin, James S. *The Voice of the People: Public Opinion and Democracy.* New Haven: Yale University Press, 1995.

Foucault, Michel. *The Archaeology of Knowledge and the Discourse on Language.* Trans. A. M. Sheridan Smith. New York: Pantheon, 1972.

———. *The History of Sexuality.* Trans. Robert Hurley. New York: Pantheon, 1976. New York: Vintage, 1990.

———. *Madness and Civilization: A History of Insanity in the Age of Reason.* Trans. Richard Howard. New York: Pantheon, 1961. New York: Vintage, 1988.

Frank, Joan. "Sketch." *San Francisco Review of Books* 16 (Fall 1991): 9–10.

Fraser, Nancy. "Rethinking the Public Sphere: A Contribution to the Critique of Actually Existing Democracy." *Habermas and the Public Sphere.* Ed. Craig Calhoun. Cambridge, Mass.: MIT Press, 1992. 109–42.

"Freedom No License." Letter by "A Reader." *Chicago Sun-Times* 26 Mar. 1962: 29.

"Freedoms Foundation Honors TV Critic Molloy." *Chicago Sun-Times* 22 Feb. 1962: 14.

Gabriel, Joseph M. "Hails Judge Epstein's Ruling." Letter. *Chicago Daily News* 6 Mar. 1962: 16.

Gardner, Marilyn. "Monsters and Their Keepers." *Christian Science Monitor* 19 Mar. 1991: 13.

Gertz, Elmer, and Felice Flanery Lewis, eds. *Henry Miller: Years of Trial and Triumph, 1962–1964.* Carbondale: Southern Illinois University Press, 1978.

Gibson, Walker. "Authors, Speakers, Readers, and Mock Readers." *College English* 11 (Feb. 1950): 265–69.

"Girl-Watching Department." Photo. *Chicago's American* 20 Aug. 1961, pictorial ed.: 3.

Giroux, Henry. *Border Crossings: Cultural Workers and the Politics of Education.* New York: Routledge, 1992.

Gitlin, Todd. *The Twilight of Common Dreams: Why America Is Wracked by Culture Wars.* New York: Holt, 1995.

Goldstein, Laurence. Introduction. Spec. issue of *Michigan Quarterly Review* 29.4 (Fall 1990): 485–89.

"The Good Old Days." Letter. *Little Review* 6.10 (Mar. 1920): 60–61.

Gordon, Rosalie M. Letter. *Chicago Tribune* 17 Aug. 1961: 16.

Graff, Gerald. *Professing Literature: An Institutional History.* Chicago: University of Chicago Press, 1987.

Grim, Jessica. Rev. of *Mercy,* by Andrea Dworkin. *Library Journal* 15 Nov. 1991: 106–7.

"Grove Press Will Fight 'Tropic' Ban in Mass." *Publishers Weekly* 31 July 1961: 23.

Gusfield, Joseph R. *The Culture of Public Problems: Drinking-Driving and the Symbolic Order.* Chicago: University of Chicago Press, 1981.

Habermas, Jürgen. *Between Facts and Norms: Contributions to a Discourse Theory of Law and Democracy.* Trans. William Rehg. Cambridge, Mass.: MIT Press, 1996.

———. *Communication and the Evolution of Society.* Trans. Thomas McCarthy. Boston: Beacon, 1979.

———. "The Public Sphere: An Encyclopedia Article." Trans. Sara Lennox and Frank Lennox. *New German Critique* 3 (Fall 1974): 49–55.

———. *The Structural Transformation of the Public Sphere: An Inquiry into a Category of Bourgeois Society.* Trans. Thomas Burger. Cambridge, Mass.: MIT Press, 1989.

Hall, Stuart. "Cultural Studies and Its Theoretical Legacies." *Cultural Studies.* Ed. Lawrence Grossberg, Cary Nelson, and Paula Treichler. New York: Routledge, 1992. 277–94.

Harris, Joseph. "The Idea of Community in the Writing Classroom." *College Composition and Communication* 40 (Fall 1989): 11–22.

Harris, Sydney J. "Strictly Personal: Pornography Stems from the Spirit." *Chicago Daily News* 30 Oct. 1961: 8.

Haugh, Rev. Joseph P. Letter. *Chicago Tribune* 20 Aug. 1961: 20.

Hauser, Gerard A. "Administrative Rhetoric and Public Opinion: Discussing the Iranian Hostages in the Public Sphere." *American Rhetoric: Context and Criticism.* Ed. Thomas W. Benson. Carbondale: Southern Illinois University Press, 1990. 323–83.

———. "Conversations with Carroll Arnold about the Epirical Attitude." *Carroll Arnold as Intellectual Force.* Ed. Roderick P. Hart. Annandale, Va.: National Communication Association, 1998. 11–13.

———. "Defining Publics and Reconstructing Public Spheres: The Final Report of the Attorney General's Commission on Pornography." *Warrenting Assent.* Ed. Edward Schiappa. Albany: State University of New York Press, 1994. 283–310.

———. *Vernacular Voices: Rhetorics of Publics and Public Spheres.* University of South Carolina Press, 1999.

Hauser, Gerard A., and Carole Blair. "Rhetorical Antecedents to the Public." *Pre/Text* 3 (Summer 1982): 139–67.

Heap, Jane. "Art and the Law." *Little Review* 7.3 (Sept.–Dec. 1920): 5–7.

———. Reply to "The Good Old Days." *Little Review* 6.10 (Mar. 1920): 61–62.

———. Reply to letter of R. McM. *Little Review* 5.2 (June 1918): 55.

———. Reply to letter of S. S. B. *Little Review* 4.2 (June 1918): 54.

———. Reply to letter of T. D. O'B. *Little Review* 5.3 (July 1918): 58.

———. Reply to Mary Widney, "The Public Taste." *Little Review* 7.2 (July–Aug. 1920): 33.

———. Reply to "'Ulysses.'" *Little Review* 7.1 (May–June 1920): 72.

Hitchens, Christopher. "Minority Report." *Nation* 7–14 Jan. 1991: 7.

Hoban, Phoebe. "'Psycho' Drama." *New York* 17 Dec. 1990: 33+.

Hohendahl, Peter Uwe. "The Public Sphere: Models and Boundaries." *Habermas and the Public Sphere.* Ed. Craig Calhoun. Cambridge, Mass.: MIT Press, 1992. 99–142.

Holland, Norman. *Five Readers Reading.* New Haven: Yale University Press, 1975.

———. "UNITY, IDENTITY, TEXT, SELF." *PMLA* 90 (Oct. 1975): 813–22.

Holub, Robert C. *Crossing Borders: Reception Theory, Poststructuralism, Deconstruction.* Madison: University of Wisconsin Press, 1992.

Hunter, Rex. "The Layman Speaks—!!" Letter. *Little Review* 5.3 (July 1918): 61–62.

Hutchison, E. R. *Tropic of Cancer on Trial: A Case History of Censorship.* New York: Grove, 1968.

"Improper Novel Costs Women $100." *New York Times* 22 Feb. 1921: 13.

Irving, John. "Pornography and the New Puritans." *New York Times Book Review* 29 Mar. 1992: 1+.

Iser, Wolfgang. *The Act of Reading.* Baltimore: Johns Hopkins University Press, 1978.

James, Caryn. "Now Starring, Killers for the Chiller 90's." *New York Times* 10 Mar. 1991, sec. 2: 1+.

Jauss, Hans Robert. *Aesthetic Experience and Literary Hermeneutics.* Trans. Michael Shaw. Minneapolis: University of Minnesota Press, 1982.

Jenefsky, Cindy. "To Remember the Pain." Rev. of *Mercy,* by Andrea Dworkin. *Women's Review of Books* Feb. 1992: 6–7.

Jenkins, Philip. *Using Murder: The Social Construction of Serial Homicide.* Hawthorne, N.Y.: Aldine de Gruyter, 1994.

Johnstone, Henry W., Jr. "From Philosophy to Rhetoric and Back." *Rhetoric, Philosophy, and Literature: An Exploration.* Ed. Don M. Burks. West Lafayette: Purdue University Press, 1978. 49–66.

Jones, Malden. "State Court Rules 'Tropic of Cancer,' Bruce Obscene." *Chicago's American* 19 June 1964: 1+.

Jones, William Powell. *James Joyce and the Common Reader.* Norman: University of Oklahoma Press, 1955.

Joost, Nicholas. *Years of Transition: The Dial, 1912–1920.* Barre, Mass.: Barre, 1967.

Jordan, Fred. Letter. *Chicago's American* 3 Mar. 1962: 12.

Joyce, James. *Ulysses.* New York: Random House, 1933.

"Judge Keeps Ban on 'Tropic' Sale." *Chicago's American* 22 Mar. 1962, 4th ed.: 10.

"Judge OKs Sale Here of 'Tropic.'" *Chicago Sun-Times* 22 Feb. 1962: 26.

"Judge Sets Full Hearing for Dec. 15 on 'Tropic of Cancer' Censorship." *Chicago Sun-Times* 25 Nov. 1961, 1st ed.: 14.

Kahn, Joseph P. "'American Psycho': Sick or Slick?" *Boston Globe* 20 Mar. 1991: 67+.

Kaplan, Esther. "Rapes of Wrath." Rev. of *Mercy,* by Andrea Dworkin. *Village Voice* 5 Nov. 1991: 76.

Kellough, Lt. B. "Duty of Police." Letter. *Chicago Sun-Times* 21 Oct. 1961: 21.

Kennedy, James A. "For Norris." Letter. *Chicago Sun-Times* 13 Mar. 1962: 29.

Kimball, Roger. "Much Less Than Zero." *Wall Street Journal* 6 Mar. 1991: A7.

"Kings, Councilors Ban 'Tropic of Cancer.'" Editorial. *Publishers Weekly* 23 Oct. 1961: 35.

Kolben, A. Letter. *Chicago Tribune* 17 Aug. 1961: 16.

Kupcinet, Erv. "Kup's Column." *Chicago Sun-Times* 14 Mar. 1962: 30.

Lanham, Richard. *Analyzing Prose.* New York: Scribner's, 1983.

———. *A Handlist of Rhetorical Terms.* 2d ed. Berkeley: University of California Press, 1991.

"Law and Press Freedom." Editorial. *Chicago's American* 1 July 1964: 14.

Lazarz, Mrs. Theodore T. "Against Norris." Letter. *Chicago Sun-Times* 13 Mar. 1962: 29.

Leff, Michael. "Hermeneutical Rhetoric." *Rhetoric and Hermeneutics in Our Time.* Ed. Walter Jost and Michael J. Hyde. New Haven: Yale University Press, 1997. 196–214.

———. "The Topics of Argumentative Invention in Latin Rhetorical Theory from Cicero to Boethius." *Rhetorica* 1.1 (1983): 23–44.

Lehmann-Haupt, Christopher. "'Psycho': Whither Death without Life?" *New York Times* 11 Mar. 1991: C18.

Lentricchia, Frank. *Criticism and Social Change.* Chicago: University of Chicago Press, 1983.

Leo, John. "Marketing Cynicism and Vulgarity." *U.S. News and World Report* 3 Dec. 1990: 23.

Lesch, Stephanie. "Make Own Decision." Letter. *Chicago Sun-Times* 19 Mar. 1962: 21.

Lewis, Felice Flanery. *Literature, Obscenity, and Law.* Carbondale: Southern Illinois University Press, 1976.

Lewis, Mrs. George. "Aid to Obscenity?" Letter. *Chicago's American* 24 Oct. 1961: 6.

"Liberties Unit Sues to Revoke Ban on 'Tropic of Cancer.'" *Chicago Sun-Times* 17 Oct. 1961, 2d ed.: 24.

Liebovich, Louis W. "Clayton Kirkpatrick." *Twentieth-Century American Newspaper Publishers.* Ed. Peter J. Ashley. Vol. 127 of *Dictionary of Literary Biography.* Detroit: Gale Research, 1993. 174–79.

Lind, Jack. "How Courts Define Book's Obscenity: 'Tropic of Cancer' Case Looks to Community Standards." *Chicago Daily News* 22 Jan. 1962: 14.

Lipuma, Phyllis. Letter. *Chicago Tribune* 24 Aug. 1961: 16.

Lockhart, William B., and Robert C. McClure. "Censorship of Obscenity: The Developing Constitutional Standards." *Minnesota Law Review* 45.5 (1960): 5–121.

———. "Literature, the Law of Obscenity, and the Constitution." *Minnesota Law Review* 38.295 (1954): 295–395.

———. "Obscenity Censorship: The Core Constitutional Issue—What Is Obscene?" *Utah Law Review* 7.3 (Spring 1961): 289–303.

Love, Robert. "Psycho Analysis." Interview with Bret Easton Ellis. *Rolling Stone* 4 Apr. 1991: 45+.

Lunsford, Andrea A., and Lisa Ede. "Representing Audience: 'Successful' Discourse and Disciplinary Critique." *College Composition and Communication* 47 (May 1996): 167–79.

Mabley, Jack. "Court Ruling to Bring New Flood of Smut." *Chicago's American* 29 Nov. 1964: 3.

———. "Flower Seed 'Jag' Newest Teen Thrill Food." *Chicago's American* 12 July 1963: 3.

———. "High School Girl Speaks Out on Smut." *Chicago's American* 7 Mar. 1962: 3.

———. "It's the Day Readers Have Their Say!" *Chicago's American* 23 Mar. 1962: 3.

———. "A Paperback Insult to Community." *Chicago's American* 13 Oct. 1961: 3.

———. "Smut Sellers' Strange Views of the Law." *Chicago's American* 24 June 1964: 3.

———. "'That Book' to Get Shock Treatment." *Chicago's American* 2 Mar. 1962: 3.

Machor, James L., ed. *Readers in History: Nineteenth-Century American Literature and the Contexts of Response.* Baltimore: Johns Hopkins University Press, 1993.

Madison, James. "Federalist No. 10." *The Federalist: A Commentary on the Constitution of the United States.* New York: Modern Library, [1980]. 53–62.

Mailer, Norman. "Children of the Pied Piper: Mailer on 'American Psycho.'" *Vanity Fair* Mar. 1991: 154+.

Mailloux, Steven. *Reception Histories*. Ithaca: Cornell University Press, 1998.

———. "Rhetorical Hermeneutics Revisited." *Text and Performance Quarterly* 11 (July 1991): 233–48.

———. *Rhetorical Power*. Ithaca: Cornell University Press, 1989.

Marks, Alvin Jasper. "Literary Masterpiece." Letter. *Chicago Sun-Times* 21 Oct. 1961: 21.

Martensen, Mrs. R. Letter. *Chicago Daily News* 2 Mar. 1962: 8.

"Mass. Moves to Ban 'Tropic of Cancer.'" *Publishers Weekly* 24 July 1961: 44.

"Mayor Lyrical over Culture Here, Lauds Our Opera, Symphony; but What about Banned Book?" *Chicago Daily News* 12 Oct. 1961: 3.

McCarthy, Thomas. Introduction. *Communication and the Evolution of Society*. By Jürgen Habermas. Boston: Beacon, 1979. vii–xxiv.

McChesney, Robert W. *Corporate Media and the Threat to Democracy*. Open Media Pamphlet Series. New York: Seven Stories Press, 1997.

———. *Telecommunications, Mass Media, and Democracy: The Battle for Control of U. S. Broadcasting, 1928–1935*. New York: Oxford University Press, 1993.

McDowell, Edwin. "NOW Chapter Seeks Boycott of 'Psycho' Novel." *New York Times* 12 Dec. 1990: C17.

———. "Vintage Buys Violent Book Dropped by Simon and Schuster." *New York Times* 17 Nov. 1990: A13.

McElroy, Edward F. "For the Record." Letter. *Chicago Sun-Times* 8 Mar. 1962: 37.

McHugh, Mrs. Paul A. Letter. *Chicago Tribune* 17 Aug. 1961: 16.

McKeon, Richard. *Rhetoric: Essays in Invention and Discovery*. Woodbridge Conn.: Ox Box Press, 1987.

McM., R. "James Joyce." Letter. *Little Review* 5.2 (June 1918): 55.

McPhaul, Jack. "Is It Pornography?" *Chicago Sun-Times* 2 June 1961, sec. 2: 6.

Miller, Henry. *Tropic of Cancer*. New York: Grove, 1961.

Miner, Brad. "S&S, Not S&M." *National Review* 31 Dec. 1990: 43.

Molloy, Paul. "He Questions the Merit of 'Tropic.'" *Chicago Sun-Times* 16 Mar. 1962: 40.

Moon, Eric. "'Problem' Fiction." *Library Journal* 1 Feb. 1962: 485+.

Morrisey, Vangie R. Letter. *Chicago Tribune* 20 Aug. 1961: 20.

"Mr. Sumner's Glorious Victory." Editorial. *New York Tribune* 23 Feb. 1921: 10.

Nelson, Ed. Letter. *Chicago Tribune* 24 Aug. 1961: 16.

Norris, Hoke. "'Cancer' in Chicago." *Evergreen Review* 6.5 (July–Aug. 1962): 41–66.

———. "Flood of Filth." *Chicago Sun-Times* 7 Mar. 1962: 14.

———. "From Norris." Letter. *Chicago Sun-Times* 13 Mar. 1962: 29.

———. "A Guest Columnist." *Chicago Sun-Times* 2 Mar. 1962: 40.

———. "Lamentable Influence." *Chicago Sun-Times* 23 Feb. 1962, sec. 2: 8.

———. "Literary Taste." *Chicago Sun-Times* 16 Feb. 1962, sec. 2: 8.

———. "Police Censor Book." *Chicago Sun-Times* 12 Oct. 1961: 15.

"Novel Ruled Obscene; Book Seller Guilty." *Chicago Tribune* 24 Feb. 1962: 7.

O'B., T. D. "In Which It Is Left to Us!" Letter. *Little Review* 5.3 (July 1918): 58.

O'Briant, Don. "Controversial Novel Shipped to Bookstores." *Atlanta Journal* 2 Mar. 1991: B8.

Oettinger, H. J. "Book Censorship." Letter. *Chicago's American* 28 June 1964: 8.

Ong, Walter J. "A Writer's Audience Is Always a Fiction." *PMLA* 90 (Jan. 1975): 6–21.

Paglia, Camille. "The Return of Carry Nation." *Playboy* Oct. 1992: 36–38.

———. "It's a Jungle out There, so Get Used to It!" *Utne Reader* Jan. 1993: 61–65. Rpt. from *Sex, Art, and American Culture*. New York: Vintage, 1992.

———. "The Joy of Presbyterian Sex." *New Republic* 21 Jan. 1991: 24–27.

Pamp, Oke G. "Word to Censors." Letter. *Chicago's American* 27 May 1963: 12.

Park, Douglas. "Analyzing Audiences." *College Composition and Communication* 37 (Dec. 1986): 478–88.

———. "The Meanings of 'Audience.'" *College English* 44 (Mar. 1982): 247–57.

Parker, Jack D. Letter. *Chicago Tribune* 18 Aug. 1961: 10.

Paul, Mrs. Henry. Letter. *Chicago Tribune* 17 Aug. 1961: 16.

Perelman, Chaim, and Lucie Olbrechts-Tyteca. *The New Rhetoric: A Treatise on Argumentation*. Trans. John Wilkinson and Purcell Weaver. South Bend, Ind.: Notre Dame University Press, 1969.

Pirie, John T., Jr. Letter. *Chicago Tribune* 20 Aug. 1961: 20.

"Police Censorship." Editorial. *Chicago Sun-Times* 21 Oct. 1961: 21.

"Police Chiefs Sued for Ban on Book Sales." *Chicago Tribune* 24 Oct. 1961: 3.

Poulet, Georges. "Criticism and the Experience of Interiority." *The Structuralist Controversy: The Language of Criticism and the Sciences of Man*. Ed. Richard A. Macksey and Eugenio Donato. Baltimore: Johns Hopkins University Press, 1972. 56–72.

Prince, Gerald. "Introduction to the Study of the Narratee." *Poetique* 14 (1973): 177–96.

Pristin, Terry. "Gruesome Novel 'American Psycho' Hits Bookstores." *Los Angeles Times* 1 Mar. 1991: B1.

Quindlen, Anna. "Publish or Perish." *New York Times* 18 Nov. 1990, sec. 4: 17.

Quintilian. *Institutio Oratoria*. Trans. H. E. Butler. 4 vols. Loeb Classical Library. Cambridge, Mass.: Harvard University Press, 1959–63.

R., F. E. "'Obscenity.'" Letter. *Little Review* 6.11 (Apr. 1920): 61.

Radway, Janice. *A Feeling for Books: The Book-of-the-Month Club, Literary Taste, and Middle-Class Desire*. Chapel Hill: University of North Carolina Press, 1997.

———. *Reading the Romance: Women, Patriarchy, and Popular Literature*. Chapel Hill: University of North Carolina Press, 1988.

Rawlinson, Nora. "Libraries Order Ellis Novel despite Furor." *Library Journal* Jan. 1991: 17.

———. Rev. of *American Psycho*, by Bret Easton Ellis. *Library Journal* Jan. 1991: 147.

Reid, Calvin. "Was It Censorship? Some Reactions." *Publishers Weekly* 30 Nov. 1990: 10.

Rekruceak, E. R. Letter. *Chicago's American* 3 Mar. 1962: 12.

Rekruciak, Edward W. Letter. *Chicago Daily News* 2 Mar. 1962: 8.

Rekruciak, Regina. "Deplores Ruling." Letter. *Chicago Sun-Times* 2 Mar. 1962: 29.

Rembar, Charles. *The End of Obscenity: The Trials of Lady Chatterley, Tropic of Cancer, and Fanny Hill*. New York: Random, 1968.

Reuter, Madalynne. "Vintage to Issue Controversial Ellis Novel after S&S Cancellation." *Publishers Weekly* 30 Nov. 1990: 8.

Richards, I. A. *Practical Criticism*. London: Paul, Trench, Trubner, 1929.

———. *Principles of Criticism*. London: Paul, Trench, Trubner, 1925.

Riffaterre, Michael. "Describing Poetic Structures: Two Approaches to Baudelaire's 'Les Chats.'" *Reader-Response Criticism: From Formalism to Post-Structuralism*. Ed. Jane P. Tompkins. Baltimore: Johns Hopkins University Press, 1981. 26–40.

Rodger, John J. "On the Degeneration of the Public Sphere." *Political Studies* 33 (June 1985): 203–17.

Rose, Don. "Why He's Attacked." Letter. *Chicago Sun-Times* 26 Mar. 1962: 29.

Rosenblatt, Louise. *Literature as Exploration*. 4th ed. New York: Modern Language Association, 1976.

———. *The Reader, the Text, the Poem: The Transactional Theory of the Literary Work*. Carbondale, Ill.: Southern Illinois University Press, 1978.

Rosenblatt, Roger. "Snuff This Book! Will Bret Easton Ellis Get Away with Murder?" *New York Times Book Review* 16 Dec. 1990: sec. 7: 3.

Rossman, Charles. Introduction. Special issue on *Ulysses*. *Studies in the Novel* 22.2 (Summer 1990): 113–17.

Royko, Mike. "No Dirty Books, No Clean Books, Just No Books." *Chicago Daily News* 22 June 1964: 8.

Russell, Diana E. H., ed. *Making Violence Sexy: Feminist Views on Pornography*. Athene Series. New York: Teachers College Press, 1993.

S., J. J. Letter. *Chicago Tribune* 18 Aug. 1961: 10.

S., M. J. Letter. *Chicago Tribune* 17 Aug. 1961: 16.

Said, Edward. *The World, the Text, and the Critic*. Cambridge, Mass.: Harvard University Press, 1983.

Savickas, E. E. "Too Much Filth." Letter. *Chicago's American* 22 Mar. 1962: 30.

Schick, Frank L. *The Paperbound Book in America*. New York: Bowker, 1958.

Schudson, Michael. *The Good Citizen: A History of American Civic Life*. New York: Free Press, 1998.

———. "Was There Ever a Public Sphere? If So, When? Reflections on the American Case." *Habermas and the Public Sphere*. Ed Craig Calhoun. Cambridge, Mass.: MIT Press, 1992. 143–63.

Schultz, W. F. Letter. *Chicago Daily News* 2 Mar. 1962: 8.

Schwarzlose, Richard Allen. *Newspapers: A Reference Guide.* Westport, Conn.: Greenwood Press, 1987.

Segall, Jeffrey. *Joyce in America: Cultural Politics and the Trials of* Ulysses. Berkeley: University of California Press, 1993.

Selleg, Richard M. "The State Department and Public Opinion." Letter. *Chicago Tribune* 28 Feb. 1962: 20.

Selzer, Jack. "More Meanings of *Audience.*" *A Rhetoric of Doing: Essays on Written Discourse in Honor of James Kinneavy.* Ed. Roger Cherry, Neil Nakedate, and Steven Witte. Carbondale: Southern Illinois University Press, 1992. 161–77.

Sennett, Richard. *The Fall of Public Man: On the Social Psychology of Capitalism.* New York: Vintage, 1974.

"Sent to the Cleaner." Editorial. *Chicago Tribune* 13 Aug. 1961: 24.

Sheppard, R. Z. "A Revolting Development." *Time* 29 Oct. 1990: 100.

Shifreen, Lawrence J. *Henry Miller: A Bibliography of Secondary Sources.* Metuchen, N.J.: Scarecrow Press, 1979.

Shorris, Earl. *The New American Blues: A Journey through Poverty to Democracy.* New York: Norton, 1997.

Smith, John Justin. "You Can Disagree with Columnist ———— and He with You." *Chicago Daily News* 1 Mar. 1962: 18.

"Smut Case Defense Motion Denied." *Chicago Sun-Times* 13 Dec. 1961, 2d ed.: 40.

Solon, Israel. Letter. *Little Review* 4.1 (May 1918): 62–64.

Spivak, Gayatri Chakravorty. "Can the Subaltern Speak?" *Marxism and the Interpretation of Culture.* Ed. Cary Nelson and Lawrence Grossberg. Urbana: University of Illinois Press, 1988. 271–313.

Spoor, Milton R. Letter. *Chicago Tribune* 18 Aug. 1961: 10.

"Statement of Support of Freedom to Read." *Evergreen Review* 6.25 (July–Aug. 1962): front cover+.

Steinberg, Sybil. Rev. of *Mercy,* by Andrea Dworkin. *Publishers Weekly* 25 July 1991: 36.

Steiner, Wendy. "Declaring War on Men." Rev. of *Mercy,* by Andrea Dworkin. *New York Times Book Review* 15 Sept. 1991: 11.

Stiles, Todd. "How Bret Ellis Turned Michael Korda into Larry Flynt." *Spy* Dec. 1990: 43.

Stoltenberg, John. "Pornography and Freedom." *Making Violence Sexy: Feminist Views on Pornography.* Ed. Diana E. H. Russell. Athene Series. New York: Teachers College Press, 1993. 65–77.

Streitfeld, David. "'Psycho' Analysis." *Washington Post* 16 Dec. 1990: WBK15.

Strunsky, Simeon. "About Books, *More or Less:* On Accepting Life." *New York Times Book Review* 16 Oct. 1927: 4.

Stumpf, [Rev.] Louis. Letter. *Chicago Tribune* 17 Aug. 1961: 16.

"Suburb Police Act to Bar Miller Book." *Chicago Sun-Times* 11 Oct. 1961, final ed.: 26.

"Taste, Not Morals, Violated." Editorial. *New York Times* 23 Feb. 1921: 12.

Taylor, Marianne, and Kenneth R. Clark. "Book's Graphic Violence Has Stores Squirming." *Chicago Tribune* 17 Nov. 1990, sec. 1: 1+.

"Ten Suburb Chiefs Sued over Book; Ask $3,900,000." *Chicago Sun-Times* 23 Oct. 1961, 2d ed.: 33.

Thelen, David. "A Round Table: What Has Changed and Not Changed in American Historical Practice?" *Journal of American History* 76.2 (1989): 393–486.

Toenies, Herbert D. Letter. *Chicago Daily News* 2 Mar. 1962: 8.

Tompkins, Jane P., ed. *Reader-Response Criticism: From Formalism to Post-Structuralism*. Baltimore: Johns Hopkins University Press, 1981.

Tooze, Mrs. Fred J. Letter. *Chicago Tribune* 24 Aug. 1961: 16.

"Top State Court Rules 'Cancer,' Bruce Obscene." *Chicago Sun-Times* 19 June 1964, 1st ed.: 2.

Treen, Joseph. "Who's behind the Axing of 'Psycho'?" *Boston Globe* 17 Nov. 1990: 12+.

"Trial Opens Tomorrow on 'THAT' Book." *Chicago's American* 19 Oct. 1961, 4th ed.: 9.

"Trial Set Jan. 10 in ACLU Suit on 'Tropic of Cancer.'" *Chicago Sun-Times* 19 Dec. 1961, 1st ed.: 18.

"'Tropic of Cancer' Reading Raided." *Chicago Sun-Times* 13 Mar. 1962: 4.

Turner, James R. Letter. *Chicago Tribune* 17 Aug. 1961: 16.

Udovitch, Mim. "Intentional Phalluses." *Village Voice* 19 Mar. 1991: 65+.

"'Ulysses.'" Letter. *Little Review* 7.1 (May–June 1920): 72.

"Vintage 'American Psycho' Has Only Minor Changes from S&S Version." *Publishers Weekly* 8 Mar. 1991: 6.

Walker, Jeffrey. *Bardic Ethos and the American Epic Poem: Whitman, Pound, Crane, Williams, Olson*. Baton Rouge: Louisiana State University Press, 1989.

Warner, Michael. "The Mass Public and the Mass Subject." *Habermas and the Public Sphere*. Ed Craig Calhoun. Cambridge, Mass.: MIT Press, 1992. 377–401.

Weisman, Alan. *Gaviotas: A Village to Reinvent the World*. White River Junction, Vt.: Chelsea Green, 1998.

Weitzel, Tony. "Books, Books Everywhere—but Not a 'Tropic.'" *Chicago Daily News* 18 Oct. 1961: 14.

———. "Good Paperbacks Can Get a Fair Shake." *Chicago Daily News* 23 Oct. 1961: 16.

Weston, Mary Ann. "Marshall Field III, Marshall Field IV, Marshall Field V." *Twentieth-Century American Newspaper Publishers*. Ed. Peter J. Ashley. Vol. 127 of *Dictionary of Literary Biography*. Detroit: Gale Research, 1993. 81–90.

Wickes, George. *Henry Miller and the Critics*. Carbondale: Southern Illinois University Press, 1963.

Widney, Mary. "The Public Taste." *Little Review* 7.2 (July–Aug. 1920): 32–33.

Williams, Lucille. Letter. *Chicago Tribune* 20 Aug. 1961: 20.

Wilson, Edmund. "Ulysses." Rev. of *Ulysses,* by James Joyce. *New Republic* 5 July 1922: 164–66.

Wise, Malcolm. "Suburbs Step Up Drive to Ban Book; City Weighs Action." *Chicago Sun-Times* 12 Oct. 1961, 1st ed.: 15.

Wojtycki, M. "Book-Snatching." Letter. *Chicago Daily News* 3 Nov. 1961: 8.

Wolf, Naomi. "The Animals Speak." *New Statesman and Society* Apr. 1991: 33+.

"Worries about a Book." Editorial. *Los Angeles Times* 16 Dec. 1990: M6.

Yardley, Jonathan. "Norman Mailer's Shock Schlock." *Washington Post* 4 Mar. 1991: B2.

Yates, Frances. *The Art of Memory.* Chicago: University of Chicago Press, 1984.

# Index

ROSA A. EBERLY is an assistant professor in the Division of Rhetoric and Composition and in the Department of English at the University of Texas at Austin.

Selling Free Enterprise: The Business Assault on Labor and
Liberalism, 1945–60   *Elizabeth A. Fones-Wolf*
Last Rights: Revisiting *Four Theories of the Press*   *Edited by
John C. Nerone*
"We Called Each Other Comrade": Charles H. Kerr &
Company, Radical Publishers   *Allen Ruff*
WCFL, Chicago's Voice of Labor, 1926–78   *Nathan Godfried*
Taking the Risk Out of Democracy: Corporate Propaganda
versus Freedom and Liberty   *Alex Carey; edited by
Andrew Lohrey*
Media, Market, and Democracy in China: Between the Party
Line and the Bottom Line   *Yuezhi Zhao*
Print Culture in a Diverse America   *Edited by James P. Danky
and Wayne A. Wiegand*
The Newspaper Indian: Native American Identity in the Press,
1820–90   *John M. Coward*
E. W. Scripps and the Business of Newspapers
*Gerald J. Baldasty*
Picturing the Past: Media, History, and Photography   *Edited by
Bonnie Brennen and Hanno Hardt*
Rich Media, Poor Democracy: Communication Politics in
Dubious Times   *Robert W. McChesney*
Silencing the Opposition: Antinuclear Movements and the
Media in the Cold War   *Andrew Rojecki*
Citizen Critics: Literary Public Spheres   *Rosa A. Eberly*

Typeset in 10/13 Sabon
with Crud display
Designed by Dennis Roberts
Composed by Jim Proefrock
at the University of Illinois Press


University of Illinois Press
1325 South Oak Street
Champaign, IL 61820-6903
www.press.uillinois.edu